# NATIONAL GEOGRAPHIC KiDS

# ALMANAC 2021

An octopus swims below the
water's surface in Maui, Hawaii, U.S.A.

# ALMANAC
## 2021

NATIONAL GEOGRAPHIC
WASHINGTON, D.C.

# National Geographic Kids Books gratefully acknowledges the following people for their help with the *National Geographic Kids Almanac*.

Bryan Howard of the National Geographic Explorer Programs

## Amazing Animals

Suzanne Braden, Director, Pandas International

Dr. Rodolfo Coria, Paleontologist, Plaza Huincul, Argentina

Dr. Sylvia Earle, National Geographic Explorer-in-Residence

Dr. Thomas R. Holtz, Jr., Senior Lecturer, Vertebrate Paleontology, Department of Geology, University of Maryland

Dr. Luke Hunter, Executive Director, Panthera

Nizar Ibrahim, National Geographic Explorer

Dereck and Beverly Joubert, National Geographic Explorers-in-Residence

"Dino" Don Lessem, President, Exhibits Rex

Kathy B. Maher, Research Editor (former), *National Geographic* magazine

Kathleen Martin, Canadian Sea Turtle Network

Barbara Nielsen, Polar Bears International

Andy Prince, Austin Zoo

Julia Thorson, Translator, Zurich, Switzerland

Dennis vanEngelsdorp, Senior Extension Associate, Pennsylvania Department of Agriculture

## Wonders of Nature

Anatta, NOAA Public Affairs Officer

Dr. Robert Ballard, National Geographic Explorer-in-Residence

Douglas H. Chadwick, Wildlife Biologist and Contributor to *National Geographic* magazine

Susan K. Pell, Ph.D., Science and Public Programs Manager, United States Botanic Garden

## Space and Earth
## Science and Technology

Tim Appenzeller, Chief Magazine Editor, *Nature*

Dr. Rick Fienberg, Press Officer and Director of Communications, American Astronomical Society

Dr. José de Ondarza, Associate Professor, Department of Biological Sciences, State University of New York, College at Plattsburgh

Lesley B. Rogers, Managing Editor (former), *National Geographic* magazine

Dr. Enric Sala, National Geographic Explorer-in-Residence

Abigail A. Tipton, Director of Research (former), *National Geographic* magazine

Erin Vintinner, Biodiversity Specialist, Center for Biodiversity and Conservation at the American Museum of Natural History

Barbara L. Wyckoff, Research Editor (former), *National Geographic* magazine

## Culture Connection

Dr. Wade Davis, National Geographic Explorer-in-Residence

Deirdre Mullervy, Managing Editor, Gallaudet University Press

## Going Green

Eric J. Bohn, Math Teacher, Santa Rosa High School

Stephen David Harris, Professional Engineer, Industry Consulting

Catherine C. Milbourn, Senior Press Officer, EPA

Brad Scriber, Senior Researcher, *National Geographic* magazine

Paola Segura and Cid Simões, National Geographic Emerging Explorers

Dr. Wes Tunnell, Harte Research Institute for Gulf of Mexico Studies, Texas A&M University–Corpus Christi

Natasha Vizcarra, Science Writer and Media Liaison, National Snow and Ice Data Center

## History Happens

Dr. Sylvie Beaudreau, Associate Professor, Department of History, State University of New York

Elspeth Deir, Assistant Professor, Faculty of Education, Queens University, Kingston, Ontario, Canada

Dr. Gregory Geddes, Professor, Global Studies, State University of New York–Orange, Middletown-Newburgh, New York

Dr. Fredrik Hiebert, National Geographic Visiting Fellow

Micheline Joanisse, Media Relations Officer, Natural Resources Canada

Dr. Robert D. Johnston, Associate Professor and Director of the Teaching of History Program, University of Illinois at Chicago

Dickson Mansfield, Geography Instructor (retired), Faculty of Education, Queens University, Kingston, Ontario, Canada

Tina Norris, U.S. Census Bureau

Parliamentary Information and Research Service, Library of Parliament, Ottawa, Canada

Karyn Pugliese, Acting Director, Communications, Assembly of First Nations

## Geography Rocks

Dr. Kristin Bietsch, Research Associate, Population Reference Bureau

Carl Haub, Senior Demographer, Conrad Taeuber Chair of Public Information, Population Reference Bureau

Dr. Toshiko Kaneda, Senior Research Associate, Population Reference Bureau

Dr. Walt Meier, National Snow and Ice Data Center

Dr. Richard W. Reynolds, NOAA's National Climatic Data Center

United States Census Bureau, Public Help Desk

# Contents

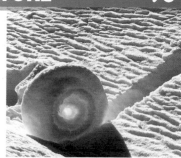

**THE RESULTS ARE IN!**
Which idea won our 2020
Visionary Almanac Challenge?
*See page 25.*
Want to become part of the 2021 Almanac
Challenge? Go to page 24 to find out more.

NATIONAL
GEOGRAPHIC
KIDS
ALMANAC
CHALLENGE
2021

Colorful kites soar above the beach during the annual International Berck-sur-Mer Kite Festival in northern France.

# Newly Discovered Animals

From an ORANGUTAN to COLORFUL FISH, here are some species recently discovered in the wild.

## Wakatobi and Wangi-Wangi White-Eyes

You can't miss the pop-out peepers of the two birds recently discovered in Sulawesi, Indonesia. Aptly named white-eyes, both of these birds are marked with a white ring around each eye. The main difference between the two? The Wakatobi white-eye (left) has a yellow belly, while the Wangi-Wangi white-eye's belly is white. Found in separate areas off the coast of Sulawesi, the birds are named for their island homes.

## Vibranium Fish

Wakanda forever! A marine biologist named a never-seen-before fish the Vibranium wrasse after one of his favorite films, *Black Panther*. This tiny purple fish, found off the coast of Zanzibar, lives near reefs and eats plankton.

## Rain Frog

A total of 11 species of rain frogs have been identified by researchers in Ecuador. This group of new hoppers is believed to be one of the biggest discoveries of amphibians in recent years. The frogs, which vary in color from bright yellow to dark brown, live in an area of less than 965 square miles (2,500 sq km) in the rainforest.

## Tapanuli Orangutan

What's the rarest great ape on the planet? Scientists say it's the Tapanuli orangutan, a new species recently identified on the island of Sumatra in western Indonesia. The Tapanuli orangutan lives exclusively in a high-elevation forest called Batang Toru, while other species are found in different parts of Sumatra and on Borneo across the Java Sea. While the discovery is exciting, it is also a reminder of just how fragile certain species are. Experts say there are just 800 of these orangutans on Earth, underlining the importance of conservation work being done to save all orangutans.

# ASTEROID
## SELF-DESTRUCTS

Some asteroids crash into Earth. Some barrel into other planets. And sometimes, they self-destruct. That's what is likely happening to one asteroid known as 6478 Gault, a space rock that's some 2.5 miles (4 km) in diameter and travels in a circular orbit in an asteroid belt between Mars and Jupiter. Images from the Hubble Space Telescope showed the giant asteroid splitting apart, leaving behind two bright, dusty tails, one of which measures a whopping 500,000 miles (805,000 km) long and 3,000 miles (4,800 km) wide. 6478 Gault, which was first spotted by astronomers in 1988, is one of some one million space rocks shooting through space. But the sight of an asteroid becoming unglued is rare: Astronomers estimate that this type of event happens just once a year.

# Town Aims for Zero Waste

The village of Kamikatsu, Japan, may be tiny, but it's making a big impact on the future of our planet. There, the 1,500 residents aim to recycle everything they use, from chopsticks to printer cartridges. In fact, 80 percent of the town's waste is recycled or composted—which is four times the rate of the country of Japan as a whole. The people of Kamikatsu sort their trash into some 40 different recycling bins set aside for items like aluminum cans, steel cans, paper cartons, and paper flyers.

Locals also get creative with their trash, like repurposing old kimonos into teddy bears. While an 80 percent recycling rate is impressive, the citizens of Kamikatsu don't want to stop there: They're hoping to produce absolutely zero waste in the near future.

# WILDLIFE CROSSINGS

Overpass in Banff, Alberta, Canada

**Eco-friendly bridges and tunnels help animals get from one side to the other—safely.**

### How did the bear cross the road?

In Banff, Canada, it walks across an overpass! Or, more specifically, a grassy bridge spanning the width of the Trans-Canada Highway. A part of a wildlife initiative meant to protect animals like bears, wolves, coyotes, and moose from getting hit by cars, Banff boasts numerous wildlife crossing structures. And they don't just keep the animals safe: The overpasses protect people, too, since they can greatly reduce the amount of animal-car collisions on the roads.

Similar overpasses have been built in different parts of the world, including western Europe and other areas in Canada. And plans are under way to construct what may be the world's largest wildlife crossing over a Southern California, U.S.A., highway for animals like mountain lions, deer, lizards, and snakes. The bridge, which will stretch some 200 feet (61 m) above 10 lanes of highway, is slated to be completed in 2023.

A toad in the U.K. crosses a road through an underground wildlife tunnel.

In some places, animals head underground to get to where they want to go. Road tunnels for wildlife in areas like Banff serve as safe ways for critters to cross busy roads. And, like the overpasses, these tunnels can curb collisions between cars and wildlife.

On one stretch of highway in the Santa Cruz Mountains in California, for example, a tunnel is being built for the many mountain lions and deer that tend to dash across the four lanes—a dangerous and often fatal mission.

# "ICE TSUNAMI"

Usually, a strong storm over Lake Erie in eastern Canada and western New York State, U.S.A., means there may be flooding along the shoreline. But when temperatures dip well below the freezing mark, something else can happen: an "ice tsunami"! This wacky phenomenon happens when strong winds push blocks of ice floating in the lake toward the water's edge. The ice surges over the lake's shoreline, creating frozen, moving walls as high as three-story buildings. An ice tsunami is a cool sight, but just like an actual tsunami, it can be damaging to anything in its path.

# Robots Comfort Kids

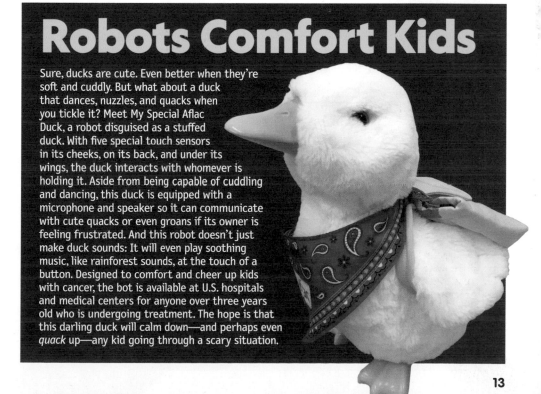

Sure, ducks are cute. Even better when they're soft and cuddly. But what about a duck that dances, nuzzles, and quacks when you tickle it? Meet My Special Aflac Duck, a robot disguised as a stuffed duck. With five special touch sensors in its cheeks, on its back, and under its wings, the duck interacts with whomever is holding it. Aside from being capable of cuddling and dancing, this duck is equipped with a microphone and speaker so it can communicate with cute quacks or even groans if its owner is feeling frustrated. And this robot doesn't just make duck sounds: It will even play soothing music, like rainforest sounds, at the touch of a button. Designed to comfort and cheer up kids with cancer, the bot is available at U.S. hospitals and medical centers for anyone over three years old who is undergoing treatment. The hope is that this darling duck will calm down—and perhaps even *quack* up—any kid going through a scary situation.

# DOGS AT THE MOVIES

**A group of adorable dogs hit the theater for a very good cause.**

This theater is for the dogs! A group of dogs recently took in a showing of *Billy Elliot* at a movie theater in Ontario, Canada. But they weren't just checking out the film for fun: They were actually in training! All of the dogs are in the process of becoming service dogs for those with special needs, and sitting through a movie was simply practice for their future gig.

A service dog attends most everyday activities with its human and needs to ignore distractions—like food and other people—so it can stay focused on its job. So, by taking the dogs to the movies, their handlers hope it will teach them to stay relaxed for a couple of hours in an environment with loud noises, flashing lights, tight spaces, and potential crowds. So how did the dogs do? The handlers were quite impressed by their four-legged friends, giving them an A+ for their behavior. Sounds like these dogs deserve a treat or two!

# HOT MOVIES in 2021*

- *Trolls World Tour*
- *The Boss Baby 2*
- *Rugrats*
- *Sing 2*
- *Tom and Jerry*
- *Mary Poppins 3*
- *Moana 2*
- *Zootopia 2*
- *The Little Mermaid*

*Release dates and titles are subject to change.

# HIGH-TECH HELP

When caretakers at the Jurong Bird Park in Singapore noticed a suspicious gash on a resident hornbill's casque—the helmet-like part atop the bill—they suspected something was seriously wrong. After all, two of their hornbills had recently been diagnosed with cancer, and this bird, named Jary, was showing similar signs.

A scan confirmed the diagnosis, and Jary underwent surgery to remove the cancerous growths—and most of his casque. But all wasn't bleak for this bird: A team of veterinary experts quickly sprang into action, using a 3D printer to create a prosthetic casque. Made to fit Jary just right, the customized casque was carefully screwed into place and sealed with a special resin so it stayed put. After some time in quarantine to recover, Jary—whose name means "warrior with a helmet" in ancient Norse—returned to his home in the bird park, healthy and cancer free.

# ECO-SHOES

One brand of shoes is taking a step in the right direction when it comes to protecting the planet. Rothy's shoes are made of discarded plastic water bottles and other recycled materials. To create the shoes, the bottles are crushed, melted into pellets, and pulled into soft fibers that are knit together to form a stretchy material. Recycled foam fills each shoe's inside. And the packaging? Even the shoe boxes are made from recycled materials. Rothy's has repurposed tens of millions of water bottles—helping stomp out the problem of too much waste on Earth.

# Cool Events 2021

## PAN-O-RAMA ST. JOHN'S FESTIVAL

The tropical sounds of steel pan drums drift through the Caribbean island of St. John as local bands compete for glory in this friendly competition.

**June**

## SPECIAL OLYMPICS WORLD WINTER GAMES

Sweden will host this weeklong event for athletes with intellectual disabilities—it's one of the largest and most inspiring sports events on the planet.

**February 6–February 12**

## WORLD GIRAFFE DAY

Stick your neck out for giraffes and raise awareness for these enchanting animals.

**June 21**

## U.S. QUIDDITCH CUP

Move over, Harry Potter! Athletes in Salt Lake City, Utah, U.S.A., will go broomstick to broomstick in this real-life version of the game, plucked from the pages of the famous books.

**April 17–18**

## RUGBY LEAGUE WORLD CUP

Men's, women's, and wheelchair rugby league teams from around the world head to England to duke it out at this epic event.

**October 23–November 27**

## WORLD LAUGHTER DAY

What's so funny? Find something to LOL about today!

**May 2**

## WORLD PASTA DAY

Did someone say spaghetti?

Pile it on your plate and eat up today!

**October 25**

## HAEUNDAE SAND FESTIVAL

This beachside fest in Busan, South Korea, featuring castle-building, sand baths, and a volleyball competition, celebrates all things sand.

**Late May/Early June**

## SANTA SUNDAY

Forget sleds: Some 250 Santas ride on skis and snowboards at this event in Maine, U.S.A., which raises money for charity.

**December**

# Rooftop POOL

Designers of this sky-high swimming spot aim for new heights.

Visitors who take a dip in the Infinity London will be able to swim *and* sightsee at the same time! This splashy see-through pool—set to be the world's first infinity pool with 360-degree views—has been designed to be built some 656 feet (200 m) atop a 55-story luxury hotel in the British capital. The pool will be accessed by a rotating spiral staircase rising from the pool floor—a concept based on the door of a submarine. And that's not the only futuristic feature: The water will be heated using waste energy from the building's air-conditioning system. Now that's one *cool* pool.

Rendering of Infinity London's planned rooftop pool

NO UMBRELLA NEEDED. WEATHER FORECASTERS DETERMINED THE LARGE GREEN "CLOUD" ON THE RADAR MAP ABOVE WAS ACTUALLY A SWARM OF LADYBUGS.

# A Chance of LADYBUGS

Residents of San Diego, California, U.S.A., were *bugging* out when a massive swarm of ladybugs recently flew high over the coastal city. Measuring about 10 miles (16 km) wide, the swarm spanned somewhere between 5,000 and 9,000 feet (1,500 and 2,700 m) in the sky. Also known as a "bloom," the group was so big that it registered on the National Weather Service's radar. While experts aren't sure what type of ladybugs formed this phenomenon, they think it was likely a mega migration. Each summer, big groups of certain ladybug species fly from the higher elevations of California to the valleys to lay eggs.

Cave divers explore a tree-lined spring that forms part of the Devil's Spring System in Florida, U.S.A.

# DARE TO EXPLORE

From listening to animals to reading the stars, three Nat Geo explorers share secrets about communicating with the world.

"Don't be afraid to take things apart. Play with them, see how they work, and experiment on your own."

TOPHER WHITE PREPARES TO MOUNT A LISTENING DEVICE TO A TREE THAT WILL HELP NAB ILLEGAL LOGGERS ON THE GROUND.

## THE ENGINEER

**Topher White** attaches recycled cell phones to trees in remote rainforests around the world, hoping to pick up the sounds of illegal loggers. He describes trying to work while being swarmed by bees.

"Even though the forests can be home to illegal loggers, sometimes what's going on in the treetops is scarier than what's on the ground. One time I was installing a phone and bees kept landing on me. Eventually I was completely covered with them! But I had to finish the job, even if it meant getting a *lot* of bee stings.

"The phones I place each have an app that turns the phone into a listening device. They capture all the sounds of the rainforest. Listening to this noise can help us pick out the sounds of things like chain saws and logging trucks. If we can pinpoint the sounds of illegal logging, we can instantly send alerts to local authorities and tribes, who are then able to stop illegal loggers on the spot. In a way, the trees are telling us when they need help."

## WANT TO BE AN ENGINEER?

| | |
|---|---|
| **STUDY** | Mathematics, physics |
| **WATCH** | The documentary series *The Trials of Life* |
| **READ** | *The Wild Trees* by Richard Preston |

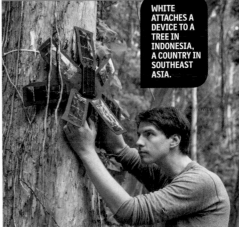

WHITE ATTACHES A DEVICE TO A TREE IN INDONESIA, A COUNTRY IN SOUTHEAST ASIA.

FROM LEFT: ASTRONOMERS HALEY FICA, MUNAZZA ALAM, AND SARA CAMNASIO STAND IN FRONT OF A 21-FOOT (6.4-M)-WIDE TELESCOPE IN CHILE.

# THE ASTRONOMER

**Munazza Alam** searches the sky for a planet that humans could live on one day. She discusses her hunt for what she calls the "Earth Twin."

"I spend a lot of my nights at observatories atop mountain ranges, using high-resolution telescopes that are sometimes the size of a school bus. I'm observing faraway planets outside our solar system called exoplanets. By analyzing these exoplanets, I hope to discover if any of them have atmospheres similar to Earth that people could one day survive in. You could say I'm searching for Earth's twin. An 'Earth Twin' would be a rocky planet with temperatures that would support liquid water. We haven't found one yet, but I do think we're getting closer. The more we study the stars and their planets, the more we can understand what they're like. As an astronomer, it's my job to keep examining the sky in the hopes that it'll reveal new things about our galaxy and beyond."

"If you have a curiosity, don't let that flame go out. Never let go of that enthusiasm, because it will inspire you forever."

## WANT TO BE AN ASTRONOMER?

| | |
|---|---|
| **STUDY** | Physics, astronomy |
| **WATCH** | *Zathura: A Space Adventure* |
| **READ** | *The Magic School Bus: Lost in the Solar System* by Joanna Cole |

# THE CONSERVATIONIST

**Hotlin Ompusunggu** works to protect the forests of Indonesia in Southeast Asia. She talks about saving orangutans and educating illegal loggers.

"I'll occasionally see orangutans frolicking in the trees above me. We've placed cameras in the forests to monitor their movements, and sometimes it looks like they might be posing for a picture—sort of like an orangutan selfie! Their population in Indonesia is decreasing, mostly because of logging, so when I see one of these photos I'm very happy. It means orangutans are still there, and it's like they're saying, 'Thank you for protecting our home.'

"People may not always agree with you, but don't let that stop you from sharing your ideas."

"The forests of Indonesia provide natural resources like fruit, meat, and wood. Often loggers will try to gain these resources illegally, which is dangerous for animals and people. By educating loggers on the impact of their actions, we can begin to create new forest guardians."

## WANT TO BE A CONSERVATIONIST?

| | |
|---|---|
| **STUDY** | Biology, ecology |
| **WATCH** | *Dr. Seuss' The Lorax* |
| **READ** | *My Life With the Chimpanzees* by Jane Goodall |

AN ORANGUTAN HANGS OUT IN THE FORESTS OF INDONESIA.

# Jamal Galves
# Manatee Man

**GALVES HOLDS A BABY MANATEE THAT WAS RESCUED AFTER BEING SEPARATED FROM ITS MOTHER.**

**A TRACKING RADIO AND ANTENNA HELP GALVES OBSERVE AND RECORD THE BEHAVIOR OF TAGGED MANATEES.**

National Geographic Explorer Jamal Galves is working so hard to save Antillean manatees in his native Belize, he's known as the "manatee man." Listed as a vulnerable species—or likely to become endangered unless its population numbers improve—all manatees are threatened by habitat loss and collisions with boats. "They could eventually go extinct," explains Galves. "My mission is to stop that from happening."

Growing up in Gales Point Manatee, a tiny village in the Central American country, Galves knew from the time he was 11 that he wanted to dedicate his life to the unique animals. Today, he spends his days either in the field observing manatees in their natural habitat or traveling the world advocating for their protection and better environmental laws.

"Manatees fall victim to boats, habitat destruction, pollution, climate change, and poaching," Galves says. "I want to bring awareness and share the issues manatees are facing locally and internationally."

Galves is the person to call whenever an Antillean manatee is in need of help. With the Clearwater Marine Aquarium Research Institute, he's rescued those massive mammals that have become tangled in fishing gear or injured by a boat. He has also saved newborn calves abandoned on the beach, taking them to a rescue facility to be nursed back to health.

"The favorite parts about my job? Hugging manatees when I rescue them, giving them names that fit their personality, bottle-feeding babies, and releasing them to the wild when they're ready," Galves says.

Manatees are already beloved animals in Belize. But Galves hopes that his work will help make them targets of conservation efforts around the world. "We need to save this species," he shares. "Because they can't save themselves."

**Bet You Didn't Know!**

# 6 marvelous facts about manatees

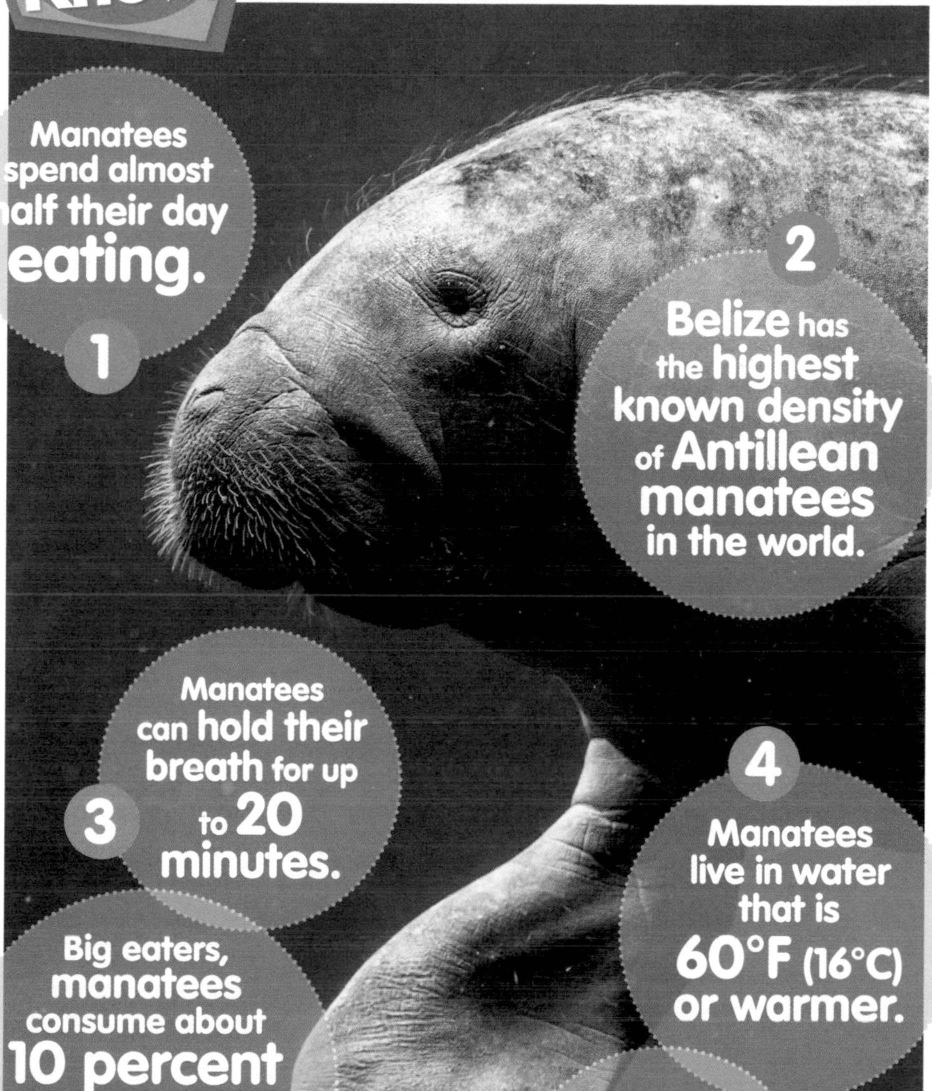

**1** Manatees spend almost half their day eating.

**2** Belize has the highest known density of Antillean manatees in the world.

**3** Manatees can hold their breath for up to 20 minutes.

**4** Manatees live in water that is 60°F (16°C) or warmer.

**5** Big eaters, manatees consume about 10 percent of their body weight in plants daily.

**6** Elephants are closely related to manatees.

ANTILLEAN MANATEE

23

# Be a Kids vs. Plastic Leader

NATIONAL GEOGRAPHIC KiDS
ALMANAC CHALLENGE 2021

**N**early nine million tons (8.1 million t) of plastic enter the ocean each year. That's the equivalent of unloading a dump truck of plastic into the ocean *every minute*. Help keep habitats healthy for humans and animals by participating in this year's Kids vs. Plastic Almanac Challenge.

Plastic water bottles, straws, and bags might be part of your everyday life. They're called "single-use plastics" because you use them once, then throw them away. But that plastic doesn't disappear when you're done with it: Most of it ends up in the ocean, where it can entangle animals or make them sick.

National Geographic explorers are working hard to raise awareness and solve this plastics problem. Check out what one explorer is doing to reduce single-use plastic in her own family and around the world.

### Meet National Geographic Explorer and Plastic Waste Activist Jenna Jambeck

An award-winning explorer and environmental engineer, Jenna Jambeck is working hard to reduce the amount of plastic piling up in the oceans and on land. Here, Jambeck shares how she got her start in this field of science—and how you can get involved, too.

**What inspired you to care about the amount of plastics in the environment?**
I grew up in a town of less than 3,000 people in Minnesota, U.S.A., where there was no trash collection. We had to take our trash to the landfill ourselves, so I saw what everyone threw away and became fascinated with it.

Plus, I've always loved the ocean. When I first heard about our waste ending up in the ocean, I knew we were doing something wrong on land. Then I became dedicated to protecting the seas.

**What are you working on now?**
As a co-leader for the Sea to Source plastic expeditions for National Geographic, we are trying to better understand how waste moves from land into our waterways, especially rivers that can lead into the ocean. Having grown up on a river, this is especially important to me. I'm also looking at how natural disasters contribute to the plastic pollution problem.

**Why is this issue so important?**
The statistics are pretty scary. The amount of plastic produced around the world over the past 60 years is equivalent to the weight of 80 blue whales. A lot of that becomes waste, but only 9 percent of that waste is recycled. The rest ends up in landfills or in our environment. It litters our ocean and our shores, and animals ingest and get entangled in the plastic.

**So how *can* kids help to reduce the amount of plastic they use at home?**
To start, pay attention to the plastic items you use. Are they all useful? Can you imagine a different way to get the same or similar food or drink without the packaging? Can you reuse it?

**Any other ways kids can get involved?**
There are many ways to make a collective difference. Start clubs and groups with friends to communicate your message about plastics. Do research to empower yourself about the topic, then communicate it to others.

You can also tap into the Marine Debris Tracker (marinedebris.engr.uga.edu), which is a great tool for collecting data on what's leaking out into the environment. You can create a map of what you find in your neighborhood—it doesn't have to be anywhere near water or the ocean—and find out what the top trash items are in your area. It's an easy way to make a big difference.

# THIS YEAR'S CHALLENGE

The good news is that kids can make a difference when it comes to plastic! Join the Kids vs. Plastic Almanac Challenge at natgeokids.com/almanac.

**Get inspired!** Check out our top 10 tips online to reduce your plastic waste.

**Take action!** Tell us how many of the tips you were able to do in one month by filling out a form and taking our online poll.

**Inspire and involve others!** Show us the creative ways you've been able to reduce plastic waste in your home, classroom, or community by sending us your stories and photos (along with your form), and your entry may appear in next year's almanac!

**Take the pledge!** Commit to using less plastic and earn your certificate.

**Be a Kids vs. Plastic leader and remember:** Awareness inspires action, which leads to change!

 Get details and official rules at **natgeokids.com/almanac.**

## LAST YEAR'S CHALLENGE

For the Almanac's 10th anniversary, we asked kids to think 10 years into the future to envision a change that would make the world better. Submissions covered a range of important issues—from finding a cure for cancer to saving endangered species—and showed how smart, creative, and caring today's kids are!

The grand prize winner of the Almanac 2020 Visionary Challenge is Kai S., from Hawaii, U.S.A., who has a revolutionary idea to rid the ocean of plastic waste and save marine life. First, ban single-use plastic. Then, create a plastic-eating enzyme (a molecule that speeds up chemical reactions) to break down any plastic left in the ocean. The enzyme would be safely deployed via a self-propelled machine that looks like a whale! The machine would find, gulp up, and "digest" the plastic.

**Check out the grand prize entry and more visionary ideas at natgeokids.com/almanac.**

MANY VISIONARY IDEAS FOCUSED ON KEEPING THE OCEAN HEALTHY AND FREE OF PLASTIC.

# Meet Your Shark Bestie

Some sharks grow more than 30,000 teeth in their lifetime.

## YOU WON'T BELIEVE THESE PREDATOR PERSONALITIES.

While diving off the Bahama Islands, National Geographic photographer Brian Skerry noticed an oceanic whitetip shark swimming toward him. Soon the nine-foot (2.7-m)-long female was gently bumping her snout against Skerry's camera.

The shark's mouth was closed, so Skerry knew she wasn't trying to bite him. Instead, she just examined his photographic equipment like a curious kid. Skerry says this type of behavior shows that sharks have all sorts of personalities. And even individuals belonging to a species that's thought to be aggressive can have a major sweet side.

### PERSONALITY POWER

Hiking in the Bahamas through a mangrove forest—a group of shrubs or trees that grow in coastal waters—Skerry arrived at a wild nursery for lemon shark pups in about a foot (0.3 m) of water. He put on his snorkel gear and scrambled onto his stomach to snap pics of the fish, watching as three shark pups swished closer to investigate. "Certain sharks are quicker to explore new things in their environment," Skerry says—meaning some sharks are also super social, while others within the same species prefer their me time.

Different sharks within the same species thrive in different situations. Social lemon sharks may do better when food is plentiful because they'll share the grub with each other. But when food is scarce, the loner lemon sharks might thrive, since they don't divide their meals.

### SUPERSIZE SHARK

On another diving trip, Skerry caught sight of a 14-foot (4.3-m)-long tiger shark in the Atlantic Ocean. Skerry admits to being nervous at first, but the shark just glided over him and actually allowed Skerry to touch her. The tiger shark, known as Emma, visited the dive site almost every day during Skerry's stay. "She was just a gentle giant," says Skerry.

Skerry hopes that by showing the different personalities of sharks, people will view them

SKERRY TOOK THIS PHOTO OF A LEMON SHARK PUP FROM THE WATERY FLOOR OF A MANGROVE FOREST.

More than 450 species of sharks exist, but at least 26 of them are endangered and at least 48 are vulnerable.

THIS PHOTO, TAKEN BY BRIAN SKERRY, SHOWS A DIVER INTERACTING WITH A TIGER SHARK OFF THE BAHAMA ISLANDS.

THE ULTIMATE BOOK OF SHARKS

Check out this book!

SKERRY READIES HIS CAMERA TO TAKE PHOTOS OF A SCHOOL OF CARIBBEAN REEF SHARKS.

less as scary animals and more as individuals that deserve our care and protection—even if they do have a lot of teeth!

## GUARDIANS OF THE SEA

Want to help keep coral reefs in good condition? Call in the sharks! Certain sharks eat animals that prey on herbivorous (or plant-eating) fish. Since herbivorous fish eat harmful algae that grow on the reefs, a break in that chain would be bad news for coral. Thank goodness for hungry sharks.

A REMORA FISH CATCHES A RIDE ON A TIGER SHARK OFF THE BAHAMA ISLANDS.

# awes8me
## EXTREME SPORTS

CLIFF JUMPERS!

### 2 ON A ROLL

Who says you can't walk on water? Water zorbing brings extra thrills to a day at the lake, ocean, or pool. Climb inside this giant inflatable orb and run or walk across the water's surface. You're sure to have a ball!

### 1 TAKE THE PLUNGE

*Cannonball!* A brave diver leaps off the La Quebrada Cliffs in Acapulco, Mexico. The height of the jump? Some 150 feet (46 m)—four times taller than most platform diving boards.

### 4 GO WITH THE FLOW

This sport is on fire. In ash boarding, you strap a wooden board onto your feet before shooting down the slope of an active volcano, reaching speeds of up to 50 miles an hour (80 km/h).

### 3 CURVE APPEAL

Cars and motorcycles drive sideways along a wall in this dizzying display in India. Thanks to centripetal force, vehicles stay stuck to the wall as they loop around the curved course.

**5**

## WHEELS UP
Rock-and-roll! A free rider sails over a steep rock wall in Moab, Utah, U.S.A. In free riding, cyclists use obstacles in nature—like rock formations and twisty trails—to do daring tricks and stunts.

**6**

## BALANCING ACT
No fear here: A daredevil tiptoes along a wire as she crosses between two cliffs in the Italian Alps. A stumble at this height would be like falling from the top of the Empire State Building.

**7**

## THROWN FOR A LOOP
Stunt cyclist Danny MacAskill seems to defy gravity by riding around a 16-foot (4.9-m)-tall loop. Here, he's shown in a time-lapsed photo making a full circle before riding away on his bike.

**8**

## BIG AIR
A snowboarder is flying high during the slopestyle event at the 2018 Winter Olympics in PyeongChang, South Korea. Slopestyle competitors race down a mountain dotted with obstacles like ramps, which allow them to catch major air.

**DUH!** Don't try these tricks on your own.

29

# SOLO TREKS
## ACROSS ANTARCTICA

It's tough enough for a team of explorers to trek across Antarctica. But imagine doing it completely on your own, towing a 300-pound (136-kg)-plus sled across the ice for nearly two months straight.

That's just what a pair of adventurers did in separate solo trips across the coldest continent. In December 2018, both Colin O'Brady and Louis Rudd completed their respective journeys just two days apart.

What began as a race between the two men turned into a journey of survival, as both faced low visibility, biting winds, and bitter cold temperatures that could drop below minus 50°F (-46°C) during their more than 900-mile (1,450-km) trek. Both men traveled with skis while dragging sleds packed with supplies. Rudd's sled weighed 330 pounds (150 kg), while O'Brady's was 375 pounds (170 kg). Both had scary stumbles while skiing over the icy surface. Still, neither used any sort of outside support, like supply drops or wind-harnessing kites that could have helped them pull their heavy loads. They slept in tents, made water out of snow, and rationed the carefully measured food they packed to make sure they had enough fuel to last the entire way.

While O'Brady eventually completed his journey first, both men emerged as winners: Collectively, their efforts raised thousands of dollars for charity.

RIGHT: SELFIE OF COLIN O'BRADY TAKEN DURING HIS EXPEDITION. BELOW: O'BRADY ARRIVES AT THE SOUTH POLE ON DAY 40 OF HIS SOLO CROSSING.

Geographic South Pole

LEFT: LOUIS RUDD ON THE FINAL DAY OF HIS SOLO CROSSING. BELOW: RUDD ON SKIS AT THE SOUTH POLE ON DAY 40 OF HIS EXPEDITION.

Geographic South Pole

# HOW TO SURVIVE A
# KILLER BEE ATTACK!

### ① Buzz Off
Killer bees—or Africanized honeybees—attack only when their hive is being threatened. If you see several bees buzzing near you, a hive is probably close by. Heed their "back off" attitude and slowly walk away.

### ② Don't Join the Swat Team
Your first instinct might be to start swatting and slapping the bees. But that just makes the buzzers angry. Loud noises have the same effect, so don't start screaming, either. Just get away.

### ③ Don't Play Hide-and-Seek
Hives are often near water, but don't even think about outlasting the bees underwater. They'll hover and attack when you come up for air, even if you try to swim for it.

### ④ Make Like Speedy Gonzalez
Killer bees will chase you, but they'll give up when you're far enough away from the hive (usually about 200 yards [183 m]). Take off running and don't stop until the buzzing does.

### ⑤ Create a Cover-Up
Killer bees often go for the face and throat, which are the most dangerous places to be stung. While you're on the run, protect your face and neck with your hands, or pull your shirt over your head.

## HOW TO SURVIVE A
## BEE STING!

### 1. De-Sting Yourself
First, get inside or to a cool place. Then, remove the stinger by scraping a fingernail over the area, like you would to get a splinter out. Do not squeeze the stinger or use tweezers unless you absolutely can't get it out any other way because squeezing it may release more venom.

### 2. Put It on Ice
Wash the area with soap and water and apply a cool compress to reduce swelling. Continue icing the spot for 20 minutes every hour. Place a washcloth or towel between the ice and your skin.

### 3. Treat It Right
With a parent's permission, take an antihistamine and gently rub a hydrocortisone cream on the sting site.

### 4. Hands Off
Make sure you don't scratch the sting. You'll just increase the pain and swelling.

### 5. Recognize Danger
If you experience severe burning and itching, swelling of the throat and/or mouth, difficulty breathing, weakness, or nausea, or if you already know you are allergic to bees, get to an emergency room immediately.

31

# PHOTO TIPS:
## Getting Started

**TAKING A PHOTO IS AS EASY AS PUSHING A BUTTON,** but taking a good photo requires patience and a general understanding of how photography works. Whether you're using a low-end smartphone or a high-end digital camera, check out National Geographic photographer Annie Griffiths' top tips and tricks for taking better pictures. With these expert pointers, you'll discover how to get the shot you want.

### TIP 1

#### Get Closer When You Photograph People

Remember, it's the face of a person that makes us love people pictures, not their shoes! So move in close and show that beautiful face!

### TIP 2

#### Take Time to Think About Your Composition

**Composition** is the way you place objects or people inside the frame. This is where you can be most creative. Remember, what is left OUT of the frame is as important as what is left in, so look carefully to see if anything in the shot will distract from your subject. If so, find a way to recompose, or rearrange, the photo so the distraction is left out.

## TIP 3
### Get Moving!

If you have taken lots of shots from one spot, try looking at the subject from another angle: above, behind, close up, far away. Professional photographers are moving all the time, always trying for a better shot.

## TIP 4
### Don't Photograph People in the Sun

Bright sun is usually the worst light for photographing people. The sun causes deep shadows and harsh light. Besides, everyone in the picture is usually squinting! It's much better to move your subjects to a shady spot where the light is softer.

## TIP 5
### Quality Not Quantity

It's far better to take fewer, more thoughtfully composed pictures, than it is to shoot like a maniac. It's not about how many pictures you take. It's about how cool those pictures are!

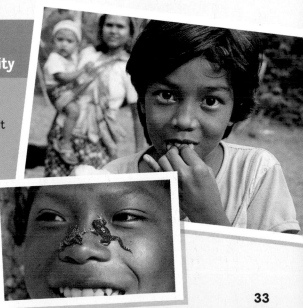

Check out this book!

# QUIZ WHIZ

**Discover just how much you know about exploration with this quiz!**

Write your answers on a piece of paper. Then check them below.

**1** Which country has the highest known density of Antillean manatees in the world?

a. Bermuda
b. Belize
c. Bahrain
d. Bolivia

**2** **True or false?** Of the 450-plus species of sharks, 26 of them are endangered.

**3** In ash boarding, people strap on a wooden board and shoot down what?

a. a ski slope
b. a sand dune
c. an active volcano
d. a waterfall

**4** Two explorers recently made history when they both completed a trek across _____.

**5** In photography, _____ is the way you place objects or people inside the frame.

a. composition
b. measurement
c. correction
d. magnification

Not **STUMPED** yet? Check out the *NATIONAL GEOGRAPHIC KIDS QUIZ WHIZ* collection for more crazy **EXPLORATION** questions!

**ANSWERS:** 1. b; 2. True; 3. c; 4. Antarctica; 5. a

## HOMEWORK HELP

# How to Write a Perfect Essay

**Need to write an essay?** Does the assignment feel as big as climbing Mount Everest? Fear not. You're up to the challenge! The following step-by-step tips will help you with this monumental task.

**1** **BRAINSTORM.** Sometimes the subject matter of your essay is assigned to you, sometimes it's not. Either way, you have to decide what you want to say. Start by brainstorming some ideas, writing down any thoughts you have about the subject. Then read over everything you've come up with and consider which idea you think is the strongest. Ask yourself what you want to write about the most. Keep in mind the goal of your essay. Can you achieve the goal of the assignment with this topic? If so, you're good to go.

**2** **WRITE A TOPIC SENTENCE.** This is the main idea of your essay, a statement of your thoughts on the subject. Again, consider the goal of your essay. Think of the topic sentence as an introduction that tells your reader what the rest of your essay will be about.

**3** **OUTLINE YOUR IDEAS.** Once you have a good topic sentence, you then need to support that main idea with more detailed information, facts, thoughts, and examples. These supporting points answer one question about your topic sentence—"Why?" This is where research and perhaps more brainstorming come in. Then organize these points in the way you think makes the most sense, probably in order of importance. Now you have an outline for your essay.

**4** **ON YOUR MARK, GET SET, WRITE!** Follow your outline, using each of your supporting points as the topic sentence of its own paragraph. Use descriptive words to get your ideas across to the reader. Go into detail, using specific information to tell your story or make your point. Stay on track, making sure that everything you include is somehow related to the main idea of your essay. Use transitions to make your writing flow.

**5** **WRAP IT UP.** Finish your essay with a conclusion that summarizes your entire essay and restates your main idea.

**6** **PROOFREAD AND REVISE.** Check for errors in spelling, capitalization, punctuation, and grammar. Look for ways to make your writing clear, understandable, and interesting. Use descriptive verbs, adjectives, or adverbs when possible. It also helps to have someone else read your work to point out things you might have missed. Then make the necessary corrections and changes in a second draft. Repeat this revision process once more to make your final draft as good as you can.

# AMAZING
## ANIMALS

A Bengal tiger, a species that is primarily found in India, leaps through the air.

# Bet You Didn't Know!

# 10 tail-wagging facts about

**1**

**A dog** can make about **100** different facial expressions.

**2**

**Dogs** have three times more **taste buds** than **cats.**

**3**

It can take up to **two months** before a newborn puppy **can wag its tail.**

**4**

**Most dogs have brown eyes.**

**5**

The **Norwegian Lundehund** has at least **six toes on each foot.**

**6**

**Bloodhounds** can follow **a scent** that is **four** days old.

# dogs

**7** Some dogs have **webbed feet.**

**8** The shortest full-grown dog stands 3.8 inches (9.65 cm) tall— as tall as a coffee mug!

**9** A greyhound can reach speeds of about **45 miles an hour** (72 km/h).

**10** Some **2,000 active-duty dogs** serve in the U.S. military.

# 5 COOL CATS

**True stories of amazing felines**

**A** black cat crossed your path? It might be your lucky day! Cat lovers know that any kitty can bring good things like comfort and companionship. That's why humans have lived with feline friends for thousands of years, and why cats are still popular pets today.

## 1 CAT DETECTIVE

**THE CAT** Snowball
**THE SPOT** Prince Edward Island, Canada
**WHY HE'S COOL** Snowball helped solve a crime—a serious one. When police found white cat hairs clinging to a jacket with blood on it., they took a hard look at Snowball and DNA from cells in his hair. Since every individual's DNA is unique, scientists were able to show the hairs were Snowball's. That way, police could connect the jacket and the crime to Snowball's owner, who turned out to be the culprit. It was the first time cat DNA was used to convict a criminal. Looks like Snowball really shed some light on this crime.

## 2 FURRY FIRE ALARM

**THE CAT** Luna
**THE SPOT** Chester, South Carolina, U.S.A.
**WHY SHE'S COOL** Around 4 a.m., Emily Chappell-Root felt her cat Luna clawing, pawing, and nipping at her feet. Thinking the cat wanted to show off a rabbit she had brought into their home, Chappell-Root went into the hallway. But instead of a rabbit, she saw flames coming from the kitchen. Thanks to Luna, she had time to get all six of her children, plus the other pets, out of the house. "Black cats have a reputation of being unlucky," Chappell-Root says. "But adopting Luna has been one of the luckiest things that happened to our family."

# 3 SURFER CAT

**THE CAT** Nānākuli
**THE SPOT** Honolulu, Hawaii, U.S.A.
**WHY HE'S COOL** Nānākuli the one-eyed cat knows exactly how to ride the waves: He lies down on his owner's surfboard with his paws hanging ten. His owners think that taking baths as a kitten helped the cat, nicknamed Kuli, get used to the water. Eventually they gave Kuli a tiny life jacket and let him float on a surfboard while gently splashing seawater on his paws. Now Kuli wears a leash as he surfs with his owners behind him on the board—as long as the water isn't too rough. *Cat*-abunga, dude!

KULI GETS READY TO CATCH SOME WAVES WITH OWNER ALEXANDRA GOMEZ-YOUNG.

WHAT A TEACHER'S PET! TOMBI "HELPS" WITH CLASSWORK.

# 4 TOP OF THE CLASS

**THE CAT** Tombi
**THE SPOT** Izmir, Turkey
**WHY HE'S COOL** One morning when the school bell rang, 33 students and one stray cat filed into Özlem Pinar Ivaşçu's third-grade classroom. "The kids started playing with him immediately," Ivaşçu says. The kitty didn't want to leave—and the students didn't want him to go. So the cat, named Tombi, was given vaccinations and a medical checkup to make sure he would be safe to have in the school. Now officially the class cat, Tombi sleeps through classes on a bookshelf and then plays with the kids during breaks. This kitty is a real class act!

# CAT IN CHARGE 5

**THE CAT** Larry
**THE SPOT** London, U.K.
**WHY HE'S COOL** Larry has his own doorman. And an official title. And a job to do. This rescue kitty is the Chief Mouser to the Cabinet Office, meaning he keeps the home of the prime minister of the United Kingdom totally mouse free. Once, Larry almost lost his position after a former prime minister spotted a rodent in his office—and Larry didn't lift a paw. The cat's still employed though. Guess Larry is too cute to be voted out of office.

LARRY GUARDS 10 DOWNING STREET, HOME TO THE UNITED KINGDOM'S PRIME MINISTER.

# Extraordinary ANIMALS

## Baby Sloths Rock Out

**San Josecito de Heredia, Costa Rica**
Huey is in school—and since he's a two-toed sloth at the Toucan Rescue Ranch, that means his classroom includes two rocking chairs connected by ropes and vines.

Rangers near Braulio Carrillo National Park found one-month-old Huey alone in the forest, too young to survive on his own. They brought him to the rescue center, where staff prepare orphaned sloths to live in the wild. That's where the rocking chairs come in—they teach the sloths how to climb in real trees. "The chairs, vines, and ropes aren't stable, so they sway like branches in the wind," says Pedro Montero, a biologist at the center.

Once he aces the rocking chairs, Huey will climb on a jungle gym made of wood and tree branches. After mastering that, he'll hang out in a larger enclosure that will get him ready for life in the wild. When Huey is about two years old, staff will put a tracking collar on him. Then his keepers will leave the enclosure door open, letting Huey "graduate" to the forest when he's ready—no cap and gown required!

You're totally rocking this.

Just call me Superpig!

## Pig Saves Owner

**Las Vegas, Nevada, U.S.A.**
Jordan Jones was playing outside when a growling dog suddenly lunged toward him. Terrified, the boy could barely react. But just in time, Jordan's potbellied pig Dasiey jumped in front of the dog, fending off the angry animal.

Jordan's mom, Kim Jones, heard Dasiey's squeals and ran outside. "Jordan was just frozen, not moving," she says. "Dasiey was backed into a corner but still standing up to the dog." At one point Dasiey's head was locked in the dog's jaws. But she refused to give up.

Jordan's dad finally untangled Dasiey and the dog. Jordan was fine, as was Dasiey after a few stitches. "If Dasiey hadn't been there, the dog would've attacked Jordan," Jones says. "Dasiey will always be our hero."

## Dog Hangs Ten

Sit? Stay? Please. I can do better than that.

**Pacifica, California, U.S.A.**
This dog knows how to catch—how to catch waves, that is! Abbie Girl the Australian kelpie took the top prize at the World Dog Surfing Championships two years in a row, by surfing the largest and longest waves. "She nailed it in every category," competition judge Charly Kayle says.

Owner Michael Uy started taking Abbie to the beach after adopting her more than a decade ago. Once the dog got used to the water, she eventually hopped on a surfboard. "Working kelpies herd sheep by running across their backs," Uy says, noting her breed's natural instinct might help Abbie balance. The dog also rides a custom board that's lighter, thinner, and soft on top so she can dig in her claws. And nobody minds the wet dog smell!

## Seal Pup Mystery

**Carnforth, England, U.K.**
The last thing anyone expected to see in the middle of a country road was a seal pup. But there was Ghost, two miles (3.2 km) away from the nearest river and about eight miles (13 km) from his ocean habitat. How did the motherless youngster get so far from home?

"You never see seals this far inland," wildlife rescuer Nick Green says. "I figured whoever reported the seal had made a mistake." Seals often hunt where rivers meet the sea, so one possibility is that Ghost swam too far upriver and got lost. But the fact that he left the river and made the difficult journey over land stunned rescuers. "They feel safest in the water," Green says. "This was extremely unusual, and we'll never know the reason."

Luckily, Ghost was healthy and unharmed, so he was released back into the Irish Sea less than two weeks later. "He swam right off," Green says. The mystery remains unsolved, but at least the story has a happy ending.

Next time I'll ask for directions.

# INCREDIBLE ANIMAL FRIENDS

Best friends fur-ever!

## DOG CALMS CHEETAH

**COLUMBUS, OHIO, U.S.A.**

For the first few weeks of his life, Emmett the cheetah cub had pneumonia and required around-the-clock care. Kind humans at the Wilds conservation center in Cumberland, Ohio, oversaw his recovery. But once Emmett was better, he moved to the Columbus Zoo and Aquarium.

Cheetahs are naturally cautious animals. But Emmett had a rough start. So the zookeepers thought it was important that he find a friend. Like people, some animals can get lonely. Having a friend—an animal to interact with, and even cuddle with—is important for development. That's where Cullen came in: This bundle of fur was destined to become Emmett's adorable puppy pal.

The pair love playing together, and they are helping the Columbus Zoo raise awareness about cheetahs to help protect this vulnerable species.

EMMETT

CULLEN

## CAT CARETAKER

Striped friends for the win.

KITTEN

EMU ▶

**TE HORO, NEW ZEALAND**

Sometimes cats have an unfriendly reputation. Not Kitten the cat. A longtime resident at Free as a Hawk Refuge, Kitten is known for being exceptionally nurturing toward other animals.

Kitten's owner thinks that because the cat was so well cared for when she was young, she might believe that all kinds of animals at the sanctuary need taking care of—including ducks, lambs, opossums, and others.

The feline has even been caring for a baby emu that hatched at the refuge. The striped pair spend most of their time snuggled together on a comfortable couch, with Kitten grooming the sleeping emu's long, feathered neck.

# FAWN BEFRIENDS RABBIT

**BUFFALO, NEW YORK, U.S.A.**

When Leondra Scherer, a wildlife rescuer and rehabilitator, got a call in late fall that a fawn needed help, she thought it was a mistake. Baby deer are typically born between May and August in upstate New York, and it would be rare for one to be born so late in the year. But sure enough, Scherer found an orphaned one-day-old fawn in desperate need of care.

Scherer named the fawn Pumpkin and brought her home to tend to her. Scherer would've loved for Pumpkin to have an animal companion she could interact with, but all of the other fawns at the farm were much older than Pumpkin and ready to be released back into the wild.

That's when Scherer adopted Chunk, a laid-back rabbit. "I wasn't sure if it would work," Scherer says. But when she introduced the two, Chunk immediately hopped over to the fawn for snuggles and a nap. "If you see a picture of Pumpkin and you can't see Chunk ... he's there, he's just burrowed beneath her!" Scherer says.

PUMPKIN

CHUNK

You make me so hoppy!

# LLAMA COMFORTS SHEEP

May the Force be with you!

YODA ▶

CLAIRE ▽

**LOS ANGELES, CALIFORNIA, U.S.A.**

Felicity the sheep was severely mistreated until she was rescued from her former living situation. At her new home, the Barbados blackbelly sheep never quite bonded with the other sheep and spent her time alone. Until she befriended a goat named Claire, that is.

Claire was rescued around the same time as Felicity; the duo were known as pals around their new home, the Farm Sanctuary. But after a while, Claire began to spend more of her time with the other goats. In Claire's absence, a gentle llama named Yoda stepped up to look after the shy sheep.

Felicity and Yoda enjoy going for walks on the hillside, grazing in the fields, and napping together. Felicity can even tuck her little body beneath Yoda's larger one when she's feeling shy or scared, which some experts say comforts the anxious sheep.

As Felicity has gotten used to her new home, she's also become less nervous around her human caregivers. She now takes treats from them, something she wouldn't have done previously. Maybe the sweet, soothing llama has more in common with a certain Jedi master than just a name!

# WHAT IS Taxonomy?

Since there are billions and billions of living things, called organisms, on the planet, people need a way of classifying them. Scientists created a system called taxonomy, which helps to classify all living things into ordered groups. By putting organisms into categories, we are better able to understand how they are the same and how they are different. There are eight levels of taxonomic classification, beginning with the broadest group, called a domain, followed by kingdom, down to the most specific group, called a species.

Biologists divide life based on evolutionary history, and they place organisms into three domains depending on their genetic structure: Archaea, Bacteria, and Eukarya. (See page 165 for "The Three Domains of Life.")

## Where do animals come in?

Animals are a part of the Eukarya domain, which means they are organisms made of cells with nuclei. More than one million species of animals have been named, including humans. Like all living things, animals can be divided into smaller groups, called phyla. Most scientists believe there are more than 30 phyla into which animals can be grouped based on certain scientific criteria, such as body type or whether or not the animal has a backbone. It can be pretty complicated, so there is another, less complicated system that groups animals into two categories: vertebrates and invertebrates.

**HEDGEHOG**

### SAMPLE CLASSIFICATION
### PHILIPPINE TARSIER

| | |
|---|---|
| Domain: | Eukarya |
| Kingdom: | Animalia |
| Phylum: | Chordata |
| Class: | Mammalia |
| Order: | Primates |
| Family: | Tarsiidae |
| Genus: | *Carlito* |
| Species: | *syrichta* |

TIP:
Here's a sentence to help you remember the classification order:
<u>D</u>id <u>K</u>ing <u>P</u>hillip <u>C</u>ome <u>O</u>ver <u>F</u>or <u>G</u>ood <u>S</u>oup?

## BY THE NUMBERS

There are 13,730 vulnerable or endangered animal species in the world. The list includes:

- **1,220 mammals**, such as the snow leopard, the polar bear, and the fishing cat.
- **1,492 birds**, including the Steller's sea eagle and the black-banded plover.
- **2,494 fish**, such as the Mekong giant catfish.
- **1,367 reptiles**, including the Round Island day gecko.
- **1,597 insects**, such as the Macedonian grayling.

- **2,157 amphibians**, such as the emperor newt.
- **And more**, including 183 arachnids, 733 crustaceans, 239 sea anemones and corals, 187 bivalves, and 2,039 snails and slugs.

**ROUND ISLAND DAY GECKO**

# Vertebrates
## Animals WITH Backbones

**Fish** are cold-blooded and live in water. They breathe with gills, lay eggs, and usually have scales.

**Amphibians** are cold-blooded. Their young live in water and breathe with gills. Adults live on land and breathe with lungs.

**Reptiles** are cold-blooded and breathe with lungs. They live both on land and in water.

**Birds** are warm-blooded and have feathers and wings. They lay eggs, breathe with lungs, and are usually able to fly. Some birds live on land, some in water, and some on both.

**Mammals** are warm-blooded and feed on their mothers' milk. They also have skin that is usually covered with hair. Mammals live both on land and in water.

BIRD: MANDARIN DUCK

AMPHIBIAN: POISON DART FROG

# Invertebrates
## Animals WITHOUT Backbones

**Sponges** are a very basic form of animal life. They live in water and do not move on their own.

**Echinoderms** have external skeletons and live in seawater.

**Mollusks** have soft bodies and can live either in or out of shells, on land or in water.

**Arthropods** are the largest group of animals. They have external skeletons, called exoskeletons, and segmented bodies with appendages. Arthropods live in water and on land.

**Worms** are soft-bodied animals with no true legs. Worms live in soil.

**Cnidaria** live in water and have mouths surrounded by tentacles.

MOLLUSK: MAGNIFICENT CHROMODORID NUDIBRANCH

SPONGE: SEA SPONGE

MOLLUSK: GARDEN SNAIL

## Cold-Blooded
### versus
## Warm-Blooded

**Cold-blooded** animals, also called ectotherms, get their heat from outside their bodies.

**Warm-blooded** animals, also called endotherms, keep their body temperature level regardless of the temperature of their environment.

# BIZARRE Insects

### Check out some of the strangest bugs on Earth!

The bright-colored head of the puss moth caterpillar warns predators to stay away. This species, one of the most toxic caterpillars in North America, can spray acid from its head when it is attacked.

**puss moth caterpillar**

**walking leaf**

This flat, green insect is a master of disguise: It's common to mistake this bug for an actual leaf, thanks to its large, feathery wings. This clever camouflage provides protection from potential predators.

**giraffe-necked weevil**

No surprise, this bug gets its name from its extra-long neck. The males have longer necks than females do, which they use to fight other males for mating rights.

**thorn bugs**

One tiny thorn bug may not be a match for a bigger predator, but when grouped together on a branch, these spiky bugs create a prickly pack no bird wants a bite of!

**spiny katydid**

This katydid is covered in sharper-than-knives spikes. If a predator attacks, this species springs into action, defending itself by jabbing an enemy with its spiny legs and arms.

## cockchafer beetle

The wild, feathery antennae on the male cockchafer may be cool to look at, but they're also helpful tools. They enable the bug to sniff for food and feel out its surrounding environment.

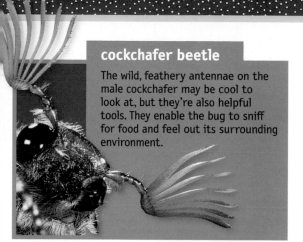

## acorn weevil

The acorn weevil's hollow nose is longer than its body, and perfect for drilling through the shells of acorns. A female will feast on the nut by sucking up its rich, fatty liquid, and then lay her eggs in the acorn.

## pink grasshopper

Though most grasshoppers are green or brown, some—like this pink nymph—are much brighter. Pink grasshoppers are rare, most likely because they are easy for predators to spot.

## man-faced stinkbug

There are more than 4,500 species of stinkbugs worldwide, including this brilliant yellow species, whose shield shaped body displays a unique pattern resembling a smiling face. Like all stink-bugs, this species secretes a foul-smelling liquid from scent glands between its legs when it feels threatened.

## rhinoceros beetle

Ounce for ounce, this insect, which gets its name from the hornlike structure on the male's head, is considered one of the world's strongest creatures. It is capable of carrying up to 850 times its own body weight.

# WELCOME to FOX Island

## How clever scientists saved these cute critters

Native Americans likely brought island foxes to the southern Channel Islands.

A MATING PAIR OF ISLAND FOXES SHOWS AFFECTION. THE SPECIES USUALLY MATES FOR LIFE.

An island fox kit emerges from its underground den and sniffs the brush on Santa Cruz Island, some 20 miles (32.2 km) off the southern coast of California, U.S.A. His brother follows, and the two foxes tumble over each other as they play fight. Decades ago, about 4,000 island foxes roamed Santa Cruz Island and two others in the Channel Islands National Park. But now, these two kits are part of the island fox's shrinking population—only about 200 of the species remain throughout the islands.

## Out of Balance

About the size of house cats, foxes were once the top predators on these islands, eating everything from insects to mice to birds to fruit. But that started changing about 80 years ago. Before, the foxes shared their island home with bald eagles, which ate mostly fish and chased away other birds of prey. In the 1940s and 1950s, though, pesticide waste began seeping into the ocean off the California coast. It poisoned sea creatures, which over time poisoned fish-eating bald eagles, too. By 1960 all the bald eagles were gone from the islands.

BALD EAGLE

The foxes, which are excellent climbers, can grab fruit from the tips of tree branches.

## Eagle Swap

Of course, the scientists still had to get the predators away from the islands. They set up bait around the island to trap the birds—but some were too smart to fall for the trick and avoided the traps. Scientists finally nabbed the last golden eagles by trapping them on the ground with a net that was shot from a helicopter. In all, the team trapped, transported, and released 32 golden eagles back to the California mainland.

Now they just had to keep the golden eagles from coming back. The plan? Raising bald eagle chicks on the islands. Scientists even fed the eagles through a door so they wouldn't bond with humans.

Today, about 60 bald eagles fly over the Channel Islands. They are helping to maintain a safe habitat for the foxes so the mammals can continue to thrive.

## Fox Island

With the golden eagle population dwindling, the wild foxes could safely breed again. Combined with pups from the captive foxes, scientists eventually increased the fox population to a healthy 250. Once the golden eagles were completely gone, scientists released the captive foxes back into their habitat.

A SCIENTIST CHECKS OUT A YOUNG BALD EAGLE, ONE OF THE FIRST HATCHED ON THE NORTHERN ISLANDS IN 50 YEARS.

Without the territorial bald eagles guarding the islands, golden eagles settled on three northern Channel Islands: San Miguel, Santa Rosa, and Santa Cruz. Unlike bald eagles, these birds hunt mammals that live on land. Island foxes became the perfect prey. Within a decade, golden eagles nearly wiped out the foxes.

## The Comeback

The foxes were in danger of disappearing from the islands forever unless someone did something—fast. Working together, scientists from the National Park Service, the Nature Conservancy, and other agencies developed an amazing plan to save the island fox.

First, scientists had to keep the critters safe from eagles. So they created special traps to help them move the foxes to safety. Biologists baited the traps with cat food and simply waited for the foxes to walk in.

Scientists kept breeding pairs in 20-by-40-foot (6-by-12-m) pens on their home islands. Inside, the foxes climbed on tree branches, rested in hammocks, and hid in wooden den boxes. Then ... success! The foxes began having kits the following year. These animals were starting their comeback.

AN ISLAND FOX KIT STAYS CLOSE TO ITS DEN. KIT DENS ARE OFTEN IN ROCKS, WOOD PILES, BRUSH, OR BURROWS.

The population on the three islands today is the same if not greater than it was before the golden eagles came to the islands. The curious, playful critters often greet human visitors when they arrive—and can get mischievous.

"They'll try to pull the zipper down on my tent and run off with my shoes and socks," says Chuck Graham, a wildlife photographer and kayak guide. "They're a part of the Channel Islands. They deserve to be here."

PREPARE TO BE
AMAZED BY THIS
**ACROBAT**
OF THE FOREST ...

# THE INCREDIBLE RED PANDA

A red panda totters along the branch of an evergreen tree, placing one paw in front of the other like a gymnast on a balance beam. But then ... whoops! The panda loses its footing. A fall from this height—about 100 feet (30 m)—could be deadly. But the panda quickly grips the branch with all four paws and some seriously sharp claws, steadies itself, and keeps moving.

Red pandas spend about 90 percent of their time in the trees, says Mariel Lally, a red panda keeper at the Smithsonian's National Zoo in Washington, D.C., U.S.A. In fact, red pandas have adapted so well to life in the trees that they're famous for their incredible acrobatic skills. Check out three ways that red pandas land a perfect score with their amazing aerial act.

ASIA

Bay of Bengal

South China Sea

INDIAN OCEAN

Where red pandas live

## BUILT-IN BALANCE

A tightrope walker is all about balance. But red pandas can't exactly extend their arms like an acrobat. Instead they hold their tails straight behind them. "If they start to swing in one direction, they can move their tails the opposite way," Lally says. "It's sort of like a tightrope walker's pole."

## UNDER FUR COVER

What's the best way to avoid a hungry snow leopard? Never let it see you in the first place! The small red panda's fiery coat sticks out at the zoo, but in the fir trees of the Himalayan mountains, the fur hides the panda in the reddish moss and white lichen (a plantlike organism) that often hang on the trees. Red pandas are so hard to spot that even scientists have trouble locating these creatures.

## FAKE THUMB

A trapeze artist needs her thumbs to wrap her whole hand around the trapeze as she swings. Otherwise she might fly off! Same idea with red pandas. They have a special thumb-like wrist bone that gives them an extra grip when climbing down trees headfirst.

## RED PANDA ON THE RUN

**Smithsonian's National Zoo, Washington, D.C.**

Ashley Wagner was out with her family when she spotted an animal crossing the street. At first Wagner's mom thought they'd seen a raccoon, but as soon as the creature turned its face toward them, Wagner knew it was a red panda. "He seemed very confident," she says.

Rusty the runaway red panda had arrived at the zoo just a few weeks before. As he scampered under a fence, Wagner snapped photos, shared them on social media, and called the zoo. Soon a team came to the rescue, eventually nabbing him from a tree.

Today, Rusty has retired from his life on the run and settled down. The father of three red panda cubs, he lives at the Smithsonian Conservation Biology Institute.

## SAVING THE RED PANDA

With their kitten-like faces, fluffy fur, and waddling walk, red pandas are adorable. But these endangered animals are also ideal targets for the illegal pet trade.

Luckily, people are trying to help them. There's the Red Panda Network, which hires local people to keep watch over the red pandas in Nepal, replant bamboo, and help paying tourists observe them without disturbing the creatures. Other organizations track poachers by using DNA samples from red pandas rescued from the black market to learn where the animals are being taken from.

You can help by asking your parents and older siblings not to "like" photos and videos of red pandas on social media unless you know that the group or person posting them is trustworthy (like a wildlife photographer or a conservation group).

# HOW TO SPEAK GORILLA

A YOUNG MOUNTAIN GORILLA IN THE DEMOCRATIC REPUBLIC OF THE CONGO REACHES FOR A CAMERA.

## Discover five surprising ways these apes communicate

Keepers entering the gorilla enclosure at the Columbus Zoo and Aquarium in Ohio, U.S.A., often hear a noise that sounds like a babbling human. But it's just Mac, a western lowland gorilla. The ape greets his caregivers by making long, low grumbling sounds, gorilla-speak for "Hi, there!" When keepers exit the area in the evening, he makes a similar sound as if to say "Good night."

Mac isn't just making noise. Gorillas like him have things to say. And if you pick up a little gorilla language, you just might understand them.

"Apes are excellent communicators," Columbus Zoo curator Audra Meinelt says. And sound isn't the only way gorillas "talk." They use movements and even body odor to get their point across. It's no wonder experts think gorillas are among the most advanced animal communicators after humans. Check out these five amazing stories.

## ① "What's in it for me?"

Nia, a western lowland gorilla, was excited when she discovered a new "toy"—a plastic cup—had been added to her habitat at the Columbus Zoo. When zookeepers came to replace the cup with another toy, Nia wouldn't give it up. So Nia's keepers offered her a treat as a reward. Nia gave up the cup—and realized that things she finds in her habitat can be valuable. The next time Nia found a cup in her space, the gorilla broke it into several pieces and only gave the keepers one piece at a time ... in exchange for a treat after every piece!

Other gorillas at the zoo caught on to Nia's trick. "They'll hold out an item they think we might want, but not all the way," zookeeper Heather Carpenter says. "If we try to get it, they'll pull it back like, 'Not so fast!' Their actions are telling us that they'll give us what we want—but only when we offer something *they* want."

A WESTERN LOWLAND GORILLA GOOFS OFF IN ITS ZOO ENCLOSURE.

## 3 "Follow me."

Kighoma the eastern lowland gorilla is the leader of his troop in the Democratic Republic of the Congo, a country in Africa. It's easy to spot the gorilla in charge, according to Sonya Kahlenberg of the Gorilla Rehabilitation and Conservation Education Center. Adult male leaders are identified by the silver fur on their backs. (They're called, well, silverbacks.) And they're often belching!

"It sounds like *na-oom*, kind of like a throat clearing. It means, 'I'm over here,'" Kahlenberg says. "And whenever Kighoma is ready to move, he'll make that grumbling sound and the other gorillas know to follow him."

## 2 "Help!"

Anthropologist Kelly Stewart wanted to see how the wild mountain gorillas she was observing would react to her new gorilla T-shirt. But when she opened her jacket to reveal the shirt to a young female, Simba, the gorilla screamed—a sound that means "I'm scared!" in young gorillas. And *that* told the older troop members that Simba needed help. The group's leader, Uncle Bert, barreled toward Stewart with a deep roar. Stewart quickly covered her shirt and stepped away from Simba, who stopped screaming. Uncle Bert backed off once Simba was quiet—the little gorilla was OK now that the unfamiliar "gorilla" was gone. "I never wore that T-shirt again!" Stewart says.

A SILVERBACK MOUNTAIN GORILLA IN RWANDA LEADS HIS TROOP.

A GORILLA GETS A WHIFF OF SOMETHING GROSS.

## 4 "I'm not happy."

When zookeepers at the Dallas Zoo in Texas, U.S.A., smell a gym-sock-like odor, they know it's time to do an extra check on the gorillas. The smell comes from the male apes' armpits, and it may mean that a squirrel has entered their exhibit, or that the males aren't getting along. Either way, the stink signifies that something's not quite right.

## 5 "You've got this!"

Fasha the wild mountain gorilla had gotten her foot caught in a poacher's trap in the forests of Rwanda, Africa. She escaped, but couldn't keep up with her troop. But Icyororo the gorilla wasn't leaving her friend behind. Arms linked, they made their way through the forest. Every few minutes Icyororo turned and patted Fasha as if to say, "We're almost there."

When the pals crossed a river together, Icyororo gave Fasha a hug, demonstrating a gorilla's amazing ability to encourage their loved ones.

You can do this!

# Surprise Party!

## Red-eyed tree frogs astonish others with their weird behavior.

L ooking for a snack, a 30-inch (76-cm)-long viper slithers down a tree in a steamy rainforest in Central America. Suddenly it sees a tasty-looking, 3-inch (7.6-cm)-long red-eyed tree frog resting on a nearby leaf. The reptile lunges forward and snatches up the tiny croaker in its fanged mouth. But the snake's in for a not-so-pleasant surprise—the frog tastes terrible! The snake immediately spits out the amphibian. Landing unharmed on the forest floor, the frog blinks its big red eyes, then hops off to safety.

Red-eyed tree frogs have some features and behaviors that surprise other animals in their rainforest home, as well as the experts who study them. Discover how these jaw-dropping jumpers turn their habitat into one big surprise party.

The red-eyed tree frog oozes stinky, slightly toxic slime through its skin when a predator is near. It also doesn't taste very good!

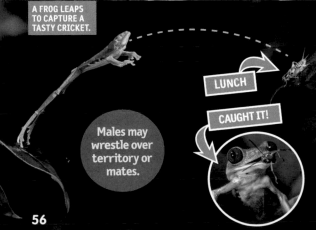

A FROG LEAPS TO CAPTURE A TASTY CRICKET.

LUNCH

CAUGHT IT!

Males may wrestle over territory or mates.

## Ambush and Eat

A red-eyed tree frog might jump through the air to get closer to an insect it wants to eat. This animal also uses the element of surprise. Known as an ambush predator, the amphibian sometimes hides among the leaves in its rainforest home. The frog waits patiently until a tasty-looking moth or cricket comes within striking distance. Then it fires out its long, sticky tongue to capture the insect and pull the meal into its mouth. Now *that's* some fast food.

## Eye Spy

These nocturnal animals may spend the day lazing on plants, but they can still spy on their habitat. Thanks to a see-through third eyelid that closes over their eyeballs when resting, the amphibian can stay on the lookout for trouble while it reenergizes. If a hunter does approach, the frog can leap away, startling its pursuer. The eyelid's stripes also may help hide the frog's bright red eyes from would-be predators.

## Stick to It

Slick surfaces aren't a problem for this frog. It can easily clamber across wet leaves. Instead of hopping, the animal takes careful steps like a pro rock climber. It also has rounded toe pads that stick to surfaces like suction cups, and its feet produce gluey mucus to help it grip slippery surfaces. It can even cling to the undersides of leaves to hide from predators—Spider-Man-style. That's a sticky surprise.

UNDERSIDE OF FOOT

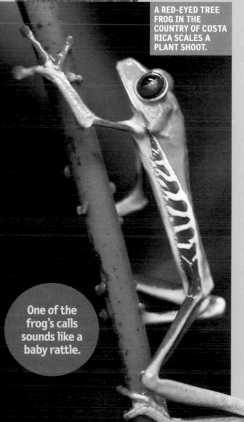

A RED-EYED TREE FROG IN THE COUNTRY OF COSTA RICA SCALES A PLANT SHOOT.

One of the frog's calls sounds like a baby rattle.

## Shake It Off

When researchers visited the country of Panama to study these frogs, they saw something that gave them a jolt: a male frog shaking the shoot of a plant with his hind legs, similar to a person strumming a guitar string! They realized that males do this when other males come too close to their turf. The shaking creates vibrations, which intruders interpret as a signal to back off.

Why not just croak loudly to ward off intruders? "They don't want to reveal their location to the entire pond, including enemies such as frog-eating bats," biologist Michael Caldwell says. That'd shake things up *way* too much.

NORTH AMERICA
ATLANTIC OCEAN
PACIFIC OCEAN
SOUTH AMERICA

Gulf of Mexico

Caribbean Sea

MEXICO

BELIZE
HONDURAS

GUATEMALA

NICARAGUA

EL SALVADOR

COSTA RICA

PANAMA

PACIFIC OCEAN

COLOMBIA

Where red-eyed tree frogs live

# MIXED-UP MARSUPIALS?

## FIND OUT WHY QUOKKAS ACT LIKE GIRAFFES, KOALAS, AND BATS.

When explorers in the late 1600s first spotted this fuzzy, friendly-looking animal in Australia, they figured they'd stumbled on a house-cat-size rat. Not even close. Quokkas might be related to kangaroos and wallabies, but they're way weirder. This marsupial has traits more often associated with other animals—and that makes it one wacky critter.

## THEY REACH FOR LEAVES LIKE KOALAS

Ground-dwelling quokkas sometimes climb five feet (1.5 m) up a tree trunk to reach a tasty-looking leaf or berry. That might not *sound* impressive, but it's something its closest relatives—kangaroos and wallabies—can't do. Tree-loving koalas have strong, large paws made for gripping branches all day. But the quokka can hold on only for a few minutes. Just enough time to swipe a snack!

## THEY HOP LIKE RABBITS

If you spot a brown fuzz ball bouncing through the brush, it's not a rabbit—it's a leaping quokka! Although they usually crawl on all fours, quokkas also use their strong back legs to jump. These animals also create passageways in the bushes and grass as they move through the brush, similar to the underground tunnels bunnies create. Furry, cute, *and* hoppy? Yes, please!

## THEY CATCH Z'S LIKE BATS

OK, quokkas don't sleep while hanging from a cave or tree, but they do sometimes nap with their heads upside down. Quokkas often sleep in a sitting position with their head resting on their feet. "It's very cute," says Cassyanna Gray, a conservation officer on Australia's Rottnest Island, one place quokkas live. Also, like most bats, quokkas are mostly nocturnal, snoozing when the hot sun is out.

## THEY CHEW LIKE GIRAFFES

Quokkas eat their food in a way that is similar to giraffes. Both animals use their large, flat molars to grind tough treats like leaves to release moisture and nutrients. The difference? Giraffes later regurgitate the food (meaning they basically throw it back up into their mouths—yuck!) and chew it some more. When a quokka swallows food, the meal enters its first stomach (yep, quokkas have two tummies!), where the food is broken down more before entering the second stomach.

## SAY "LEAVES"!

Quokkas have smiley faces and are sometimes friendly around people, so tourists to Australia's Rottnest Island often get too close. The extra attention could put quokkas in danger—or it might help the species survive.

Authorities on Rottnest Island protect the critters with rules against touching or feeding the quokkas. Human food can make them sick, plus giving them snacks (and even water) can make the quokkas too dependent on people. But by following the rules and keeping a safe distance, island tourists help give authorities more power to support the quokka's habitat. For instance, conservationists can use the money generated from tourism to protect the island and monitor the quokka population.

So if you want to protect the quokkas *and* get an epic picture, just use a selfie stick!

Rottnest Island, one of the places quokkas live, got its name after explorers thought quokkas were rats. (Get it? *Rat* nest? Rottnest?)

# SCALY SUPERHEROES

## Discover the hidden powers of the pangolin.

Clark Kent and Peter Parker—the alter egos of Superman and Spider-Man—don't really stand out. And neither do pangolins in the tropical forests or grasslands of Africa and Asia where they live. But like your favorite movie heroes, this animal has a few hidden superpowers. Check them out here.

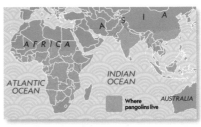

## SPIDER-MAN STICKINESS!

SPIDER-MAN

Spider-Man shoots out sticky strands of webbing from his wrists to swing from one sky-scraper to another. When a pangolin is hungry, it shoots out its sticky tongue, which extends up to 16 inches (41 cm) past its mouth. Coated in gluey saliva, the licker scoops up ants and termites, the pangolin's favorite snacks. In all, the mammal can eat some 70 million insects a year. Makes sense that this superhero-like creature would have a super appetite.

## WOLVERINE CLAWS!

WOLVERINE

During fights with villains, Wolverine defends himself with long, sharp claws that pop out of his knuckles. Pangolins have claws on each of their front feet used to rip up ant and termite nests as they search for dinner. Claws also help them clutch on to branches or dig burrows for sleeping. Whether you're a superhero or a pangolin, claws really come in handy.

Eight species of pangolins exist in all.

The animal emits a stinky odor when threatened.

## IRON MAN ARMOR!

CLOSE-UP OF SCALES

IRON MAN

Iron Man sports a high-tech suit of armor that shields the superhero from weapons hurled by enemies. Pangolins wear armor, too. Their "suits" consist of rows of overlapping scales that resemble a pine cone. Made out of keratin—the same substance in your fingernails—the pangolin's armor is so tough that predators such as lions can't bite through it. It's too bad that this armor doesn't come with built-in jets!

## ANT-MAN MOVES!

ANT-MAN

When he senses trouble, Ant-Man shrinks to the size of, well, an ant. Pangolins, which can be almost six feet (1.8 m) long from head to tail tip, have their own way of shrinking. If the mammal notices a nearby predator, it'll curl into a small ball less than half its normal size and shield its stomach and face. Unable to find a vulnerable part of the pangolin to strike, many enemies give up. Tiny can be tough.

## TONGUE TIME

Up to 28 inches (71 cm) in all, a pangolin's tongue can be almost as long as its body (minus the tail)! How does it fit inside the mammal? The tongue runs from its mouth down its sternum (or breastbone). The back end curves around organs in the lower abdomen, arching toward the backbone. At rest, the tongue's front end is coiled inside the pangolin's mouth. The animal flicks out its licker to snag grub.

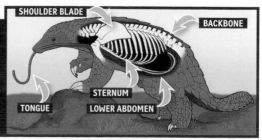

SHOULDER BLADE

BACKBONE

TONGUE

STERNUM

LOWER ABDOMEN

# THE SECRET LIVES OF

Orcas don't often dive very deep—their food is usually near the surface, so they are as well.

You'd need more than 650 cans of tuna to keep an orca full!

# Orcas

## "FRIENDING" OTHER DOLPHINS. "LIKING" FUN ACTIVITIES. "CHATTING." ORCAS MIGHT HAVE THE BEST SOCIAL NETWORK EVER.

A bottlenose dolphin flips its tail as it swims with its dolphin friends. A baby chimpanzee watches closely as its mom shows it how to crack a nut. A male wolf howls to gather the pack for a hunt.

Playing, teaching, and working together are known as "social skills." Humans, of course, are social animals. So are bottlenose dolphins, chimps, and wolves. And according to scientists, it's time to move one animal higher up the list: orcas!

Orcas are dolphins, so scientists already know about some of their social behaviors. "We knew orcas travel in pods," says biologist Janice Waite of the National Oceanic and Atmospheric Administration (NOAA), in the United States. But new research shows that the school-bus-size swimmers have more complex social behaviors than previously understood.

Could orcas be among the most social animals of all? Here are five stories to help you decide.

### Orcas "adopt" orphans.

Springer watched curiously as a boat approached her. The young orca had been orphaned as a calf, so no one had taught her that boat propellers could injure her. Wanting to take a closer look, Springer swam closer until ... *whoosh!* An older female orca called Nodales forcefully shoved her away from danger.

"Nodales took Springer under her wing, even though they weren't related," says Paul Spong, co-director of OrcaLab, a research station in Canada. "It didn't take long for the young orca to understand she should keep away from boats." Today, Springer is a mother herself—and she stays out of water traffic.

## Orcas "babysit" other orcas.

One day a female named Sharky moved close to a group of newborn orcas and their mothers. Sharky swam near a calf, then led it away to play with her—giving the moms a break. Waite observed Sharky behave like that with other calves as well. "She's not the only young female we've seen 'babysit' other orcas," Waite says. "We think they do it as practice for when they have calves of their own."

ORCAS APPROACH A WEDDELL SEAL, HOPING TO MAKE IT THEIR MEAL.

## Orcas are team players.

A Weddell seal lies on a sheet of floating ice in Antarctica. Suddenly five orcas begin nudging the ice. Then, a large female orca begins to make whistling and clicking noises. It's like a signal: The other orcas line up, swim toward the ice, and create a wave that knocks the seal into the water. Oddly, the orcas let the seal escape.

Some experts believe that the female orca was teaching hunting and teamwork to her calves. And as with any new skill, practice makes perfect!

## Orcas put family first.

Researchers rarely spotted Plumper and Kaikash apart. But when older bro Plumper got sick, the researchers worried that he wouldn't be able to keep up with his younger sibling. But the brothers were inseparable. Kaikash would swim a short distance, then wait for Plumper to catch up. "This went on for hours," Spong says. "Kaikash didn't seem to mind. Like human brothers, these two had each other's backs."

Researchers now know that orca families spend most of their days together. Although adults—especially males—sometimes split from the group to hunt, they stay close enough to hear family members. Says Waite: "They're probably as close with their families as we are with ours."

## Orcas play together.

Orcas are known for breaching—or leaping out of the water—to show their playful side. "They get most excited when they meet up in groups," says biologist Candice Emmons of NOAA. She's seen orcas from different pods brush against each other to say hello. She's also watched orcas smacking their tails against the water (called lobbing) to show excitement. But Emmons's favorite thing to observe is "pec slapping."

"That's when they touch each other with their pectoral fins, which are like their arms," Emmons says. Sort of like orca high fives!

An orca's diet consists of whales, sea lions, penguins, seals, walruses, and a variety of fish and squid. *Chomp!*

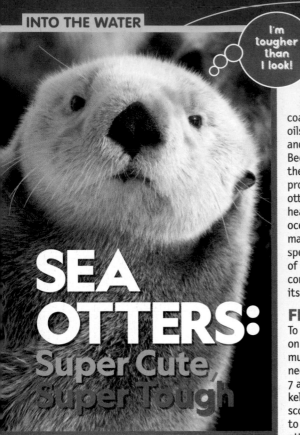

I'm tougher than I look!

# SEA OTTERS:
## Super Cute, Super Tough

## ULTIMATE FUR COAT

A sea otter wears a luxurious fur coat made up of about 800 million hairs. A shield from the sea, the coat is covered in natural oils that keep the skin and underfur dry. Because its fur is the only thing protecting a sea otter from the heat-stealing ocean water, the marine mammal spends nearly half of its day cleaning, combing, and fluffing its coat.

Only a female and her pups will hunt in groups or share food.

## FEEDING FRENZY

To stay warm, an otter also relies on a super-revved metabolism. It must eat three times more calories than a kid needs in order to survive. A daily menu might be 7 abalone, 37 cancer crabs, 50 sea urchins, or 157 kelp crabs—that's about equal in calories to 42 scoops of chocolate ice cream! Otters also have to work for their food: To eat 150 kelp crabs, the otter needs to make at least 150 dives!

S ea otters may look like cute, gentle balls of fur, but they're actually rugged, resilient predators that battle prey, the environment, and other otters every day. Here's why they deserve a reputation as the tough guys of the ocean.

## SEA SURVIVOR

A sea otter is about the same size as an 11-year-old kid—but a whole lot tougher. A human would be lucky to last 20 minutes in an otter's home just beyond the breaking waves before hypothermia— a drop in body temperature—set in and their body shut down. Unlike whales and walruses, otters don't have blubber (a thick layer of fat) to keep them warm. So how do they survive?

Sea otters are related to skunks, weasels, badgers, and river otters.

## SUPER STRENGTH

Sea otters are like superheroes when it comes to strength. A hard clam or mussel shell is no match for an otter's extremely powerful jaws and strong teeth. A person would have to use a special sharp tool to pry a firmly anchored abalone from its rock. An otter has only its paws and an occasional rock. The otter also uses its strong paws to snatch and overpower large crabs while avoiding their dangerous claws.

Super swimmers, super eaters, super divers— sea otters definitely deserve their rep as supertough marine mammals.

# Incredible Powers of the OCTOPUS!

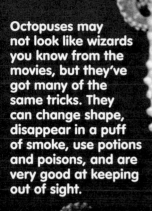

Octopuses may not look like wizards you know from the movies, but they've got many of the same tricks. They can change shape, disappear in a puff of smoke, use potions and poisons, and are very good at keeping out of sight.

## POTIONS AND POISONS

Blue-ringed octopuses make one of the deadliest poisons in the world. They have enough poison in their saliva to kill a human, though these mollusks mostly use their venom to paralyze prey or to defend themselves from enemies.

## TRICK ARMS

When faced with danger, some octopuses will break off an arm and scoot away. The arm keeps wriggling for hours, sometimes crawling all over an attacker and distracting it. The octopus grows a new arm out of the stump.

## DISAPPEARING ACT

To confuse attackers, an octopus will squirt a concentrated ink out of its backside that forms a smokelike cloud. This allows enough time for the octopus to escape.

THE OCTOPUS IS THE TALLER LUMP ON THE RIGHT. THAT'S BRAIN CORAL ON THE LEFT.

## MAGICAL MOVES

Octopuses can squeeze through tiny holes as if they were moving from room to room through keyholes. Some can even swim through the sand, sticking an eye up like a periscope to see if the coast is clear.

# OCEAN SUPERSTARS

The fascinating lives of 6 sea turtle species

Think all sea turtles are the same? Think again! Each of these species stands out in its own way.

**1  GREEN SEA TURTLE: THE NEAT FREAK**

In Hawaii, U.S.A., green sea turtles choose a "cleaning station"—a location where groups of cleaner fish groom the turtles by eating ocean gunk, like algae and parasites, off their skin and shells. In Australia, the turtles rub against a favorite sponge or rock to scrub themselves. Neat!

**2  KEMP'S RIDLEY: THE LITTLE ONE**

They may be the smallest sea turtles (babies shown here), but they're not so tiny: Adults weigh as much as many 10-year-old kids, and their shell is about the size of a car tire. They're speedy, too: It takes them less than an hour to dig a nest, then lay and bury their eggs.

### 3  OLIVE RIDLEY: THE ULTRA-MOM

Every year, hundreds of thousands of female olive ridley sea turtles take over beaches to lay their eggs and then bury them before disappearing back into the sea. Call it safety in numbers: With thousands of turtles swarming the shoreline, they're sure to overwhelm any predator.

### 4  LEATHERBACK: THE MEGA-TURTLE

These giants among reptiles have shells about as big as a door and weigh as much as six professional football players! Their size doesn't slow them down, though. A leatherback can swim as fast as a bottlenose dolphin.

### 5  HAWKSBILL: THE HEARTY EATER

What's the hawksbill's favorite snack? Sponges! These turtles gobble about 1,200 pounds (544 kg) of sponges a year. The turtles can safely eat this sea life, which is toxic to other animals. That means there are plenty of sponges to snack on!

### 6  LOGGERHEAD: THE TOUGH GUY

The loggerhead sea turtle's powerful jaws can easily crack open the shells of lobsters, conchs, and snails to get at the meat inside. Some loggerheads swim a third of the way around the world to find food.

An Amur leopard can leap up to 10 feet (3 m) in the air.

# THE WORLD'S RAREST LEOPARD

## THESE BIG CATS GET A NEW CHANCE AT SURVIVAL.

SOFT, DENSE FUR KEEPS AMUR LEOPARDS WARM IN THE BITTER COLD.

**S**talking down the snowy hillside, the Amur leopard watches its prey through the trees. In the clearing below, a sika deer munches on tree bark. The leopard crouches, then suddenly springs forward, tackling the deer from 10 feet (3 m) away. With a deadly combination of speed, strength, and stealth, the Amur leopard seems like it has everything it needs for survival. But after decades of habitat loss and poaching, these endangered cats almost went extinct. Thanks in part to a newly established national park, Amur leopards are coming back from the brink.

### Disappearing Act

Amur leopards live along the Russian–Chinese border, where they've adapted to their chilly climate with bushier fur and longer legs to trudge through the deep snow. But as hearty as they are, the leopards couldn't fight off the humans moving into their habitat or the poachers who killed them to sell their coats. At one point, there were only about 30 left in the world. They were going extinct.

### Saving the Leopards

To protect these cats, scientists had to convince the government that this was something worth doing. The first step was to show where the leopards spent their time—and what land needed protection most. Using camera traps and devices that automatically take photos and videos of passing animals, experts were

AMUR LEOPARDS OFTEN DRAG THEIR PREY UP INTO A TREE BEFORE EATING.

Armed with this information, scientists approached the Russian government about coming up with a plan to protect the big cats. After proving how few leopards were left in the wild and what was needed to save them, scientists persuaded officials to take action to save the world's most endangered big cat from extinction.

able to get more information about the Amur leopards in the area. And, because a leopard's spots—called rosettes—are as unique as human fingerprints, scientists could identify individual leopards to figure out where each leopard spent most of its time.

## New Territory

The camera trap footage also revealed that their home ranges were up to twice the distance of leopards in other parts of the world—and that they traveled very far to find food. That meant larger pieces of land needed to be protected for both the leopard and its prey. Better-protected prey meant more food for the leopards and their cubs.

AMUR LEOPARDS GIVE BIRTH TO ONE TO FOUR CUBS AT A TIME.

Amur leopards are named after the Amur River, a body of water that runs along the border of Russia and China.

The result: Land of the Leopard National Park. The 647,400-acre (261,994-ha) refuge—about two and a half times bigger than where the leopards had been living—added newly protected areas to pre-existing reserves. New laws on hunting animals such as sika deer meant the big cats wouldn't run out of food. Millions of dollars were spent on anti-poaching patrols and other efforts, including a "Leopard Tunnel" built on a stretch of busy highway so that Amur leopards and Amur tigers didn't have to dodge speeding cars.

## Bouncing Back

After Land of the Leopard National Park was created in 2012, the Amur leopard population grew to 84 by 2015. Since then, more new cubs have been spotted. Throughout the forest, young leopards are now crouching nearby as their mom teaches them how to hunt. They're learning from her how to survive. And one day, some of those cubs will have babies of their own to teach.

AN AMUR LEOPARD'S LARGE PAWS WORK LIKE SNOWSHOES, LETTING THE CAT WALK ON SNOW WITHOUT SINKING.

**69**

# RISE
## OF THE
# TIGER

An adult male tiger can weigh the same as eight 10-year-old kids.

Tigers live in both cold and hot climates.

## Scientists find good news with the help of secret snaps.

Recently, scientists have worked to get a current global estimate of how many wild tigers exist. As part of the effort, experts in countries throughout the tiger's range, including Russia, Bangladesh, Bhutan, India, and Nepal, trekked to forests and grasslands where the cats live to set up camera traps—motion-sensing or remote-controlled cameras that snap wildlife pics. They hoped the photos would give clues about the number of tigers in each nation.

### Cats on Camera

To track down tigers, researchers focused on water holes and areas with boar and other tiger prey. There, they fixed multiple camera traps to trees to catch the cats from different angles. The cameras' treelike disguise made them less likely to be destroyed by curious animals. After setting up the traps, the researchers journeyed home.

### Take a Number

The cameras snapped pictures of any animal that walked in front of them, using night vision to get good photos in the dark, when tigers are most active. The researchers returned to collect the devices a few months later and uploaded their pictures to computers, which analyzed each tiger's coat pattern and recognized when a certain tiger appeared more than once. The computers then counted how many individuals appeared overall in the photos.

Using this data and other information, teams were able to estimate how many tigers live in the countries studied. The final tally surprised them all.

### Tiger Time

Researchers estimated that about 4,000 wild tigers exist on the planet. That's up from as few as 3,200, the estimated population in 2010. Experts say this bump may be partly due to conservation efforts made by several of the countries where tigers live, such as laws to protect the cats' habitats.

Still, experts emphasize that the rise in numbers doesn't mean that tigers are out of danger. In fact, it's possible that better technology may have allowed researchers to photograph more tigers than before, making it seem as if the population is increasing. Still, analyzing these "selfies" is certainly a step in the right direction for the future of wild tigers.

A TIGER CUB INVESTIGATES A CAMERA THAT'S MOUNTED ON WHEELS AND CONTROLLED REMOTELY BY A RESEARCHER.

# MARGAYS: OUT ON A LIMB

**M**eet the margays! These small wild cats, about the size of a house cat, are native to rainforests of Central and South America. Because of their secretive lifestyle—they spend a lot of their lives in trees, even hunting among the branches—catching a glimpse of these acrobatic cats in their natural habitat is no easy task.

## BUILT TO CLIMB

With a body uniquely adapted to life in the treetops, a margay moves through the canopy like a feline gymnast. Unlike most wild cats, it can go down a tree headfirst. The margay's ankles can rotate all the way around to face backward, which allows the cat to quickly change direction while climbing.

A margay's feet are wide and soft, with flexible toes that allow it to grab branches. Its 17-inch (43-cm)-long tail provides balance as it moves around in the treetops.

## TRACKING MARGAYS

Because margays can stay hidden in the trees, experts use radio collars to track these cats and shed some light on their daily activities. As a result, the margay's characteristics and habits aren't a complete secret. Experts have observed that these solitary animals are active mostly at night (their huge eyes help them see in the dark), hunting for birds, snakes, rodents, and even small monkeys. It takes skillful climbing to accomplish that hunting feat.

## SAVING MARGAY HABITAT

Though the overall margay population isn't in immediate danger, the cats are vulnerable. Margays need tropical forests to survive. Habitat destruction, especially clearing forests for farms and ranches, is their biggest threat. Today, scientists are working hard to save the habitat of these acrobats of the rainforest.

**Climbing skills make margays the acrobats of the rainforest.**

CLIMBING HEADFIRST DOWN A TREE IS A RARE ABILITY MARGAYS HAVE MASTERED.

# Prehistoric TIMELINE

**HUMANS HAVE WALKED** on Earth for some 200,000 years, a mere blip in the planet's 4.5-billion-year history. A lot has happened during that time. Earth formed, and oxygen levels rose in the millions of years of the Precambrian time. The productive Paleozoic era gave rise to hard-shelled organisms, vertebrates, amphibians, and reptiles.

Dinosaurs ruled Earth in the mighty Mesozoic. And 65 million years after dinosaurs became extinct, modern humans emerged in the Cenozoic era. From the first tiny mollusks to the dinosaur giants of the Jurassic and beyond, Earth has seen a lot of transformation.

## THE PRECAMBRIAN TIME

### 4.5 billion to 541 million years ago

- Earth (and other planets) formed from gas and dust left over from a giant cloud that collapsed to form the sun. The giant cloud's collapse was triggered when nearby stars exploded.
- Low levels of oxygen made Earth a suffocating place.
- Early life-forms appeared.

## THE PALEOZOIC ERA

### 541 million to 252 million years ago

- The first insects and other animals appeared on land.
- 450 million years ago (mya), the ancestors of sharks began to swim in the oceans.
- 430 mya, plants began to take root on land.
- More than 360 mya, amphibians emerged from the water.
- Slowly, the major landmasses began to come together, creating Pangaea, a single supercontinent.
- By 300 mya, reptiles had begun to dominate the land.

## What Killed the Dinosaurs?

It's a mystery that's boggled the minds of scientists for centuries: What happened to the dinosaurs? While various theories have bounced around, a recent study confirms that the most likely culprit is an asteroid or comet that created a giant crater. Researchers say that the impact set off a series of natural disasters like tsunamis, earthquakes, and temperature swings that plagued the dinosaurs' ecosystem and disrupted their food chain. This, paired with intense volcanic eruptions that caused drastic climate changes, is thought to be why half of the world's species—including the dinosaurs—died in a mass extinction.

# DINO TIMES

## THE MESOZOIC ERA

**252 million to 66 million years ago**

The Mesozoic era, or the age of the reptiles, consisted of three consecutive time periods (shown below). This is when the first dinosaurs began to appear. They would reign supreme for more than 150 million years.

## TRIASSIC PERIOD

**252 million to 201 million years ago**

- Appearance of the first mammals. They were rodent-size.
- The first dinosaur appeared.
- Ferns were the dominant plants on land.
- The giant supercontinent of Pangaea began breaking up toward the end of the Triassic.

## JURASSIC PERIOD

**201 million to 145 million years ago**

- Giant dinosaurs dominated the land.
- Pangaea continued its breakup, and oceans formed in the spaces between the drifting landmasses, allowing sea life, including sharks and marine crocodiles, to thrive.
- Conifer trees spread across the land.

## CRETACEOUS PERIOD

**145 million to 66 million years ago**

- The modern continents developed.
- The largest dinosaurs developed.
- Flowering plants spread across the landscape.
- Mammals flourished, and giant pterosaurs ruled the skies over small birds.
- Temperatures grew more extreme. Dinosaurs lived in deserts, swamps, and forests from the Antarctic to the Arctic.

## THE CENOZOIC ERA—TERTIARY PERIOD

**66 million to 2.6 million years ago**

- Following the dinosaur extinction, mammals rose as the dominant species.
- Birds continued to flourish.
- Volcanic activity was widespread.
- Temperatures began to cool, eventually ending in an ice age.
- The period ended with land bridges forming, which allowed plants and animals to spread to new areas.

# DINO Classification

**Classifying dinosaurs and all other living things** can be a complicated matter, so scientists have devised a system to help with the process. Dinosaurs are put into groups based on a very large range of characteristics.

Scientists put dinosaurs into two major groups: the bird-hipped ornithischians and the lizard-hipped saurischians.

## Ornithischian

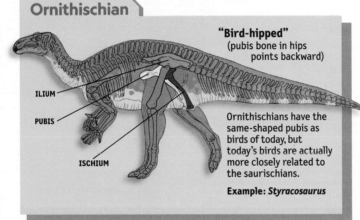

ILIUM

PUBIS

ISCHIUM

**"Bird-hipped"**
(pubis bone in hips points backward)

Ornithischians have the same-shaped pubis as birds of today, but today's birds are actually more closely related to the saurischians.

**Example: *Styracosaurus***

## Saurischian

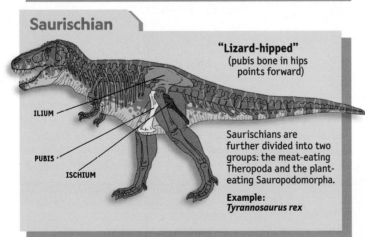

ILIUM

PUBIS

ISCHIUM

**"Lizard-hipped"**
(pubis bone in hips points forward)

Saurischians are further divided into two groups: the meat-eating Theropoda and the plant-eating Sauropodomorpha.

**Example:
*Tyrannosaurus rex***

**Within these two main divisions,** dinosaurs are then separated into orders and then families, such as Stegosauria. Like other members of the Stegosauria, *Stegosaurus* had spines and plates along the back, neck, and tail.

THE FIERCE *ALLOSAURUS* HAD NEARLY **70** TEETH.

CORYTH-OSAURUS LIVED IN BIG HERDS LIKE MODERN BUFFALO.

*BRACHIO-SAURUS* WAS TALLER THAN **TWO** GIRAFFES.

THE *SPINOSAURUS* ATE SHARKS.

# ③ NEWLY DISCOVERED DINOS

**H**umans have been searching for—and discovering—dinosaur remains for hundreds of years. In that time, at least 1,000 species of dinos have been found all over the world, and thousands more may still be out there waiting to be unearthed. Recent discoveries include *Suskityrannus hazelae.* Found in the western United States, the jaguar-size cousin of *T. rex* was discovered by a 16-year-old on a high school dig trip.

### ① Suskityrannus hazelae
(Saurischian)

**Name Meaning:** coyote tyrant

**Length:** 9 feet (2.7 m)

**Time Range:** Mid-Cretaceous

**Where:** New Mexico, U.S.A.

### ② Mnyamawamtuka moyowamkia
(Saurischian)

**Name Meaning:** animal of the Mtuka (with) a heart-shaped tail

**Length:** 25 feet (7.6 m)

**Time Range:** Mid-Cretaceous

**Where:** Tanzania

### ③ Bajadasaurus pronuspinax
(Saurischian)

**Name Meaning:** bent over forward spine

**Length:** 30 feet (9.1 m)

**Time Range:** Early Cretaceous

**Where:** Argentina

# Dynamite DINO AWARDS

**Spiky body armor. Razor-sharp teeth. Unimaginable strength.** No doubt, all dinos are cool. But whether they were the biggest, the fiercest, or the biggest-brained of the bunch, some stand out more than others. Here are seven of the most amazing dinos ever discovered.

**Supersize Appetite**

**Big Brain**

Scientists think that *Tyrannosaurus rex* could gulp down 500 pounds (227 kg) of meat at a time—that's like eating 2,000 hamburger patties in one bite!

*Troodon*, a meat-eater the size of a man, had a brain as big as an avocado pit—relatively large for a dinosaur of its small stature. Because of its big brain, scientists think *Troodon* may have been the smartest dino and as intelligent as modern birds.

**Cool Camo**

The birdlike *Sinornithosaurus* had feathers similar to those of modern birds. It may have also had reddish brown, yellow, and black coloring that kept this turkey-size raptor camouflaged as it hunted in the forest.

**Heavy-weight**

The heaviest of all dinosaurs, *Argentinosaurus* is believed to have weighed 220,000 pounds (99,790 kg)—more than 15 elephants.

**Pint-Size Predator**

*Microraptor zhaoianus*, the smallest meat-eating dinosaur, measured just 16 inches (40 cm) tall. With long toe tips for grasping branches, it's thought to be closely related to today's birds.

**Built for Speed**

**Ornithomimids**, a group of dinosaurs that resembled ostriches, would have given the world's fastest man a run for his money. Some of these long-limbed, toothless meat-eaters are thought to have clocked speeds of 50 miles an hour (80 km/h).

**Super Spines**

Known as the "spine lizard," *Spinosaurus* had huge spines sticking out of its back, some taller than a fourth grader! Weighing up to 22 tons (20 t), it may have been the biggest meat-eating dinosaur.

77

# DINO DEFENSES

Scientists don't know for sure whether plant-eating dinos used their amazing attributes to battle their carnivorous cousins, but these herbivores were armed with some pretty wicked ways they could have used to defend themselves.

## ARMOR: *GASTONIA*
## (GAS-TONE-EE-AH)

Prickly *Gastonia* was covered in heavy, defensive armor. To protect itself from the strong jaws of meat-eaters it had four horns on its head, thick layers of bone shielding its brain, rows of spikes sticking out from its back, and a tail with triangular blades running along each side.

## SPIKES: *KENTROSAURUS*
## (KEN-TROH-SORE-US)

Stand back! This cousin of *Stegosaurus* had paired spikes along its tail, which it could swing at attackers with great speed. One paleontologist estimated that *Kentrosaurus* could have swung its treacherous tail fast enough to shatter bones!

## CLUB TAIL:
### *ANKYLOSAURUS*

## (AN-KYE-LOH-SORE-US)

Steer clear! *Ankylosaurus* possessed a heavy, knobby tail that it could have used to whack attackers. It may not have totally protected the tanklike late Cretaceous dino from a determined *T. rex*, but a serious swing could have generated enough force to do some real damage to its rival reptile.

## WHIP TAIL:
### *DIPLODOCUS*

## (DIH-PLOD-UH-KUS)

Some scientists think this late Jurassic giant's tail—about half the length of its 90-foot (27-m) body—could have been used like a whip and swished at high speeds, creating a loud noise that would send potential predators running.

## HORNS:
### *TRICERATOPS*

## (TRI-SER-UH-TOPS)

There's no evidence *Triceratops* ever used its horns to combat late Cretaceous snack-craving carnivores. But scientists do believe the famous three-horned creature used its frills and horns in battle with other members of its species.

# 21 CUTEST ANIMALS OF 2021

From roly-poly pandas to scuttling crabs, there's no shortage of cute creatures on Earth. Here's Nat Geo Kids' roundup of cuddly critters that are sure to make you say *awww*.

## 1 HEADS OR TAILS

Ring-tailed lemurs are named for their unique striped appendages, which are as long as their bodies and help them balance as they climb and leap among the tree branches. They live exclusively on the African island of Madagascar.

## 2 TASTY TREAT

Eat up! A Galápagos land iguana gets ready to feast on a flower. These spiky lizards live on the Galápagos Islands, off the coast of Ecuador in South America. There, they spend their days lounging in the sun and searching for their next meal, like bright blooms, chunks of cacti, and insects.

### 3 HAVING A BALL

When the Tierpark Berlin in Germany launched a contest to name their new female polar bear cub, more than 5,000 suggestions came streaming in. The eventual winner? Hertha, a name honoring Berlin's professional soccer team. And by chasing balls around her enclosure, the fluffy cub sure lives up to her sporty name!

### 5 CUB LOVE

For about the first two years of their lives, tiger cubs stay close to their mom. From birth, she feeds them and protects them, and eventually teaches them how to hunt. By the time the cubs turn two, they're ready to tackle the real world on their own—all thanks to mom.

### 4 DECKED OUT

That's one colorful camel! This accessorized ungulate is dressed up for the Desert Festival in Jaisalmer, India. Camels are the stars of the show at the three-day festival, which celebrates local culture. The humped mammals participate in polo matches, foot races, and parades.

# 6

## LOOKING UP

A member of the antelope family native to Africa, gerenuks have wackily long necks. Why so stretchy? All that height helps them reach the tall plants they snack on.

# 8

## UP A TREE

Giant pandas—they're like adventurous kids! These roly-poly animals love to climb trees, too. They learn to climb at just a few months old, their extra-sharp claws helping them to grip the bark. And once they reach the top? A panda may lounge in the branches before heading back down.

# 7

## GLOW ON

Creepy crawler—or beautiful jewel? When basking in the glow of ultraviolet (UV) light, this scorpion dazzles with a blue-green sheen. Actually brownish in color, scorpions tend to blend into the deserts and other hot, dry places they call home.

## 9 JUST DUCKY

Mandy the mandarin duck made quite a splash! Visitors flocked to Central Park in New York City, U.S.A., to catch a glimpse of the attractive visitor. Because mandarin ducks are native to Asia, experts think this duck was once a pet who was abandoned—or simply flew the coop.

## 10 FOR THE DOG

Luigi Maestro is one pampered pooch! The dog scoots around his hometown of New York City in a variety of luxury vehicles, including a pint-size Porsche and a mini Ferrari. The cost of this car collection? More than $1,500. Bow *wow!*

83

## 11

## ON THE LOOKOUT

Native to parts of Africa, meerkats are constantly on alert for predators such as jackals and falcons. Clever critters, meerkats share the group's work—including guard duty and babysitting. Everything gets taken care of by working as a team. *Hakuna matata!* No worries!

## BY A WHISKER

What long whiskers you have! A harbor seal sports extra-long face fringe, which helps this swimmer see and hear. The supersensitive whiskers are packed with nerves and act as underwater antennae. Studies show a seal could still successfully find fish even if it were blindfolded and wearing headphones.

## 12

## 13

### EARS TO YOU

This young goat—also known as a kid—is all ears! And better to hear you with: Goats are super sensitive to a range of sound and can even move their ears to locate the source of various noises.

## BOLD BILL

This isn't your typical toucan! With a beak featuring a blend of green, red, yellow, and orange, the keel-billed toucan—also known as the rainbow-billed toucan—has one of the most colorful beaks in the bird world. It's native to Latin America and is the national bird of Belize.

## 14

## IN BLOOM

Everything's just *dandy*-lion for this guinea pig! Known for being cuddly, smart, and sweet, guinea pigs make popular pets. Actually part of the rodent family, one possible reason for their name is the piglike squeaking noises they make.

## 16

## 15

### STICK TO IT

A red-eyed tree frog's striking eyes aren't the only thing that makes this creature stand out: Sticky toe pads let it climb up just about any surface. Paired with this tiny amphibian's awesome jumping skills, it's no wonder they're often called monkey frogs!

## FUR REAL

Thanks to its bright white coat, an arctic fox blends into its icy surroundings. Its thick, fuzzy fur also acts like a warm sleeping bag, keeping the fox cozy as temperatures dip well below freezing in its chilly habitat.

**17**

**18**

## FISH FRIENDS

Nemo, is that you? Like the fish from the famous film, these bright orange clownfish live in sea anemones in warm, tropical waters. The fish clean and protect the anemone while receiving food and shelter in return.

**19**

## STAR KITTY

Lil BUB was one cool cat! This Instagram-famous feline had more than two million followers. Fans fell for Lil BUB's sweet features, the result of an extreme case of dwarfism. Sadly, BUB passed away in 2019, but she'll be remembered for more than just cute pics. She was also an author, the star of a hit documentary, and a supporter of special-needs pets.

## TRICK OR TREAT

The Halloween crab is named for its *boo*-tiful coloring, from its black body to its blood-orange legs to its purple claws. Also known as the moon crab, it's often spotted scuttling along sand dunes or in the rainforests of the Pacific coast, from Mexico to Panama.

# 20

## CROWN JEWELS

Forget glittering jewels: This caiman has a crown of butterflies! So what's up with the funky headpiece? Experts say the insects feed on the salty reptile tears when minerals like sodium are otherwise hard to find.

# 21

# QUIZ WHIZ

**Explore just how much you know about animals with this quiz!**

Write your answers on a piece of paper. Then check them below.

**1** What type of armor did the dinosaur *Gastonia* sport?
a. horns on its head
b. a super-thick skull
c. rows of spikes on its back
d. all of the above

**2** Which country is the quokka native to?
a. Argentina
b. Armenia
c. Australia
d. Angola

**3** True or false? An Amur leopard's large paws help it walk on snow without sinking.

**4** When faced with danger, some octopuses will _____.
a. dig a hole and hide in the sand
b. break off an arm and scoot away
c. shoot red-hot liquid from their eyes
d. scream and swim away

**5** What does an orca's diet mostly consist of?
a. smaller mammals and fish
b. sea grass
c. jellyfish
d. plankton

Not **STUMPED** yet? Check out the *NATIONAL GEOGRAPHIC KIDS QUIZ WHIZ* collection for more crazy **ANIMAL** questions!

**ANSWERS:** 1. d; 2. c; 3. True; 4. b; 5. a

# HOMEWORK HELP

# Wildly Good Animal Reports

Seahorse

**Your teacher wants** a written report on the seahorse. Not to worry. Use these organizational tools so you can stay afloat while writing a report.

**STEPS TO SUCCESS:** Your report will follow the format of a descriptive or expository essay (see page 35 for "How to Write a Perfect Essay") and should consist of a main idea, followed by supporting details and a conclusion. Use this basic structure for each paragraph, as well as the whole report, and you'll be on the right track.

## 1. Introduction
State your **main idea.**
*Seahorses are fascinating fishes with many unique characteristics.*

## 2. Body
Provide **supporting points** for your main idea.
*Seahorses are very small fishes.*
*Seahorses are named for their head shape.*
*Seahorses display behavior that is rare among almost all other animals on Earth.*

Then **expand** on those points with further description, explanation, or discussion.
*Seahorses are very small fishes.*
*Seahorses are about the size of an M&M at birth, and most adult seahorses would fit in a teacup.*
*Seahorses are named for their head shape.*
*With long, tubelike snouts, seahorses are named for their resemblance to horses.*
*A group of seahorses is called a herd.*
*Seahorses display behavior that is rare among almost all other animals on Earth.*
*Unlike most other fish, seahorses stay with one mate their entire lives. They are also among the only species in which dads, not moms, give birth to the babies.*

## 3. Conclusion
Wrap it up with a **summary** of your whole paper.
*Because of their unique shape and unusual behavior, seahorses are among the most fascinating and easily distinguishable animals in the ocean.*

# KEY INFORMATION

**Here are some things you should consider including in your report:**
What does your animal look like?
**To what other species is it related?**
How does it move?
**Where does it live?**
What does it eat?
**What are its predators?**
How long does it live?
**Is it endangered?**
Why do you find it interesting?

**SEPARATE FACT FROM FICTION:** Your animal may have been featured in a movie or in myths and legends. Compare and contrast how the animal has been portrayed with how it behaves in reality. For example, penguins can't dance the way they do in *Happy Feet*.

**PROOFREAD AND REVISE:** As you would do with any essay, when you're finished, check for misspellings, grammatical mistakes, and punctuation errors. It often helps to have someone else proofread your work, too, as he or she may catch things you have missed. Also, look for ways to make your sentences and paragraphs even better. Add more descriptive language, choosing just the right verbs, adverbs, and adjectives to make your writing come alive.

**BE CREATIVE:** Use visual aids to make your report come to life. Include an animal photo file with interesting images found in magazines or printed from websites. Or draw your own! You can also build a miniature animal habitat diorama. Use creativity to help communicate your passion for the subject.

**THE FINAL RESULT:** Put it all together in one final, polished draft. Make it neat and clean, and remember to cite your references.

The turquoise water of the Kuang Si Waterfall glistens in Luang Prabang, Laos.

# WONDERS of NATURE

# THE OC

## PACIFIC OCEAN

### STATS

Surface area
**65,436,200 sq mi (169,479,000 sq km)**

Portion of Earth's water area
**47 percent**

Greatest depth
**Challenger Deep
(in the Mariana Trench)
-36,070 ft (-10,994 m)**

Surface temperatures
**Summer high: 90°F (32°C)
Winter low: 28°F (-2°C)**

Tides
**Highest: 30 ft (9 m) near Korean Peninsula
Lowest: 1 ft (0.3 m) near Midway Islands**

Cool creatures: **giant Pacific octopus,
bottlenose whale, clownfish, great
white shark**

Clownfish

## ATLANTIC OCEAN

### STATS

Surface area
**35,338,500 sq mi (91,526,300 sq km)**

Portion of Earth's water area
**25 percent**

Greatest depth
**Puerto Rico Trench
-28,232 ft (-8,605 m)**

Surface temperatures
**Summer high: 90°F (32°C)
Winter low: 28°F (-2°C)**

Tides
**Highest: 52 ft (16 m)
Bay of Fundy, Canada
Lowest: 1.5 ft (0.5 m)
Gulf of Mexico and Mediterranean Sea**

Cool creatures: **blue whale, Atlantic spotted
dolphin, sea turtle, bottlenose dolphin**

Bottlenose dolphin

# EANS

## INDIAN OCEAN

### STATS

Surface area
**28,839,800 sq mi (74,694,800 sq km)**

Portion of Earth's water area
**21 percent**

Greatest depth
**Java Trench
-23,376 ft (-7,125 m)**

Surface temperatures
**Summer high: 93°F (34°C)
Winter low: 28°F (-2°C)**

Tides
**Highest: 36 ft (11 m)
Lowest: 2 ft (0.6 m)
Both along Australia's west coast**

Cool creatures: **humpback whale, Portuguese man-of-war, dugong (sea cow), leatherback turtle**

## ARCTIC OCEAN

### STATS

Surface area
**5,390,000 sq mi (13,960,100 sq km)**

Portion of Earth's water area
**4 percent**

Greatest depth
**Molloy Deep
-18,599 ft (-5,669 m)**

Surface temperatures
**Summer high: 41°F (5°C)
Winter low: 28°F (-2°C)**

Tides
**Less than 1 ft (0.3 m) variation throughout the ocean**

Cool creatures: **beluga whale, orca, harp seal, narwhal**

Leatherback turtle

Narwhal

To see the major oceans and bays in relation to landmasses, look at the map on pages 256 and 257.

**Bet You Didn't Know!**

# 10 cool facts about

Cold-water coral reef near Norway

**1** Coral reefs are home to **one-third** of the **world's fish species.**

There's a heart-shaped coral reef in **Australia.** **2**

**3** A reef fish called a **fang blenny** feeds on the **mucus of other fish.**

**4** **Cryptobenthics—** small, often jelly-bean-size fish—make up **half the fish species** living on a reef.

**5** **The Bermuda Islands** and the **Bahamas** are really **ancient coral reefs.**

# coral reefs

**6** Some deep-sea corals near Hawaii, U.S.A., are more than **4,000** years old.

**7** Coral reefs are found in less than **one percent** of the ocean.

**8** Fire coral can cause your **skin to burn** and break out in a **red rash if you touch it.**

**9** Cold-water coral reefs can be found off the coasts of the U.K., Ireland, and Norway.

**10** Coral reefs act as a barrier against **tsunamis,** protecting coasts from the huge waves and floods.

# Biomes

**A BIOME, OFTEN CALLED A MAJOR LIFE ZONE,** is one of the natural world's major communities where plants and animals adapt to their specific surroundings. Biomes are classified depending on the predominant vegetation, climate, and geography of a region. They can be divided into six major types: forest, freshwater, marine, desert, grassland, and tundra. Each biome consists of many ecosystems.

Biomes are extremely important. Balanced ecological relationships among biomes help to maintain the environment and life on Earth as we know it. For example, an increase in one species of plant, such as an invasive one, can cause a ripple effect throughout a whole biome.

## FOREST

Forests occupy about one-third of Earth's land area. There are three major types of forests: tropical, temperate, and boreal (taiga). Forests are home to a diversity of plants, some of which may hold medicinal qualities for humans, as well as thousands of animal species, some still undiscovered. Forests can also absorb carbon dioxide, a greenhouse gas, and give off oxygen.

**The rabbit-size royal antelope lives in West Africa's dense forests.**

## FRESHWATER

Most water on Earth is salty, but freshwater ecosystems—including lakes, ponds, wetlands, rivers, and streams—usually contain water with less than one percent salt concentration. The countless animal and plant species that live in freshwater biomes vary from continent to continent, but they include algae, frogs, turtles, fish, and the larvae of many insects.

**The place where freshwater and salt water meet is called an estuary.**

## MARINE

The marine biome covers almost three-fourths of Earth's surface, making it the largest habitat on our planet. Oceans make up the majority of the saltwater marine biome. Coral reefs are considered to be the most biodiverse of any of the biome habitats. The marine biome is home to more than one million plant and animal species.

**Estimated to be up to 100,000 years old, sea grass growing in the Mediterranean Sea may be the oldest living thing on Earth.**

## DESERT

Covering about one-fifth of Earth's surface, deserts are places where precipitation is less than 10 inches (25 cm) per year. Although most deserts are hot, there are other kinds as well. The four major kinds of deserts are hot, semiarid, coastal, and cold. Far from being barren wastelands, deserts are biologically rich habitats.

**Some sand dunes in the Sahara are tall enough to bury a 50-story building.**

## GRASSLAND

Biomes called grasslands are characterized by having grasses instead of large shrubs or trees. Grasslands generally have precipitation for only about half to three-fourths of the year. If it were more, they would become forests. Grasslands can be divided into two types: tropical (savannas) and temperate. Some of the world's largest land animals, such as elephants, live there.

**Grasslands in North America are called prairies; in South America, they're called pampas.**

## TUNDRA

The coldest of all biomes, a tundra is characterized by an extremely cold climate, simple vegetation, little precipitation, poor nutrients, and a short growing season. There are two types of tundra: Arctic and alpine. A tundra is home to few kinds of vegetation. Surprisingly, though, there are quite a few animal species that can survive the tundra's extremes, such as wolves, caribou, and even mosquitoes.

**Formed 10,000 years ago, the Arctic tundra is the world's youngest biome.**

# Weather and Climate

Weather is the condition of the atmosphere—temperature, wind, humidity, and precipitation—at a given place at a given time. Climate, however, is the average weather for a particular place over a long period of time. Different places on Earth have different climates, but climate is not a random occurrence. It is a pattern that is controlled by factors such as latitude, elevation, prevailing winds, the temperature of ocean currents, and location on land relative to water. Climate is generally constant, but evidence indicates that human activity is causing a change in its patterns.

## WOW-WORTHY WEATHER

**SEEING ORANGE:** Dark orange snow sometimes falls on parts of Europe, the result of storms blowing dust from the Sahara into the atmosphere, where it mixes with the white stuff.

**DEEP FREEZE:** In January 2019, temperatures in Mount Carroll, Illinois, U.S.A., dipped down to minus 38°F (-38.9°C), the city's and the state's coldest recorded temperature ever.

**THINK PINK:** "Watermelon snow" recently appeared in the mountains of the Pacific Northwest in the United States, the result of algae that turn snow pink.

# GLOBAL CLIMATE ZONES

Climatologists, people who study climate, have created different systems for classifying climates. One that is often used is called the Köppen system, which classifies climate zones according to precipitation, temperature, and vegetation. It has five major categories—tropical, dry, temperate, cold, and polar—with a sixth category for locations where high elevations override other factors.

ARCTIC OCEAN

ARCTIC CIRCLE

ATLANTIC OCEAN

PACIFIC OCEAN

TROPIC OF CANCER

EQUATOR

PACIFIC OCEAN

INDIAN OCEAN

TROPIC OF CAPRICORN

ANTARCTIC CIRCLE

**Climate**

■ Tropical ■ Dry ■ Temperate ■ Cold ■ Polar

# EXTREME CLIMATES

**Talk about a temperature swing!** The difference between the coldest place on Earth—east Antarctica—and the hottest—Death Valley, in Nevada and California, U.S.A.—is a whopping 270°F (150°C). Though they are both deserts, these two opposites are neck and neck in the race for world's most extreme climate.

## HOT
### DEATH VALLEY

| | |
|---|---|
| **CRAZY TEMPS** | Hottest temperature ever recorded: **134°F (57°C)** |
| **RAINFALL** | Death Valley is the driest place in North America. The average yearly rainfall is about **2 inches (5 cm)**. |
| **ELEVATION** | At **282 feet (86 m) below sea level**, Death Valley is the lowest point in North America. |
| **STEADY HEAT** | In 2001, Death Valley experienced **160 consecutive days** of temperatures **100°F (38°C)** or hotter. |

## COLD
### EAST ANTARCTIC PLATEAU

| | |
|---|---|
| **CRAZY TEMPS** | Coldest temperature ever recorded: **minus 135.8°F (-93°C)** |
| **RAINFALL** | East Antarctica gets less than **2 inches (5 cm)** of precipitation in a year. |
| **ELEVATION** | The record low temperature was recorded just below the plateau's **13,000-foot (3,962-m)** ridge. |
| **DARKNESS** | During parts of winter, there is **24 hours** of darkness. |

# Freaky Weather

Nature can be unbelievably powerful. A major earthquake can topple huge buildings and bring down entire mountainsides. Hurricanes, blizzards, and tornadoes can paralyze major cities. But as powerful as these natural disasters are, here are five other episodes of wacky weather that will really blow you away!

## 1 FIRE RAINBOW

Can clouds catch fire? No, but it may look like it when you spot a circumhorizontal arc, also known as a "fire rainbow." This rare sight occurs when the sun travels through wispy, high-altitude cirrus clouds—and only when the sun is very high in the sky. The result? The entire cloud lights up in an amazing spectrum of colors, sometimes extending for hundreds of miles in the sky.

## 2 SNOWBALL FACTORY

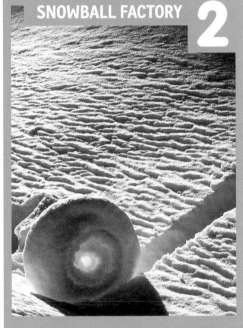

You head outside after a snowstorm and see dozens of log- or drum-shaped snowballs. These rare creations are called snow rollers, formed when wet snow falls on icy ground, so snow can't stick to it. Pushed by strong winds, the snow rolls into logs. Maybe this is nature's way of saying it's time for a snowball fight.

## 3 MYSTERY WAVES

Imagine you're on an ocean liner when a wall of water 10 stories tall races toward you like an unstoppable freight train. It's a rogue wave, also called a freak wave, which can appear without warning at any time in the open sea. These waves were once considered myths, but scientists now know they are very real—and very dangerous to even the largest ships.

## HOLE PUNCH CLOUDS 4

Nope, that's not a UFO—it's a rare formation in the sky called a hole punch cloud. This wild sight usually occurs when patches of high clouds freeze and fall away as ice crystals, eventually leaving a huge hole. Once unable to solve the mystery, researchers now believe that airplanes taking off or landing are the likely cause of these cloud holes.

## 5 THE MOTHER OF ALL TORNADOES

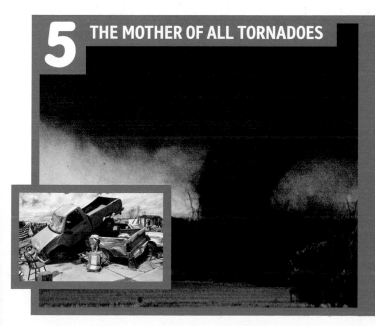

The fastest wind speed ever recorded—318 miles an hour (512 km/h)—occurred during a tornado near Oklahoma City, Oklahoma, U.S.A., in 1999. Scientists classify tornadoes by the damage they can do. With wind speeds of 70 miles an hour (113 km/h), a tornado can tear branches from trees. A tornado with wind speeds of more than 300 miles an hour (483 km/h) has the power to derail train cars, tear grass from the ground, and even rip pavement from the street.

# WATER CYCLE

Precipitation falls

Water storage in ice and snow

Water vapor condenses in clouds

Water filters into the ground

Meltwater and surface runoff

Freshwater storage

Evaporation

Groundwater discharge

Water storage in ocean

## The amount of water on Earth is more or less constant—

only the form changes. As the sun warms Earth's surface, liquid water is changed into water vapor in a process called **evaporation**. Water on the surface of plants' leaves turns into water vapor in a process called **transpiration**. As water vapor rises into the air, it cools and changes form again. This time, it becomes clouds in a process called **condensation**. Water droplets fall from the clouds as **precipitation**, which then travels as groundwater or runoff back to the lakes, rivers, and oceans, where the cycle (shown above) starts all over again.

To a meteorologist—a person who studies the weather—a "light rain" is less than 1/48 inch (0.5 mm). A "heavy rain" is more than 1/6 inch (4 mm).

**You drink the same water as the dinosaurs! Earth has been recycling water for more than four billion years.**

# Types of Clouds

If you want a clue about the weather, look up at the clouds. They'll tell a lot about the condition of the air and what weather might be on the way. Clouds are made of both air and water. On fair days, warm air currents rise up and push against the water in clouds, keeping it from falling. But as the raindrops in a cloud get bigger, it's time to set them free. The bigger raindrops become too heavy for the air currents to hold up, and they fall to the ground.

## How Much Does a Cloud Weigh?

A light, fluffy cumulus cloud typically weighs about 216,000 pounds (98,000 kg). That's about the weight of 18 elephants. A rain-soaked cumulonimbus cloud typically weighs 105.8 million pounds (48 million kg), or about the same as 9,000 elephants.

**1 STRATUS** These clouds make the sky look like a bowl of thick gray porridge. They hang low in the sky, blanketing the day in dreary darkness. Stratus clouds form when cold, moist air close to the ground moves over a region.

**2 CIRRUS** These wispy tufts of clouds are thin and hang high up in the atmosphere where the air is extremely cold. Cirrus clouds are made of tiny ice crystals.

**3 CUMULONIMBUS** These are the monster clouds. Rising air currents force fluffy cumulus clouds to swell and shoot upward, as much as 70,000 feet (21,000 m). When these clouds bump against the top of the troposphere, or the tropopause, they flatten out on top like tabletops.

**4 CUMULUS** These white, fluffy clouds make people sing, "Oh, what a beautiful morning!" They form low in the atmosphere and look like marshmallows. They often mix with large patches of blue sky. Formed when hot air rises, cumulus clouds usually disappear when the air cools at night.

103

# HURRICANE
# HAPPENINGS

**A storm is coming!** But is this a tropical cyclone a hurricane or a typhoon? These weather events go by different names depending on where they form and how fast their winds get. Strong tropical cyclones are called hurricanes in the Atlantic and parts of the Pacific Ocean; in the western Pacific they are called typhoons. But any way you look at it, these storms pack a punch.

## 1,380 MILES (2,221 km)

diameter of the most massive tropical cyclone ever recorded, 1979's Typhoon Tip

## 82°F (27.8°C)

water surface temperature necessary for a tropical cyclone to form

## 16.6

average number of tropical storms each year in the Northeast and Central Pacific Basins

## 10

number of Hurricane Sandy–related pictures uploaded every second to Instagram on October 29, 2012

## 31

number of days Hurricane John lasted in 1994

# 12.1
average number of tropical storms in the Atlantic Basin each year

# 254 MPH
(408 km/h)
strongest gust of storm wind ever recorded

# 12-25 MILES
(20–40 km)
diameter of a hurricane eye

## HURRICANE NAMES FOR 2021

Hurricane names come from six official international lists. The names alternate between male and female. When a storm becomes a hurricane, a name from the list is used, in alphabetical order. Each list is reused every six years. A name "retires" if that hurricane caused a lot of damage or many deaths. Check out the names for Atlantic hurricanes in 2021.

| | | |
|---|---|---|
| Ana | Henri | Odette |
| Bill | Ida | Peter |
| Claudette | Julian | Rose |
| Danny | Kate | Sam |
| Elsa | Larry | Teresa |
| Fred | Mindy | Victor |
| Grace | Nicholas | Wanda |

## SCALE OF HURRICANE INTENSITY

| CATEGORY | ONE | TWO | THREE | FOUR | FIVE |
|---|---|---|---|---|---|
| DAMAGE | Minimal | Moderate | Extensive | Extreme | Catastrophic |
| WINDS | 74–95 mph (119–153 km/h) | 96–110 mph (154–177 km/h) | 111–129 mph (178–208 km/h) | 130–156 mph (209–251 km/h) | 157 mph or higher (252+ km/h) |
| (DAMAGE refers to wind and water damage combined.) | | | | | |

105

# Avalanche!

A million tons (907,184 t) of snow rumble eight miles (13 km) downhill, kicking up a cloud of snow dust visible a hundred miles (161 km) away.

This is not a scene from a disaster movie—this describes reality one day in April 1981. The mountain was Mount Sanford in Alaska, U.S.A., and the event was one of history's biggest avalanches. Amazingly, no one was hurt, and luckily, avalanches this big are rare.

An avalanche is a moving mass of snow that may contain ice, soil, rocks, and uprooted trees. The height of a mountain, the steepness of its slope, and the type of snow lying on it all help determine the likelihood of an avalanche. Avalanches begin when an unstable mass of snow breaks away from a mountainside and moves downhill. The growing river of snow picks up speed as it rushes down the mountain. Avalanches have been known to reach speeds of 155 miles an hour (249 km/h)—about the same as the record for downhill skiing.

To protect yourself and stay safe when you play in the mountains, follow our safety tips.

**90 percent of AVALANCHE INCIDENTS are triggered by humans.**

## Safety TIPS

**SAFETY FIRST**
Before heading out, check for avalanche warnings.

**EQUIPMENT**
When hiking, carry safety equipment, including a long probe, a small shovel, and an emergency avalanche rescue beacon that signals your location.

**NEVER GO IT ALONE**
Don't hike in the mountain wilderness without a companion.

**IF CAUGHT**
If caught in the path of an avalanche, try to get to the side of it. If you can't, grab a tree as an anchor.

# What Is a Tornado?

## THE ENHANCED FUJITA SCALE

The Enhanced Fujita (EF) Scale, named after tornado expert T. Theodore Fujita, classifies tornadoes based on wind speed and the intensity of damage that they cause.

**EF0**
65–85 mph winds
(105–137 km/h)
Slight damage

**EF1**
86–110 mph winds
(138–177 km/h)
Moderate damage

**EF2**
111–135 mph winds
(178–217 km/h)
Substantial damage

**EF3**
136–165 mph winds
(218–266 km/h)
Severe damage

**EF4**
166–200 mph winds
(267–322 km/h)
Massive damage

**EF5**
More than 200 mph winds
(322+ km/h)
Catastrophic damage

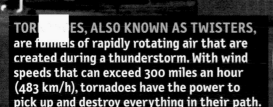

TORNADOES, ALSO KNOWN AS TWISTERS, are funnels of rapidly rotating air that are created during a thunderstorm. With wind speeds that can exceed 300 miles an hour (483 km/h), tornadoes have the power to pick up and destroy everything in their path.

THIS ROTATING FUNNEL OF AIR, formed in a cumulus or cumulonimbus cloud, became a tornado when it touched the ground.

TORNADOES HAVE OCCURRED IN ALL 50 U.S. STATES AND ON EVERY CONTINENT EXCEPT ANTARCTICA.

# Wildfire
## ANIMAL RESCUE!

In November 2018, Jeff Hill went to check on a friend's house in the woods of Paradise, California, U.S.A. The home was part of an area that, days before, had been engulfed by the Camp Fire, the deadliest and most destructive wildfire in California history to date. As Hill got closer to the home, he stumbled upon a shocking sight: There was a horse in the backyard pool!

Shivering and struggling in the water, the horse—which likely leapt into the pool to escape the flames—was weakened but alive. After Hill helped the animal out of the water, "it shook off, loved on us for a few minutes as a thank-you, and walked off assuring us that she was OK," Hill posted on Facebook. Later, animal rescue workers escorted the horse to safety.

The horse was just one of thousands of animals that were in peril during the two weeks in which the Camp Fire ravaged Northern California, burning nearly 154,000 acres (62,300 ha) and 19,000 structures. As the fire roared toward homes, people were forced to quickly evacuate and had no choice but to leave their pets and farm animals behind. Sadly, some animals perished in the fire, but a menagerie of displaced animals, from potbellied pigs to alpacas, were rescued by caring humans like Hill. Even injured wild animals, like bear cubs and foxes, were taken in to rescue centers, where they were treated and then released back into the woods.

Rescuing the animals was one thing, but reuniting them with their owners proved to be another challenge. While some humans were able to collect their pets right away, it took months for others to connect with their four-legged friends. Several local animal hospitals and other organizations posted albums of the animals online to help owners identify their missing pets.

The hope? That as the residents of Paradise continue to rebuild and recover from Camp Fire, they'll be able to do so with their beloved animals by their side.

# Terrible Tornado

In March 2019, a tornado touched down in the town of Beauregard, Alabama, U.S.A. But this was no ordinary tornado. First, there was its size: At nearly a mile (1.6 km) wide, the funnel cloud was nearly four times larger than the average tornado. Then, there was its speed: With winds spinning at about 170 miles an hour (274 km/h), it ripped homes from their foundations and trees from the ground. And finally, there was the length of its path: On the ground for a total of 70 miles (113 km), it was about 20 times as long-lasting as a typical tornado.

All told, this particular twister took out thousands of homes, killing 23 people and injuring at least 100 others. Part of a system of 40 twisters to hit the southeastern United States over the course of six hours that day, the tornado in Beauregard was the most powerful and the deadliest to hit the United States in almost six years.

The destruction was beyond devastating: Homes, cars, trees, and other structures were reduced to rubble. But slowly, the quiet country town with a population of some 10,000 is recovering. As donations poured in from near and far and the community came together determined to help each other, Beauregard began to rebuild—and heal.

# Wicked Heat Wave

Imagine a day so hot that fruit growing on trees begin to cook from the inside out. That's just what happened in parts of South Australia during a wicked heat wave in January 2019, when temperatures in some towns soared to 120°F (49°C). The hottest known weather since record-keeping began, the extreme temps caused the pits in stone fruit like peaches and nectarines to grow so hot, they burned the flesh inside the fruit. An estimated 30 percent of the stone fruit crop was destroyed as a result.

And it wasn't just fruit that took the brunt of the weather: Hundreds of flying foxes—a type of bat—died during the heat wave after succumbing to the sizzling temperatures. Thousands of fish faced the same fate due to low river levels caused by a drought. Asphalt roads melted, and dozens of brush fires broke out throughout the parched countryside.

Ultimately, the summer of 2019 set a new mark as the continent's hottest on record. And after weeks of having to keep cool by staying inside or hanging by the pools and beaches, Australians were finally given a break from the heat with rain, and lots of it: Soon after summer ends in Australia, monsoon season begins.

# QUIZ WHIZ

## Quiz yourself to find out if you're a natural when it comes to nature knowledge!

Write your answers on a piece of paper. Then check them below.

**1** **True or false?** Grasslands in North America are called pampas.

**2** Coral reefs are found in less than _____ percent of the ocean.
a. one
b. 50
c. 90
d. 20

**3** 90 percent of avalanche incidents are triggered by _____.
a. tsunamis
b. animal stampedes
c. earthquakes
d. human activity

**4** **True or false?** Tornadoes have occurred on every continent except Antarctica.

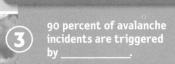

**5** You'd find leatherback turtles in which body of water?
a. Nile River
b. Indian Ocean
c. Chesapeake Bay
d. Arctic Ocean

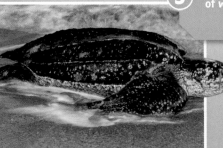

Not **STUMPED** yet? Check out the *NATIONAL GEOGRAPHIC KIDS QUIZ WHIZ* collection for more crazy **NATURE** questions!

**ANSWERS:** 1. False. They're called prairies in North America and pampas in South America.; 2. a; 3. d; 4. True; 5. b

110

# Oral Reports Made Easy

**TIP:**
Make sure you practice your presentation a few times. Stand in front of a mirror or have a parent record you so you can see if you need to work on anything, such as eye contact.

**Does the thought of public speaking** start your stomach churning like a tornado? Would you rather get caught in an avalanche than give a speech?

Giving an oral report does not have to be a natural disaster. The basic format is very similar to that of a written essay. There are two main elements that make up a good oral report—the writing and the presentation. As you write your oral report, remember that your audience will be hearing the information as opposed to reading it. Follow the guidelines below, and there will be clear skies ahead.

## Writing Your Material

Follow the steps in the "How to Write a Perfect Essay" section on page 35, but prepare your report to be spoken rather than written.
Try to keep your sentences short and simple. Long, complex sentences are harder to follow. Limit yourself to just a few key points. You don't want to overwhelm your audience with too much information. To be most effective, hit your key points in the introduction, elaborate on them in the body, and then repeat them once again in your conclusion.

### AN ORAL REPORT HAS THREE BASIC PARTS:

• **Introduction**—This is your chance to engage your audience and really capture their interest in the subject you are presenting. Use a funny personal experience or a dramatic story, or start with an intriguing question.

• **Body**—This is the longest part of your report. Here you elaborate on the facts and ideas you want to convey. Give information that supports your main idea, and expand on it with specific examples or details. In other words, structure your oral report in the same way you would a written essay, so that your thoughts are presented in a clear and organized manner.

• **Conclusion**—This is the time to summarize the information and emphasize your most important points to the audience one last time.

## Preparing Your Delivery

1 **Practice makes perfect.** Practice! Practice! Practice! Confidence, enthusiasm, and energy are key to delivering an effective oral report, and they can best be achieved through rehearsal. Ask family and friends to be your practice audience and give you feedback when you're done. Were they able to follow your ideas? Did you seem knowledgeable and confident? Did you speak too slowly or too fast, too softly or too loudly? The more times you practice giving your report, the more you'll master the material. Then you won't have to rely so heavily on your notes or papers, and you will be able to give your report in a relaxed and confident manner.

2 **Present with everything you've got.** Be as creative as you can. Incorporate videos, sound clips, slide presentations, charts, diagrams, and photos. Visual aids help stimulate your audience's senses and keep them intrigued and engaged. They can also help to reinforce your key points. And remember that when you're giving an oral report, you're a performer. Take charge of the spotlight and be as animated and entertaining as you can. Have fun with it.

3 **Keep your nerves under control.** Everyone gets a little nervous when speaking in front of a group. That's normal. But the more preparation you've done—meaning plenty of researching, organizing, and rehearsing—the more confident you'll be. Preparation is the key. And if you make a mistake or stumble over your words, just regroup and keep going. Nobody's perfect, and nobody expects you to be.

# SPACE and EARTH

Instruments aboard the spacecraft Cassini, shown approaching Saturn in this artist's rendition, have helped scientists map how textures, colors, and temperatures vary in Saturn's rings.

# A LOOK INSIDE

The distance from Earth's surface to its center is 3,963 miles (6,378 km) at the Equator. There are four layers: a thin, rigid crust; the rocky mantle; the outer core, which is a layer of molten iron; and finally the inner core, which is believed to be solid iron.

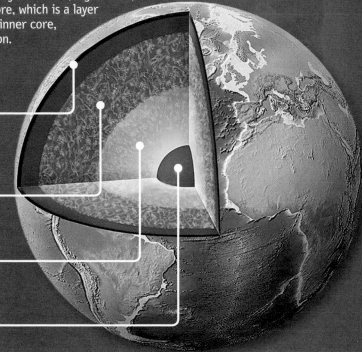

The **CRUST** includes tectonic plates, landmasses, and the ocean. Its average thickness varies from 5 to 25 miles (8 to 40 km).

The **MANTLE** is about 1,800 miles (2,900 km) of hot, thick, solid rock.

The **OUTER CORE** is liquid molten rock made mostly of iron and nickel.

The **INNER CORE** is a solid center made mostly of iron and nickel.

## What would happen if Earth had rings like Saturn?

It's good that Earth *doesn't* have rings. Saturn's rings are made of countless pieces of rock and ice that can be as tiny as a grain of sand or as big as a house. If Earth had similar rings, they'd be positioned in a way that would block sunlight and cast a shadow over the Northern and Southern Hemispheres during each region's winter. (That's when the hemispheres are tilted away from the sun.) Both areas would be darker and colder at these times. With less light coming in, crops and plants that depend on the sun to survive the season might die out. No thanks!

# ROCK STARS

Rocks and minerals are everywhere on Earth! And it can be a challenge to tell one from the other. So what's the difference between a rock and a mineral? A rock is a naturally occurring solid object made mostly from minerals. Minerals are solid, nonliving substances that occur in nature—and the basic components of most rocks. Rocks can be made of just one mineral or, like granite, of many minerals. But not all rocks are made of minerals: Coal comes from plant material, while amber is formed from ancient tree sap.

## Igneous

Named for the Greek word meaning "from fire," igneous rocks form when hot, molten liquid called magma cools. Pools of magma form deep underground and slowly work their way to Earth's surface. If they make it all the way, the liquid rock erupts and is called lava. As the layers of lava build up, they form a mountain called a volcano. Typical igneous rocks include obsidian, basalt, and pumice, which is so chock-full of gas bubbles that it actually floats in water.

ANDESITE

GRANITE PORPHYRY

## Metamorphic

Metamorphic rocks are the masters of change! These rocks were once igneous or sedimentary, but thanks to intense heat and pressure deep within the Earth, they have undergone a total transformation from their original form. These rocks never truly melt; instead, the heat twists and bends them until their shapes substantially change. Metamorphic rocks include slate as well as marble, which is used for buildings, monuments, and sculptures.

MICA SCHIST

BANDED GNEISS

## Sedimentary

When wind, water, and ice constantly wear away and weather rocks, smaller pieces called sediment are left behind. These are sedimentary rocks, also known as gravel, sand, silt, and clay. As water flows downhill, it carries the sedimentary grains into lakes and oceans, where they get deposited. As the loose sediment piles up, the grains eventually get compacted or cemented back together again. The result is new sedimentary rock. Sandstone, gypsum, limestone, and shale are sedimentary rocks that have formed this way.

LIMESTONE

HALITE

# Identifying Minerals

With so many different minerals in the world, it can be a challenge to tell one from another. Fortunately, each mineral has physical characteristics that geologists and amateur rock collectors use to tell them apart. Check out the physical characteristics below: color, luster, streak, cleavage, fracture, and hardness.

## Color

When you look at a mineral, the first thing you see is its color. In some minerals, this is a key factor because their colors are almost always the same. For example, azurite, below, is always blue. But in other cases, impurities can change the natural color of a mineral. For instance, fluorite, above, can be green, red, violet, and other colors as well. The change makes it a challenge to identify by color alone.

FLUORITE

AZURITE

## Luster

"Luster" refers to the way light reflects from the surface of a mineral. Does yours appear metallic, like gold or silver? Or is it pearly like orpiment, or brilliant like diamond? "Earthy," "glassy," "silky," and "dull" are a few other terms used to describe luster.

ORPIMENT

DIAMOND

## Streak

The "streak" is the color of the mineral's powder. When minerals are ground into powder, they often have a different color than when they are in crystal form. For example, the mineral pyrite usually looks gold, but when it is rubbed against a ceramic tile called a "streak plate," the mark it leaves is black.

PYRITE

## Cleavage

"Cleavage" describes the way a mineral breaks. Since the structure of a specific mineral is always the same, it tends to break in the same pattern. Not all minerals have cleavage, but the minerals that do, like this microcline, break evenly in one or more directions. These minerals are usually described as having "perfect cleavage." But if the break isn't smooth and clean, cleavage can be considered "good" or "poor."

MICROCLINE

GOLD

## Fracture

Some minerals, such as gold, do not break with cleavage. Instead, geologists say that they "fracture." There are different types of fractures, and depending on the mineral, the fracture may be described as jagged, splintery, even, or uneven.

## Hardness

The level of ease or difficulty with which a mineral can be scratched refers to its "hardness." Hardness is measured using a special chart called the Mohs hardness scale. The Mohs scale goes from 1 to 10. Softer minerals, which appear on the lower end of the scale, can be scratched by the harder minerals on the upper end of the scale.

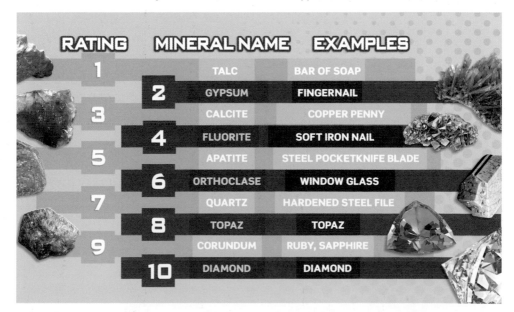

| RATING | MINERAL NAME | EXAMPLES |
|---|---|---|
| 1 | TALC | BAR OF SOAP |
| 2 | GYPSUM | FINGERNAIL |
| 3 | CALCITE | COPPER PENNY |
| 4 | FLUORITE | SOFT IRON NAIL |
| 5 | APATITE | STEEL POCKETKNIFE BLADE |
| 6 | ORTHOCLASE | WINDOW GLASS |
| 7 | QUARTZ | HARDENED STEEL FILE |
| 8 | TOPAZ | TOPAZ |
| 9 | CORUNDUM | RUBY, SAPPHIRE |
| 10 | DIAMOND | DIAMOND |

# MYSTERY SOLVED!

## Sailing Stones in Death Valley

### SO WHAT TOOK SO LONG?

Why did it take half a century or more for scientists to figure out what was moving the stones? Several factors make observing them in action difficult to near impossible.

**LOCATION:** Racetrack Playa sits more than 3,600 feet (1,100 m) above sea level and is a three-hour drive from the closest town.

ROCK TRAILS IN THE DRY LAKE BED

For decades, the remote rocks that seemed to move on their own had mostly mystified scientists and laypersons alike. The stones would sit in the same spot for years and then suddenly be found somewhere else—with long, unexplained trails behind them in the dried mud. How did these "sailing stones" move from one place to another?

Wind, water, and ice were considered the most likely explanations for the paths across Racetrack Playa—a three-mile (4.8-km)-long dry lake bed in the mountains above Death Valley, California, U.S.A., whose surface is covered with hundreds of rocks ranging from pebbles to mammoth stones weighing more than 600 pounds (272 kg). The rock trails could be up to 800 feet (244 m) long—zigging and zagging across the playa and sometimes showing

THE ROCKS ZIG AND ZAG PARALLEL TO EACH OTHER.

parallel tracks with turns in the same places. What was going on?

In 2014 scientists fitted 15 stones with motion-activated GPS units (to record their position and speed as soon as they began moving) and used time-lapse imaging and video to capture the stones' movements. What they discovered was positively earth-shattering!

After a winter storm dropped snow and rain onto the playa, the precipitation created a shallow pond about an inch (2.5 cm) deep. Freezing temperatures at night caused a thin layer of ice to form on top of it, which the next day began to melt in the sun and break up into sheets. When the floating ice panels were blown by the wind, they pushed the rocks across the playa.

So, why is this remarkable? Theories to this point had assumed that the ice needed to push these huge stones would have to be very thick and that the winds needed to push the rocks would have to be hurricane-force gusts. But what the scientists observed was that the ice sheets pushing these heavy rocks were actually very thin—less than a fifth of an inch (5 mm) thick! And the wind gusts? No hurricanes here: All it took was a light breeze. The rocks moved more easily than they ordinarily would because the ground had been softened by the water— almost like the rocks were hydroplaning. After a few months, when the pond had completely dried out, the playa was marked by a new set of trails.

This riddle had finally been "rocked" by science!

**SPEED:** Scientists estimate the sliding stones move maybe only a few minutes out of a million. When they eventually do move, the rocks move very slowly (almost too slowly even to be noticed)—one of the reasons this event wasn't easily detected before this recent use of time-lapse photography and custom-fitted rock GPS.

**OCCURRENCE:** The moving rocks are a rare phenomenon. Because the playa is dry the vast majority of the time, it could be a decade or longer before there is enough rain to make a pond deep enough to form the ice that pushes the rocks and, thus, create new trails—trails that form out of sight in the soft mud underneath the floating ice.

# A HOT TOPIC

## WHAT GOES ON
### INSIDE A STEAMING, BREWING VOLCANO?

If you could look inside a volcano, you'd see something that looks like a long pipe, called a conduit. It leads from inside the magma chamber under the crust up to a vent, or opening, at the top of the mountain. Some conduits have branches that shoot off to the side, called fissures.

When pressure builds from gases inside the volcano, the gases must find an escape, and they head up toward the surface! An eruption occurs when lava, gases, ash, and rocks explode out of the vent.

**CRATER**

**VENT**

**CONDUIT**

**FISSURE**

**MAGMA CHAMBER**

**HARDENED LAVA AND ASH LAYERS**

# TYPES OF VOLCANOES

## CINDER CONE VOLCANO
### Eve's Cone, Canada

Cinder cone volcanoes look like an upside-down ice-cream cone. They spew cinder and hot ash. Some of these volcanoes smoke and erupt for years at a time.

## COMPOSITE VOLCANO
### Licancábur, Chile

Composite volcanoes, or stratovolcanoes, form as lava, ash, and cinder from previous eruptions harden and build up over time. These volcanoes spit out pyroclastic flows, or thick explosions of hot ash that travel at hundreds of miles an hour.

## SHIELD VOLCANO
### Mauna Loa, Hawaii, U.S.A.

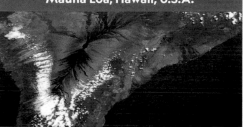

The gentle, broad slopes of a shield volcano look like an ancient warrior's shield. Its eruptions are often slower. Lava splatters and bubbles rather than shooting forcefully into the air.

## LAVA DOME VOLCANO
### Mount St. Helens, Washington, U.S.A.

Dome volcanoes have steep sides. Hardened lava often plugs the vent at the top of a dome volcano. Pressure builds beneath the surface until the top blows.

**HOT SPOTS** Some volcanoes form at hot spots, or holes beneath Earth's crust in the middle of a tectonic plate. As lava pushes up through the hole and forms a volcanic island, the plate keeps moving. More volcanoes form as it moves. Some hot spots are big enough to create a chain of volcanic islands, such as the Hawaiian Islands.

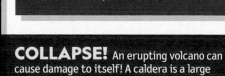

**COLLAPSE!** An erupting volcano can cause damage to itself! A caldera is a large bowl-like depression caused by the collapse of a magma chamber during an eruption. Crater Lake in Oregon, U.S.A., is a caldera that has filled with rainwater and snowfall.

# Bet You Didn't Know!

# 10 far-out facts about

**1** Luke Skywalker's **lightsaber** from *Star Wars: A New Hope* flew to the International Space Station in 2007.

**2** As many as **13 people** have been in space simultaneously.

**3** Astronauts say the moon smells like **wet ashes.**

**4** A spacecraft **glows red hot** as it returns to Earth from space.

**5** **Spiders** have traveled **into space.**

**6** A Russian rocket delivered **a pizza** to the International Space Station.

# space travel

**7** The International Space Station circles Earth every **90 minutes.**

**8** Astronauts **can grow two inches (5 cm) taller** while in space.

**A missing** European spacecraft was found on the **surface of Mars** after it vanished from contact **11 years earlier.** **9**

**10** Measuring just **1,650 feet** (500 m) wide, asteroid Bennu is the **smallest object** ever orbited by a spacecraft.

International Space Station

# A Universe of Galaxies

## 5 COOL FACTS TO RECORD

When astronauts first journeyed beyond Earth's orbit in 1968, they looked back to their home planet. The big-picture view of our place in space changed the astronauts' lives—and perhaps humanity. If you could leave the universe and similarly look back, what would you see? Remarkably, scientists are mapping this massive area. They see ... bubbles. Not literal soap bubbles, of course, but a structure that looks like a pan full of them. Like bubble walls, thin surfaces curve around empty spaces in an elegantly simple structure. Zoom in to see that these surfaces are groups of galaxies. Zoom in farther to find one galaxy, with an ordinary star—our sun—orbited by an ordinary planet—Earth. How extraordinary.

### DIGITAL TRAVELER!

Take a simulated flight through our universe, thanks to the data collected by the Sloan Digital Sky Survey. Ask an adult to help you search the internet for "APOD flight through universe sdss." Sit back and enjoy the ride!

## 2 DARK MATTER

The universe holds a mysterious source of gravity that cannot be properly explained. This unseen matter—the ghostly dark ring in this composite Hubble telescope photo— seems to pull on galaxy clusters, drawing galaxies toward it. But what is this strange stuff? It's not giant black holes, planets, stars, or anti-matter. These would show themselves indirectly. For now, astronomers call this source of gravity "dark matter."

## 1 GALAXY CLUSTERS AND SUPERCLUSTERS

Gravity pulls things together—gas in stars, stars in galaxies. Galaxies gather, too, sometimes by the thousands, form-ing galaxy clusters and superclusters with tremendously superheated gas. This gas can be as hot as 180 million degrees Fahrenheit (100 million degrees Celsius), filling space between them. These clusters hide a secret. The grav-ity among the galaxies isn't enough to bring them together. The source of the extra gravity is a dark secret.

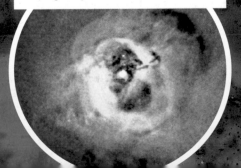

# 3 IT STARTED WHEN ...
**The Big Bang**

Long ago, the universe was compressed: It was hotter, smaller, denser than now, and completely uniform—almost. Extremely minor unevenness led to a powerful energy release that astronomers call the big bang. In a blip of time, the universe expanded tremendously. The first particles formed. Atoms, galaxies, forces, and light ... all developed from this. Today's great filaments (see fact 4) may be organized where those first uneven patches existed.

# 4 FILAMENTS AND SHEETS
**Bubbles of space**

What is the universe like at its grandest scale? The biggest big-picture view is jaw-dropping. Clusters and superclusters of galaxies—red and yellow areas in this illustration—along with dark matter, string together to form structures that are millions and billions of light-years long. These so-called walls, sheets, or filaments surround vast voids, or "bubbles," of nearly empty space—the blue areas. The universe has a structure, nonrandom and unexpected.

# 5 COLLISION ZONE

Saying that galaxies form clusters and superclusters is like saying two soccer teams simply meet. During a game, there's a lot of action and energy. Similarly, as clusters and superclusters form, there's lots going on—as evidenced by the super-high-energy x-rays that are detected (pink in this colorized image).

# PLANETS

CERES

MARS

EARTH

VENUS

MERCURY

JUPITER

SUN

## MERCURY
Average distance from the sun:
  35,980,000 miles (57,900,000 km)
Position from the sun in orbit: 1st
Equatorial diameter: 3,030 miles (4,878 km)
Length of day: 59 Earth days
Length of year: 88 Earth days
Known moons: 0
**Fun fact: Mercury is home to one of the largest craters in the solar system.**

## VENUS
Average distance from the sun:
  67,230,000 miles (108,200,000 km)
Position from the sun in orbit: 2nd
Equatorial diameter: 7,520 miles (12,100 km)
Length of day: 243 Earth days
Length of year: 224.7 Earth days
Known moons: 0
**Fun fact: It never rains on Venus.**

## EARTH
Average distance from the sun:
  93,000,000 miles (149,600,000 km)
Position from the sun in orbit: 3rd
Equatorial diameter: 7,900 miles (12,750 km)
Length of day: 24 hours
Length of year: 365 days
Known moons: 1
**Fun fact: Earth traveled more than 5,000 miles (8,047 km) in the past five minutes.**

## MARS
Average distance from the sun:
  141,633,000 miles (227,936,000 km)
Position from the sun in orbit: 4th
Equatorial diameter: 4,221 miles (6,794 km)
Length of day: 25 Earth hours
Length of year: 1.9 Earth years
Known moons: 2
**Fun fact: Iron-rich soil gives Mars its reddish appearance.**

This artwork shows the eight planets and five dwarf planets in our solar system. The relative sizes and positions of the planets are shown but not the relative distances between them.

SATURN

URANUS

NEPTUNE

PLUTO
HAUMEA
MAKEMAKE
ERIS

## JUPITER
Average distance from the sun:
483,682,000 miles (778,412,000 km)
Position from the sun in orbit: 6th
Equatorial diameter: 88,840 miles (142,980 km)
Length of day: 9.9 Earth hours
Length of year: 11.9 Earth years
Known moons: 79*
Fun fact: Jupiter is the fastest spinning planet in the solar system.

## SATURN
Average distance from the sun:
890,800,000 miles (1,433,600,000 km)
Position from the sun in orbit: 7th
Equatorial diameter: 74,900 miles (120,540 km)
Length of day: 10.7 Earth hours
Length of year: 29.5 Earth years
Known moons: 82*
Fun fact: Scientists believe that Saturn's rings will eventually disappear.

## URANUS
Average distance from the sun:
1,784,000,000 miles (2,871,000,000 km)
Position from the sun in orbit: 8th
Equatorial diameter: 31,760 miles (51,120 km)
Length of day: 17.2 Earth hours
Length of year: 84 Earth years
Known moons: 27
Fun fact: Summer on Uranus lasts 42 years.

## NEPTUNE
Average distance from the sun:
2,795,000,000 miles (4,498,000,000 km)
Position from the sun in orbit: 9th
Equatorial diameter: 30,775 miles (49,528 km)
Length of day: 16 Earth hours
Length of year: 164.8 Earth years
Known moons: 14
Fun fact: Large, dark spots on Neptune's surface are believed to be enormous storms.

*Includes provisional moons, which await confirmation and naming from the International Astronomical Union.

For information about dwarf planets—Ceres, Pluto, Haumea, Makemake, and Eris—see page 128.

# DWARF PLANETS

Haumea

Eris

Pluto

**Thanks to advanced technology,** astronomers have been spotting many never-before-seen celestial bodies with their telescopes. One new discovery? A population of icy objects orbiting the sun beyond Pluto. The largest, like Pluto itself, are classified as dwarf planets. Smaller than the moon but still massive enough to pull themselves into a ball, dwarf planets nevertheless lack the gravitational "oomph" to clear their neighborhood of other sizable objects. So, while larger, more massive planets pretty much have their orbits to themselves, dwarf planets orbit the sun in swarms that include other dwarf planets as well as smaller chunks of rock or ice.

So far, astronomers have identified five dwarf planets: Ceres, Pluto, Haumea, Makemake, and Eris. There are many more newly discovered dwarf planets that will need additional study before they are named. Astronomers are observing hundreds of newly found objects in the frigid outer solar system. As time and technology advance, the family of known dwarf planets will surely continue to grow.

## CERES
Position from the sun in orbit: 5th
Length of day: 9.1 Earth hours
Length of year: 4.6 Earth years
Known moons: 0

## PLUTO
Position from the sun in orbit: 10th
Length of day: 6.4 Earth days
Length of year: 248 Earth years
Known moons: 5

## HAUMEA
Position from the sun in orbit: 11th
Length of day: 3.9 Earth hours
Length of year: 282 Earth years
Known moons: 2

## MAKEMAKE
Position from the sun in orbit: 12th
Length of day: 22.5 Earth hours
Length of year: 305 Earth years
Known moons: 1*

## ERIS
Position from the sun in orbit: 13th
Length of day: 25.9 Earth hours
Length of year: 561 Earth years
Known moons: 1

*Includes provisional moons, which await confirmation and naming from the International Astronomical Union.

# BLACK HOLES

**BLACK HOLE** ▶

**A black hole** really seems like a hole in space. Most black holes form when the core of a massive star collapses, falling into oblivion. A black hole has a stronger gravitational pull than anything else in the known universe. It's like a bottomless pit, swallowing anything that gets close enough to it to be pulled in. It's black because it pulls in light. Black holes come in different sizes. The smallest known black hole has a mass about three times that of the sun. The biggest one scientists have found so far has a mass about three billion times greater than the sun's. Really big black holes at the centers of galaxies probably form by swallowing enormous amounts of gas over time. In 2019, scientists released the first image of a black hole's silhouette (left). The image, previously thought impossible to record, was captured using a network of telescopes.

# SPACED OUT

**THE CAT** Félicette
**THE SPOT** Space
**WHY SHE'S COOL** The fur really flew on October 18, 1963, when Félicette became the first cat in space. The French feline rocketed toward the stars to help researchers learn whether animals could survive the challenges of space travel. After soaring more than 100 miles (160 km) above Earth, the high-flying feline safely returned home the same day. We bet she was seeing stars.

# Sky Calendar 2021

Jupiter

Leonid meteor shower

Supermoon

- **JANUARY 3–4**
  QUADRANTIDS METEOR SHOWER PEAK. Featuring up to 40 meteors an hour, it is the first meteor shower of every new year.

- **APRIL 26–27**
  SUPERMOON, FULL MOON. The moon will be full and at a close approach to Earth, likely appearing bigger and brighter than usual. A supermoon will be visible April 26 in North and South America and April 27 in other continents. Look for two more supermoons on May 26 and June 24.

- **MAY 6–7**
  ETA AQUARIDS METEOR SHOWER PEAK. View about 30 to 60 meteors an hour.

- **MAY 17**
  MERCURY AT GREATEST EASTERN ELONGATION. Visible low in the western sky just after sunset, Mercury will be at its highest point above the horizon.

- **MAY 26**
  TOTAL LUNAR ECLIPSE. Look for the moon to darken and then take on a deep red color as it passes completely through Earth's umbra—or dark shadow. Visible in parts of western North America, eastern Asia, Japan, and Australia and throughout the Pacific Ocean.

- **AUGUST 2**
  SATURN AT OPPOSITION. This is your best chance to view the ringed planet in 2021. Saturn will appear bright in the sky and be visible throughout the night.

- **AUGUST 12–13**
  PERSEID METEOR SHOWER PEAK. One of the best! Up to 90 meteors an hour. Best viewing is in the direction of the constellation Perseus.

- **AUGUST 22**
  BLUE MOON, FULL MOON. You won't see this full moon turn colors. When there are four full moons in a season, such as there are this summer, the third one is called a blue moon. The second full moon in a month is also known as a blue moon. Both events are considered rare, happening only once every two or three years.

- **OCTOBER 21–22**
  ORIONID METEOR SHOWER PEAK. View up to 20 meteors an hour. Look toward the constellation Orion for the best show.

- **DECEMBER 13–14**
  GEMINID METEOR SHOWER PEAK. A spectacular show! Up to 120 multicolored meteors an hour.

- **2021—VARIOUS DATES**
  VIEW THE INTERNATIONAL SPACE STATION. Visit spotthestation.nasa.gov to find out when the ISS will be flying over your neighborhood.

Dates may vary slightly depending on your location. Check with a local planetarium for the best viewing time in your area.

# SUPER SUN!

**THE SUN IS 99.8 PERCENT OF ALL THE MASS IN OUR SOLAR SYSTEM.**

The SUN'S surface is about 10,000°F (5500°C)!

Even from 93 million miles (150 million km) away, the sun's rays are powerful enough to provide the energy needed for life to flourish on Earth. This 4.6-billion-year-old star is the anchor of our solar system and accounts for more than 99 percent of the mass in the solar system. What else makes the sun so special? For starters, it's larger than one million Earths and is the biggest object in our solar system. The sun also converts about four million tons (3,628,739 t) of matter to energy every second, helping to make life possible here on Earth. Now that's *sun*-sational!

There is **REAL GOLD** in the **SUN.**

# Storms on the Sun!

Solar flares are 10 million times more powerful than a volcanic eruption on Earth.

Solar storm

With the help of specialized equipment, scientists have observed solar flares—or bursts of magnetic energy that explode from the sun's surface as a result of storms on the sun. Solar storms occur about 2,000 times every 11 years, or once every two days. Most solar storms are minor and do not impact Earth. But the fiercer the flare, the more we may potentially feel its effects, as it could disrupt power grids or interfere with GPS navigation systems. Solar storms can also trigger stronger-than-usual auroras, light shows that can be seen on Earth.

Some solar storms travel at speeds of **THREE MILLION MILES AN HOUR** (4.8 million km/h).

131

# QUIZ WHIZ

Are your
space and Earth smarts
out of this world?
Take this quiz!

Write your answers
on a piece of paper.
Then check them below.

**1** **True or false?** Earth's mantle is made of hot, thick, solid rock.

**2** **How often do solar storms occur?**
a. once every 2 days
b. once every 200 years
c. once every 2 minutes
d. once every 2,000 years

**3** **Fill in the blank.**
A rocket delivered a _____ to the International Space Station.

**4** **What is a mineral's "streak"?**
a. its color when it is ground into powder
b. its weight
c. how it reflects light
d. how hard it is

**5** **True or false?** Some volcanoes are shaped like upside-down ice-cream cones.

Not **STUMPED** yet? Check out the
*NATIONAL GEOGRAPHIC KIDS QUIZ WHIZ* collection
for more crazy **SPACE AND EARTH** questions!

**ANSWERS:**
1. True; 2. a; 3. pizza; 4. a; 5. True

## HOMEWORK HELP

# ACE YOUR SCIENCE FAIR

**You can learn a lot about** science from books, but to really experience it firsthand, you need to get into the lab and "do" some science. Whether you're entering a science fair or just want to learn more on your own, there are many scientific projects you can do. So put on your goggles and lab coat, and start experimenting.

Most likely, the topic of the project will be up to you. So remember to choose something that is interesting to you.

**THE BASIS OF ALL SCIENTIFIC INVESTIGATION AND DISCOVERY IS THE SCIENTIFIC METHOD. CONDUCT YOUR EXPERIMENT USING THESE STEPS:**

**Observation/Research**—Ask a question or identify a problem.

**Hypothesis**—Once you've asked a question, do some thinking and come up with some possible answers.

**Experimentation**—How can you determine if your hypothesis is correct? You test it. You perform an experiment. Make sure the experiment you design will produce an answer to your question.

**Analysis**—Gather your results, and use a consistent process to carefully measure the results.

**Conclusion**—Do the results support your hypothesis?

**Report Your Findings**—Communicate your results in the form of a paper that summarizes your entire experiment.

## Bonus!

Take your project one step further. Your school may have an annual science fair, but there are also local, state, regional, and national science fair competitions. Compete with other students for awards, prizes, and scholarships!

## EXPERIMENT DESIGN
There are three types of experiments you can do.

**MODEL KIT**—a display, such as an "erupting volcano" model. Simple and to the point.

**DEMONSTRATION**—shows the scientific principles in action, such as a tornado in a wind tunnel.

**INVESTIGATION**—the home run of science projects, and just the type of project for science fairs. This kind demonstrates proper scientific experimentation and uses the scientific method to reveal answers to questions.

# FUN and GAMES

Young elephant seals in Antarctica

What did the elephant seal think of his new home?
He gave it a seal of approval!

# WE GAVE IT A SWIRL

Use the clues below to figure out which animals appear in these swirled pictures.

ANSWERS ON PAGE 338

**HINT!** Pink never goes out of style for this leggy creature.

**HINT!** Falsely known as a master of camouflage, this animal may actually change color to communicate, not to blend in.

**HINT!** This teddy bear look-alike isn't really a bear.

**HINT!** This gentle giant likes to *moo*-ve in a herd.

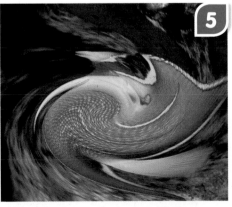

**HINT!** This animal doesn't mind spending its entire life in a school.

# WHAT IN THE WORLD?

## ALOHA SPIRIT

These photographs show close-up and faraway views of things you could see in Hawaii, U.S.A. On a separate sheet of paper, unscramble the letters to identify what's in each picture.

ANSWERS ON PAGE 338

**EPPIEPLSNA**

**SELI**

**TOCNCOU**

**AIWAAHIN SIRHT**

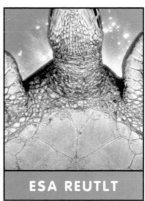

**ESA REUTLT**

**NVLAOOC**

**DAUSRFOBR**

**EKUULLE**

# GALAXY QUEST

Trace with your finger the path that Zorg the alien needs to take to get back to the mother ship. **ANSWER ON PAGE 338**

SPACE JUNK REMOVAL

BURGER HEAVEN

START

ZORG

Black
Hole
1,000,000
miles

ORBIT
INN

CAUTION!
BLACK
HOLE
#76972

# FUNNY FILL-IN

Ask a friend to give you words to fill in the blanks in this story and write them on a separate sheet of paper. Then read the story out loud and fill in the words for a laugh.

I was going to be rich! I had just invented the first electric _____. Using
                                                                    noun

a(n) _____ from _____ 's toolbox, I built it out of old _____
         tool              relative's name                                    noun, plural

and rubber _____. The first time I turned it on, the machine worked
               noun, plural

_____. I couldn't believe it! "_____!" I quickly invited
adverb ending in -ly                        exclamation

a(n) _____ billionaire to check out my invention. I couldn't wait to sell it for
          adjective

_____ million dollars and live like _____. But when
large number                                    name of a celebrity

I turned it on, something went terribly wrong. The machine started _____
                                                                      verb ending in -ing

and _____. Suddenly, it spewed _____ and shot slices of
      verb ending in -ing                    something slimy

_____ in all directions. The billionaire started screaming at the top of his
     food

_____ and ran out of my lab. Good thing I still get my weekly allowance.
body part, plural

# BARK
# PARK

Have you ever seen a dog that resembles its owner? Look for clues in the dog park to figure out which canine belongs to which owner. **ANSWERS ON PAGE 338**

# WHAT IN THE WORLD?

## COLOR YOUR WORLD

These images show close-up and faraway views of rainbow-colored objects. On a separate sheet of paper, unscramble the letters to identify what's in each picture.

**ANSWERS ON PAGE 338**

**TWSASREE**

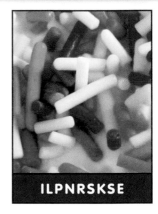

**NBRWAOI**

**ILPNRSKSE**

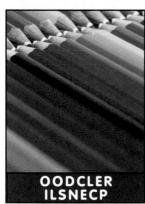

**OODCLER ILSNECP**

**LRBUEALM**

**HOUSETRTBSHO**

**RICCELOI**

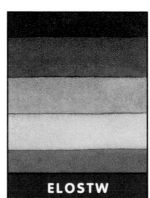

**ELOSTW**

**AESHFRTE**

# Just Joking

COW

**KNOCK, KNOCK.**

Who's there?
Olive.
Olive who?
Olive you.

**Q**

## Why do birds fly south in the winter?

It's easier than walking.

**A**

EMILY: Did you know you were built upside down?
ADAM: What do you mean?
EMILY: Your nose runs and your feet smell.

Wait! I'm not nuts! I'm just nuts for you!

You've **got** to be joking ...

# UNDERSEA STARS

This underwater band is jamming onstage, but it looks as if their instruments have disappeared. Or have they? Find the 10 instruments hidden in the scene. **ANSWERS ON PAGE 338**

1. piano
2. drums
3. flute
4. saxophone
5. triangle
6. violin
7. accordion
8. guitar
9. maracas
10. tambourine

# LAUGH OUT LOUD

"WHAT'S IT LIKE TO
GO FOR A WALK AND ACTUALLY
GO SOMEWHERE?"

"IT'S 'BRING YOUR IMAGINARY MONSTER
UNDER THE BED TO SCHOOL' DAY!"

"I DON'T CARE WHAT YOU SAY...
NEXT YEAR WE MIGRATE EARLIER."

"LOVE YOUR TURTLENECK!"

"IT'S GREAT YOU GOT A JOB AND ALL,
BUT YOU DIDN'T TELL ME YOU
WENT OVER TO THE DARK SIDE."

# FIND THE HIDDEN ANIMALS

Animals often blend in with their environments for protection. Find each animal listed below in one of the pictures. On a separate sheet of paper, write the letter of the correct picture and the animal's name.

**ANSWERS ON PAGE 338**

1. pygmy seahorses
2. Brazilian long-nosed bats
3. stone grasshopper
4. gray wolf
5. lion
6. European hares

# FUNNY FILL-IN

Ask a friend to give you words to fill in the blanks in this story and write them on a separate sheet of paper. Then read the story out loud and fill in the words for a laugh.

You'll never believe what happened when my family went on a(n) _____ safari in
<sub>adjective</sub>

_____ . We were having a great time snapping photos of the _____ wildlife.
<sub>country</sub> <sub>adjective</sub>

We saw _____ cubs, a(n) _____ -striped _____ that could run faster
<sub>animal</sub> <sub>color</sub> <sub>different animal</sub>

than _____ , and a(n) _____ _____ in a tree. Then our
<sub>famous athlete</sub> <sub>different animal</sub> <sub>verb ending in -ing</sub>

safari vehicle suddenly _____ to a stop. The wheels had become stuck in the mud.
<sub>past-tense verb</sub>

I turned around and saw a(n) _____ the size of _____ _____
<sub>different animal</sub> <sub>movie monster</sub> <sub>verb ending in -ing</sub>

toward us and making a sound like a(n) _____ . It was so close I could smell its foul-
<sub>musical instrument</sub>

scented breath. I thought the animal was going to flatten us like _____ ; instead,
<sub>breakfast food, plural</sub>

it just _____ the vehicle out of the muck with its _____ and
<sub>past-tense verb</sub> <sub>animal body part</sub>

_____ away. I couldn't wait to post these pictures on _____ .
<sub>past-tense verb</sub> <sub>website</sub>

**Play more Funny Fill-In!**
natgeokids.com/ff

147

# Just Joking

JAVAN GLIDING TREE FROG

**KNOCK, KNOCK.**

Who's there?
Annie.
Annie who?
Annie body home?

**Q** Why did the **police** stake out the baseball field?

**A** They heard that players were stealing bases.

**Q** Why couldn't the teddy bear eat his dessert?

**A** He was stuffed.

**Q** What do you get if **your parakeet** flies into the **blender?**

**A** Shredded tweet.

Just Joking

Check out this book!

148

# SIGNS OF THE TIMES

Seeing isn't always believing. One of these funny signs is not real. Can you figure out which one is fake?
**ANSWER ON PAGE 338**

1. JAIL. SCHOOL.

2. Nowhere ↓ Somewhere ↓

3. Leprechaun crossing

4. CEMETERY LANE ← DEAD END

5. SKY

6. THE OTHER ST THIS ST

7. WHOA

149

# WINDY JUMBLE

A powerful wind has whipped through this neighborhood park. Some visitors' belongings have blown away and ended up with someone else. Figure out which items belong to the people listed on the right. On a separate piece of paper, match the correct letter with the names. We've done the first one for you.   **ANSWERS ON PAGE 338**

**A** Eleanor  ___ Steve  ___ Jill
___ Sam  ___ Carlos  ___ Isabel
___ Nicole  ___ Zak  ___ Daniel
___ Ava

# Just Joking

SEA OTTER

**KNOCK, KNOCK.**

*Who's there?*
Cash.
*Cash who?*
No thanks.
I prefer peanuts.

Q

What do you call a **grizzly bear** with **no teeth?**

A gummy bear.

A

Say this three times:

**Rolling red wagons race wildly down roads.**

**TWO SNAKES ARE TALKING.**

You've **got** to be joking ...

SNAKE 1:
"Are we venomous?"

SNAKE 2:
"Yes, why?"

SNAKE 1:
"I just bit my lip."

151

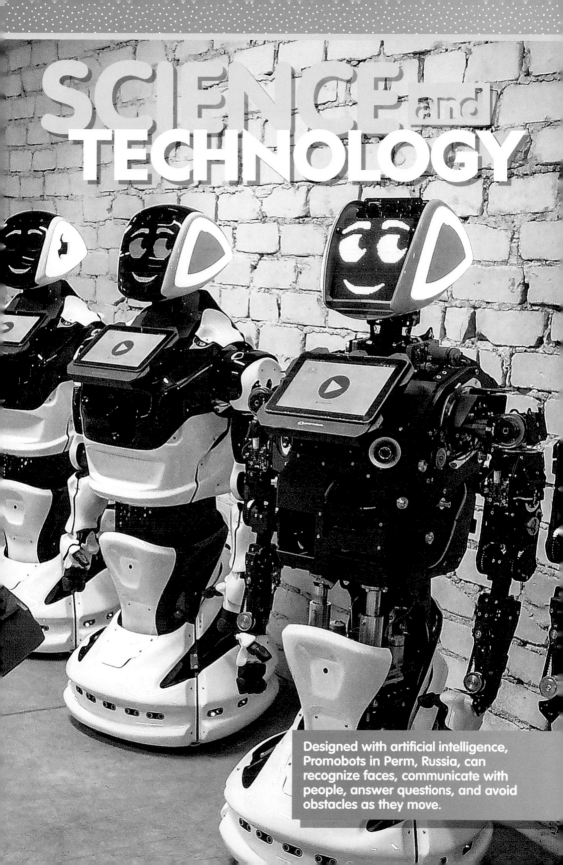

# SCIENCE and TECHNOLOGY

Designed with artificial intelligence, Promobots in Perm, Russia, can recognize faces, communicate with people, answer questions, and avoid obstacles as they move.

# JUNGLE DISCOVERY!

**National Geographic Explorer Albert Lin uses modern technology to find clues to the past.**

LASER SCANS HAVE UNCOVERED 60,000 PREVIOUSLY UNKNOWN MAYA STRUCTURES.

ANCIENT MAYA RUINS HIDDEN BENEATH THE FOREST CANOPY

I n northern Guatemala, thick green jungles extend for as far as the eye can see. It's hard to imagine that any humans could ever live beneath the dense jungle canopy, let alone establish an entire city. But as National Geographic Explorer Albert Lin recently discovered, this was once indeed the site of a thriving and sophisticated civilization some 1,500 years ago.

As an explorer and engineer, Lin has carved a career out of blending cutting-edge technology with uncovering the past. In Guatemala, seeking to uncover clues from the past, he used an aerial scanning technology called LiDAR, which stands for Light Detection and Ranging. Lin and his crew fired off pulses of laser light from an airplane to penetrate the dense canopy, then measured how long it took for each pulse to bounce back from the ground. A shorter return could mean that the beams bounced off of something elevated, like a temple. A longer measurement may indicate there's something much lower lurking beneath the treetops, like a deep riverbed. Then, with the help of GPS technology, Lin combined the data to create a detailed 3D map of the terrain. The result? A sprawling Maya "megalopolis"—several large, connected cities—about the size of Italy hidden in the dense tropical forest.

And Lin didn't stop there: With his "treasure map" in hand, Lin and his crew then trekked for hours in the jungle before locating the ancient ruins of the Maya people.

"We just followed a map created by lasers in the sky, using a helicopter to get into the jungle ... and found this,"

A NEWLY DISCOVERED MAYA PYRAMID MEASURES SEVEN STORIES HIGH.

people—did fight in major wars with nearby civilizations. Causeways—roads built on top of bodies of water—show that they likely traded with other regions.

Lin's breakthrough casts new light on the mysterious Maya world, which reached its height between A.D. 250 and 950 before its collapse. While no one truly knows what brought about the Maya's downfall, Lin's work brings us one step closer to understanding—and appreciating—the impressively complex and sophisticated civilization.

recalls Lin of the 100-foot (30-m)-tall ancient pyramid he discovered, which was previously mistaken by archaeologists to be a small mountain.

Among the other discoveries in the ancient Maya ruins? More than 60,000 structures, including pyramids, palaces, houses, farms, and roadways linking distant cities and towns. This suggests that the Maya civilization was much bigger than originally thought, with a population hovering between 10 and 15 million—a number much higher than previous estimates.

More LiDAR data uncovered extensive fortresses and defensive walls, which supports one theory that the Maya— previously thought to be mostly peaceful

Says Lin: "This LiDAR data is essentially rewriting the history of the Maya."

THE NAKED EYE SEES ONLY JUNGLE (ABOVE), BUT LIN'S TECHNOLOGY HAS REVEALED AN ANCIENT MAYA PYRAMID (BELOW).

LiDAR TECHNOLOGY HAS SHOWN THAT SOME MAYA CITIES WERE MUCH LARGER THAN RESEARCHERS PREVIOUSLY THOUGHT.

**Bet You Didn't Know!**

# 10 high-tech facts about

**1** **Robotic luggage** can follow **travelers** as they walk.

**2** A team of Swiss researchers built a robot small enough to **swim** through human arteries.

**3** The word **"robot"** first appeared in a play **written in 1929.**

**4** You can compete against a robot in **Ping-Pong.**

**5** **The first robot debuted in 1961** and worked in a **General Motors** automobile factory.

**6** **Some robots** can identify different **cheeses.**

# robots

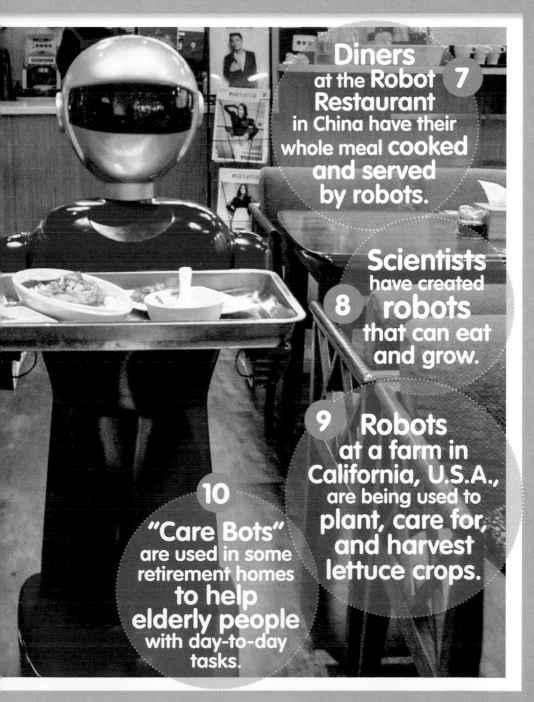

**Diners** at the **Robot Restaurant** in China have their whole meal **cooked and served by robots.** 7

**Scientists** have created 8 **robots** that can eat and grow.

9 **Robots** at a farm in California, U.S.A., are being used to **plant, care for, and harvest lettuce crops.**

10 **"Care Bots"** are used in some retirement homes **to help elderly people** with day-to-day tasks.

# FUTURE WORLD:

The year is 2070, and it's time to get dressed for school. You step in front of a large video mirror that projects different clothes on you. After you decide on your favorite T-shirt, a robot fetches your outfit. No time is lost trying to find matching socks! Chores? What chores? Get ready for a whole new home life.

## STAY CONNECTED

Whether your future home is an urban skyscraper or an underwater pod, all buildings will one day be connected via a central communications hub. Want to check out a *T. rex* skeleton at a faraway museum? You can virtually connect to it just as though you were checking it out in person. But you're not just seeing something miles away. Connect to a beach house's balcony and smell the salt water and feel the breeze. Buildings might also share information about incoming weather and emergencies to keep you safe.

## CUSTOM COMFORT ▼

Soon, your house may give you a personal welcome home. No need for keys—sensors scan your body and open the door. Walk into the living room, and the lighting adjusts to your preferred setting. Thirsty? A glass of water pops up on the counter. Before bed, you enter the bathroom and say, "Shower, please." The water starts flowing at exactly the temperature you want.

## ON LOCATION ▶

Your room has a spectacular view of the ocean ... because your house is suspended above it. New technologies will allow us to build our homes in unusual spots. In the future, "floating" structures elevated by supporting poles above water or other hard-to-access spots (think mountain peaks) will be more common as cities become more crowded. And this won't be limited to dry land on Earth. That means that one day your family could even live in space!

# Homes

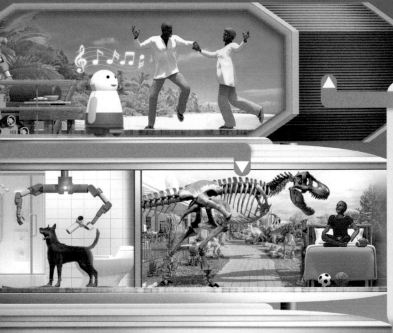

## ON THE GO

Homes of the future will always be on the move. Walls will be capable of expanding and contracting, and houses will rotate with the sun's movements to conserve energy. Buildings will also be capable of changing size depending on who's inside. Grandparents could "move in" by attaching a modular section to the front, back, or top of the house.

## BRING ON THE BOTS

While you were outside playing with your friends, your house robot did the laundry, vacuumed, and cleaned the bathroom. Meanwhile, a drone just delivered groceries for the home-bot to put away. Minutes later, lunch is ready. The service is great ... but how will you earn your allowance? Instead of taking out the garbage or setting the table, you'll earn money by helping clean and maintain the robots.

# FUTURE WORLD:

**A** buzzer goes off, marking the start of a race. Your heart is pounding—not that you can hear it over the sound of revving engines. Your car weaves through the other vehicles, making its way to the front of the pack. Peering through the windshield, you see the finish line ahead. Your car crosses first! The crowd roars.

You aren't actually in the car. But thanks to a pair of smart glasses you're wearing in the stands, you experienced exactly what the real driver did on the course.

"In the future, advanced technology will enable us to feel as if we're part of the event," says Aymeric Castaing, founder of Umanimation, a future-tech media company. Take a peek at more ways we'll be entertained by 2060 and beyond—but first, check out two terms to know.

1. Augmented reality (AR): Technology that layers computer-generated images onto things in the real world (like in Pokémon GO)

2. Virtual reality (VR): A computer-generated experience that makes you feel as if you're inside a totally different world

## SUPER STADIUMS

Didn't see that catch? No worries: In the future, 3D holograms could appear in midair above the field to show replays of sports moments. For some events, you'll even get a seat in a flying pod that can put you close to the action. (The pod even flies you home afterward!) Meanwhile, say goodbye to long lines for food or team jerseys. Through an app, flying drones will deliver anything you order right to your seat.

## GAME ON

A colorful alien zooms directly toward you, attempting to knock you aside with its spaceship. You put your hands in front of you, blocking the alien with a powerful force field. A crowd cheers your dramatic victory.

To the group assembled in front of you in the park, it looks like you just took down an alien spaceship—thanks to virtual reality (VR) goggles and a suit with motion sensors. Everything you saw through your goggles was projected onto a video screen at a virtual gaming playground. There the audience can watch and cheer as you go up against the aliens. They can also wear headsets and feel as if they're in outer space, too!

# Entertainment

### MUSEUMS TO GO

Museums of the future will blend real life with augmented and virtual reality. For example, you can check out a sculpture at an art museum with AR glasses, getting details about the artist and style. Then, using your VR headset, you can draw your own masterpiece inspired by what you saw. Not feeling creative? "Using your in-home VR headset and a 3D printer, you can create what you saw in the museum in your bedroom," Castaing says. It's like taking the museum home with you—sort of.

### THE BIG SCREEN

There won't be a bad seat in the house at movie theaters in the future. Films will surround the audience with 3D screens in every direction ... including the floor and ceiling. You'll feel like you're underwater at the latest ocean adventure blockbuster. Plus, robots will deliver the snacks you've ordered from your seat's tablet directly to your rotating chair.

### DROID BEATS

Ready to rock out to your favorite band? Whether it's pop-star robots or a robot orchestra conductor, future music may be in nonhuman hands. And audiences won't just hear music played by robots—they'll be able to see it. Augmented reality (AR) glasses will allow audiences to see which notes are coming out of the instruments in front of them. "AR glasses could even enable beginning musicians to take their lessons on the go," Castaing says. "The glasses could essentially become their teacher."

# WHAT IS LIFE?

**T**his seems like such an easy question to answer. Everybody knows that singing birds are alive and rocks are not. But when we start studying bacteria and other microscopic creatures, things get more complicated.

## SO WHAT EXACTLY IS LIFE?
Most scientists agree that something is alive if it can do the following: reproduce; grow in size to become more complex in structure; take in nutrients to survive; give off waste products; and respond to external stimuli, such as increased sunlight or changes in temperature.

## KINDS OF LIFE
Biologists classify living organisms by how they get their energy. Organisms such as algae, green plants, and some bacteria use sunlight as an energy source. Animals (like humans), fungi, and some single-celled microscopic organisms called Archaea use chemicals to provide energy. When we eat food, chemical reactions within our digestive system turn our food into fuel.

Living things inhabit land, sea, and air. In fact, life also thrives deep beneath the oceans, embedded in rocks miles below Earth's crust, in ice, and in other extreme environments. The life-forms that thrive in these challenging environments are called extremophiles. Some of these draw directly upon the chemicals surrounding them for energy. Since these are very different forms of life than what we're used to, we may not think of them as alive, but they are.

## HOW IT ALL WORKS
To try and understand how a living organism works, it helps to look at one example of its simplest form—the single-celled bacterium called *Streptococcus*. There are many kinds of these tiny organisms, and some are responsible for human illnesses. What makes us sick or uncomfortable are the toxins the bacteria give off in our bodies.

A single *Streptococcus* bacterium is so small that at least 500 of them could fit on the dot above this letter *i*. These bacteria are some of the simplest forms of life we know. They have no moving parts, no lungs, no brain, no heart, no liver, and no leaves or fruit. Yet this life-form reproduces. It grows in size by producing long chain structures, takes in nutrients, and gives off waste products. This tiny life-form is alive, just as you are alive.

What makes something alive is a question scientists grapple with when they study viruses, such as the ones that cause the common cold and smallpox. They can grow and reproduce within host cells, such as those that make up your body. Because viruses lack cells and cannot metabolize nutrients for energy or reproduce without a host, scientists ask if they are indeed alive. And don't go looking for them without a strong microscope— viruses are a hundred times smaller than bacteria.

Scientists think life began on Earth some 4.1 to 3.9 billion years ago, but no fossils exist from that time. The earliest fossils ever found are from the primitive life that existed 3.6 billion years ago. Other life-forms, some of which are shown below, soon followed. Scientists continue to study how life evolved on Earth and whether it is possible that life exists on other planets.

## MICROSCOPIC ORGANISMS

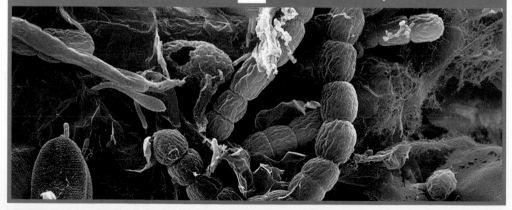

# The Three Domains of Life

Biologists divide all living organisms into three domains, or groups: Bacteria, Archaea, and Eukarya. Archaea and Bacteria cells do not have nuclei—cellular parts that are essential to reproduction and other cell functions—but they are different from each other in many ways. Because human cells have a nucleus, we belong to the Eukarya domain.

**1** BACTERIA

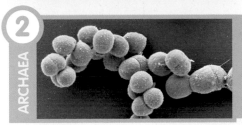

**DOMAIN BACTERIA:** These single-celled microorganisms are found almost everywhere in the world. Bacteria are small and do not have nuclei. They can be shaped like rods, spirals, or spheres. Some of them are helpful to humans, and some are harmful.

**2** ARCHAEA

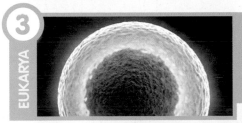

**DOMAIN ARCHAEA:** These single-celled microorganisms are often found in extremely hostile environments. Like Bacteria, Archaea do not have nuclei, but they have some genes in common with Eukarya. For this reason, scientists think the Archaea living today most closely resemble the earliest forms of life on Earth.

**3** EUKARYA

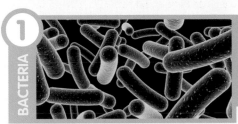

**DOMAIN EUKARYA:** This diverse group of life-forms is more complicated than Bacteria and Archaea, as Eukarya have one or more cells with nuclei. These are the tiny cells that make up your whole body. Eukarya are divided into four groups: fungi, protists, plants, and animals.

**WHAT IS A DOMAIN?** Scientifically speaking, a domain is a major taxonomic division into which natural objects are classified (see page 46 for "What Is Taxonomy?").

**FYI**

**FUNGI**

**KINGDOM FUNGI (about 100,000 species):** Mainly multicellular organisms, fungi cannot make their own food. Mushrooms and yeast are fungi.

**PROTISTS**

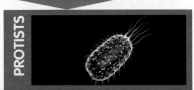

**PROTISTS (about 250,000 species):** Once considered a kingdom, this group is a "grab bag" that includes unicellular and multicellular organisms of great variety.

**PLANTS**

**KINGDOM PLANTAE (about 400,000 species):** Plants are multicellular, and many can make their own food using photosynthesis (see page 166 for "Photosynthesis").

**ANIMALS**

**KINGDOM ANIMALIA (about 1,000,000 species):** Most animals, which are multicellular, have their own organ systems. Animals do not make their own food.

# HOW DOES YOUR GARDEN GROW?

The plant kingdom is about 400,000 species strong, growing all over the world: on top of mountains, in the sea, in frigid temperatures—everywhere. Without plants, life on Earth would not be able to survive. Plants provide food and oxygen for animals and humans.

**Plants have three distinct characteristics:**

**1.** Most have chlorophyll (a green pigment that makes photosynthesis work and turns sunlight into energy), while some are parasitic. Parasitic plants don't make their own food—they take it from other plants.

**2.** Plants cannot change their location on their own.

**3.** Their cell walls are made from a stiff material called cellulose.

# Photosynthesis

Plants are lucky—most don't have to hunt or shop for food. Most use the sun to produce their own food. In a process called photosynthesis, a plant's chloroplast (the part of the plant where the chemical chlorophyll is located) captures the sun's energy and combines it with carbon dioxide from the air and nutrient-rich water from the ground to produce a sugar called glucose.

Plants burn the glucose for energy to help them grow. As a waste product, plants emit oxygen, which humans and other animals need to breathe. When we breathe, we exhale carbon dioxide, which the plants then use for more photosynthesis—it's all a big, finely tuned system. So the next time you pass a lonely houseplant, give it thanks for helping you live.

# Plant a BUTTERFLY GARDEN

**TAILED JAY**

**BUCKEYE**

**SPICEBUSH SWALLOWTAIL**

## BENEFITS OF BUTTERFLIES

Sure, butterflies are pretty. But they're also pollinators. Like bees, they travel to flowers seeking nectar. In the process, they spread pollen from one area to another, helping other plants grow. That's why "nectar plants" are an important part of your butterfly garden. They help spread the growth of valuable plants to many other places.

### SUPPLY LIST
- BUTTERFLY-FRIENDLY PLANTS
- HOST PLANTS TO LAY EGGS ON

**MONARCH**

**RED-SPOTTED PURPLE**

**EASTERN TIGER SWALLOWTAIL**

**1** Choose a spot for your garden. Butterflies like lots of sun, so make sure you plant your garden in an area that gets at least six hours of direct sunlight a day.

**2** Besides sun, butterflies need protection from wind and rain. Make sure trees or shrubs are part of your butterfly garden.

**3** Find out what butterflies you should attract. Look in a field guide or ask a ranger at a local park which butterfly species are common in your area.

**4** Certain butterflies like certain types of plants. Your local nursery can help guide you to the right ones. Many butterflies are attracted to coneflower, lilac, and purple verbena. Try to pick plants that are native to the area where you are planting, and that bloom at different times of the year. That way, butterflies are always attracted to your garden.

**5** Butterflies will also need some host plants, such as milkweed, to lay their eggs on. Your nursery can help you select the best ones.

**6** Set up some chairs or a bench and watch your garden. Butterflies are less shy than birds and usually don't mind people being around them.

# Your Amazing Body!

The human body is a complicated mass of systems—nine systems, to be exact. Each system has a unique and critical purpose in the body, and we wouldn't be able to survive without all of them.

The **NERVOUS** system controls the body.

The **MUSCULAR** system makes movement possible.

The **SKELETAL** system supports the body.

The **CIRCULATORY** system moves blood throughout the body.

The **RESPIRATORY** system provides the body with oxygen.

The **DIGESTIVE** system breaks down food into nutrients and gets rid of waste.

The **IMMUNE** system protects the body against disease and infection.

The **ENDOCRINE** system regulates the body's functions.

The **REPRODUCTIVE** system enables people to produce offspring.

Weird but true!

YOUR **BRAIN** CAN HOLD **100 TIMES** MORE INFORMATION THAN AN AVERAGE **COMPUTER**.

A speck of **blood** contains about **5 million red blood cells.**

Your hands and wrists contain 26 percent of the bones in your body.

# BY the NUMBERS

## BRAIN POWER

**Your brain is the tops—literally.** It's the most complex organ in your body, an amazing supercomputer that controls everything you do. Check out some incredible info behind the numbers that nourish your noggin.

YOUR BRAIN CAN HOLD
**1 MILLION**
GIGABYTES OF DATA.
IF YOUR BRAIN WERE LIKE
A DVR, IT COULD HOLD
**3 MILLION** HOURS OF
TELEVISION SHOWS.

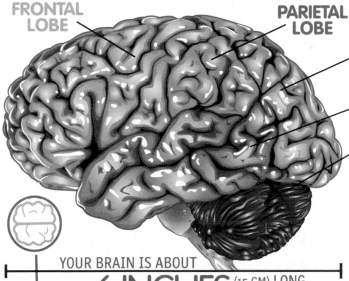

FRONTAL LOBE

PARIETAL LOBE

OCCIPITAL LOBE

TEMPORAL LOBE

CEREBELLUM

YOUR BRAIN IS ABOUT
**6 INCHES** (15 CM) LONG.

YOUR BRAIN
WEIGHS ABOUT
**3 POUNDS**
(1.3 KG).

LIKE THE EARTH, YOUR BRAIN IS DIVIDED INTO
**2**
HEMISPHERES.

YOUR BRAIN CONTAINS
**BILLIONS**
OF NERVE CELLS.

ABOUT
**2/3**
OF YOUR BRAIN IS MADE UP OF SPECIALIZED FATS.

THE BRAIN HAS
**12**
NERVE PAIRS THAT CONTROL THINGS LIKE TASTE AND HEARING.

# LOOK OUT!

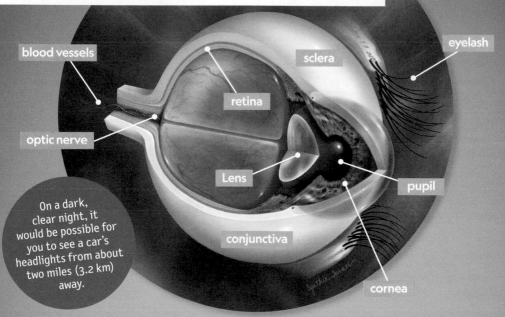

blood vessels

sclera

eyelash

retina

optic nerve

Lens

pupil

On a dark, clear night, it would be possible for you to see a car's headlights from about two miles (3.2 km) away.

conjunctiva

cornea

## Your eyes are two of the most amazing organs in your body.

These small, squishy, fluid-filled balls have almost three-quarters of your body's sensory receptors. They're like two supersmart cameras, but more complex.

So how do you see the world around you? It begins when you open the protective cover of your eyelid and let in the light. Light enters your eye through the window of your cornea and passes through the aqueous humor, a watery fluid that nourishes the eye tissue. It enters the black circle in the iris (the colored part of your eye), called the pupil. Because people need to be able to see in both bright and low light, muscles in the iris automatically make the pupil smaller when the light is strong and wider when the light is dim. Light then travels to the lens, whose muscles adjust it to be able to see objects both near and far. Then the light goes through the vitreous humor (a clear jellylike substance) to the retina. The retina, a layer of about 126 million light-sensitive cells, lines the back of your eyeball. When these cells absorb the light, they transform it into electrical signals that are sent along the optic nerve to the brain. The brain then makes sense of what you are seeing.

## A TOPSY-TURVY WORLD

Turn this over in your mind: You're looking at the world topsy-turvy, and you don't even know it. Like a camera lens, your lens focuses light, creates an image, and turns it upside down. Yep, when your lens focuses light inside your eye, it flips the image so it lands on your retina upside down. But, your brain knows to flip the image automatically to match your reality. But what if your reality suddenly

CAMERA LENS

changed? A well-known experiment in the mid-20th century in which a person wore special light-inverting goggles showed that his brain actually adjusted to the new, inverted world by eventually seeing the reversed view as normal! It is thought that newborns see the world upside down for a short while, until their brains learn how to turn things right-side up.

# AWESOME
# OPTICAL ILLUSIONS

## Ready to work your brain and show your visual alertness? Ponder these puzzling pictures to see what you see!

## WHICH CIRCLE IS **BIGGER?**

Both of these circle clusters have an orange circle surrounded by purple ones. But which orange circle is bigger? The answer may surprise you: neither! The two orange circles are the same size. The one on the right may appear bigger because it's surrounded by purple circles that are smaller than it is. The one on the left seems smaller because it's surrounded by purple circles that are larger than it is.

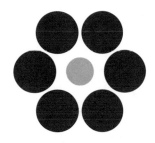

## RABBIT **OR** DUCK?

It's a duck! Or is it a rabbit? Can you see it both ways? A recent study using this illusion suggests that the more easily people can switch back and forth between the two images, the more creative they are.

## SPINNING CIRCLES

Do you see all the spinning circles? Don't look too long, or you might get dizzy! This illusion plays with your peripheral vision (vision from the sides of your eyes, not the middle). Sometimes when you look out the sides of your eyes, you see movement where really there are only patterns.

# MUSCLE POWER

## With its strong bones and flexible joints, your skeleton is built to be on the go.

But without muscles, it won't go anywhere! You need muscle power to make your body walk, run, skip, rub your nose, or even just sit up without toppling over.

The muscles that do these jobs are called skeletal muscles. You have about 650 of them, and you can control what they do. Sometimes, it takes a lot of skeletal muscles to make even a simple move. Your tongue alone contains eight muscles!

You also have muscles that work without your having to do a thing. Most of these muscles are called smooth muscles. Sheets of smooth muscle line your blood vessels, throat, stomach, intestines, lungs, and other organs. They are hard at work keeping your blood circulating and your food digesting while you're busy doing other things. And there's also that mighty muscle, your heart. It pumps thanks to cardiac muscles, which are found only in the heart.

### THE HIBERNATION MYSTERY

Very sick people often lie in bed for a long time as they recover. This lack of exercise weakens muscles—a process called "muscle atrophy." Preventing atrophy may be possible someday thanks to researchers who study hibernating animals.

Bears, for example, spend winter sleeping but do not suffer severe atrophy. When they wake up in the spring, they're as strong as—well, bears! Scientists are studying the muscles and blood of bears, ground squirrels, and other hibernators to find out how they stay in shape while sleeping. The answers may one day help people suffering from muscle atrophy when they're sick or in the hospital for a long time.

Bet You Didn't Know!

Some of your body's strongest muscles aren't in your arms or legs. They're in your jaws! These strong muscles are called the masseters. They help you chew by closing your lower jaw. Clenching your teeth will make your masseters bulge so you can feel them.

# BODY ELECTRIC

The nerve signal that tells your muscles to move is superfast! It zooms at 250 miles an hour (402 km/h), as fast as the fastest race car.

## Your body is just humming with electricity.

Nerve cells from head to toe speak to each other through electrical signals. The electrical signals zap down each nerve cell and, when they get to the end, jump across a tiny gap called a synapse (see image below). How does the signal jump across the gap?

The nerve produces special chemicals that can flow across the gap to the next cell. There,  a new electrical charge travels down the next nerve. Messages jump from neuron to neuron in a chain of electrical-chemical-electrical-chemical signals until they reach their destination.

Because nerves don't actually touch, they can change the path of their signals easily. They can make new connections and break old ones. This is how your brain learns and stores new information.

## BUNDLE OF NERVES

A 1.2-inch (3-cm) section of your brain stem (called the medulla oblongata) controls some of your body's most important functions, such as breathing and heart rate. Amazingly, it also contains your body's motor and sensory nerves and is where nerves from the left and right sides of your body cross each other on their journey toward your cerebrum.

**SENSORY NERVES** pull in information from nerve endings in your eyes, ears, skin, hands, and other parts of your body and then send this information to your brain.

**MOTOR NERVES** send messages from your brain to your muscles, telling them to contract, to run, or to walk.

**Bet You Didn't Know!**

A reflex is a nerve message that doesn't go through your brain. When you touch a hot stove, for example, a sensory neuron picks up the message ("Hot!") and passes it to a motor neuron in your spinal cord. The motor neuron then sends a message to your hand, telling it to move ("Quick!").

# THE INVADERS ARE COMING!

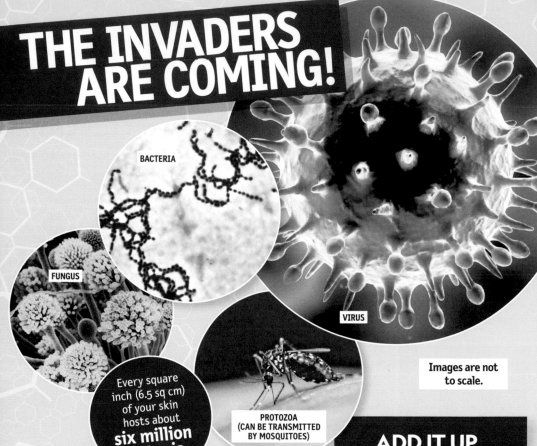

BACTERIA

FUNGUS

VIRUS

Images are not to scale.

Every square inch (6.5 sq cm) of your skin hosts about **six million bacteria.**

PROTOZOA (CAN BE TRANSMITTED BY MOSQUITOES)

**Some microorganisms (tiny living things) can make your body sick.** They are too small to see with the naked eye. These creatures—bacteria, viruses, fungi, and protozoa—are what you may know as germs.

Bacteria are microscopic organisms that live nearly everywhere on Earth, including on and in the human body. "Good" bacteria help our digestive systems work properly. Harmful bacteria can cause ailments, including ear infections and strep throat.

A virus, like a cold or the flu, needs to live inside another living thing (a host) to survive; then it can grow and multiply throughout the host's body.

Fungi get their food from the plants, animals, or people they live on. Some fungi can get on your body and cause skin diseases such as ringworm.

Protozoa are single-celled organisms that can spread disease to humans through contaminated water and dirty living conditions. Protozoa can cause infections such as malaria, which occurs when a person is bitten by an infected mosquito.

## ADD IT UP

So you know that you have bacteria on your skin and in your body. But do you know how many? Trillions. That's more than 1,000,000,000,000! Most are harmless and some are pretty friendly, keeping more dangerous bacteria at bay, protecting you from some skin infections, and helping your cuts heal.

# GERM **SHOWDOWN**

Scientists in Wales studied three greeting styles to determine which was the cleanest. Find out which one has the upper hand.

## HANDSHAKE

AN AVERAGE HANDSHAKE TRANSFERRED **MORE THAN 5 TIMES AS MUCH BACTERIA** AS A FIST BUMP. (A STRONG HANDSHAKE TRANSFERRED **10 TIMES** AS MUCH.)

## HIGH FIVE

A HIGH FIVE PASSED **TWICE AS MANY** GERMS AS A FIST BUMP.

## FIST BUMP

WINNER:

FIST BUMPS HAVE THE **LEAST SKIN-TO-SKIN CONTACT** OF THE GREETINGS, WHICH MAKES IT LESS LIKELY FOR MICROBES TO JUMP **FROM ONE HAND TO ANOTHER.**

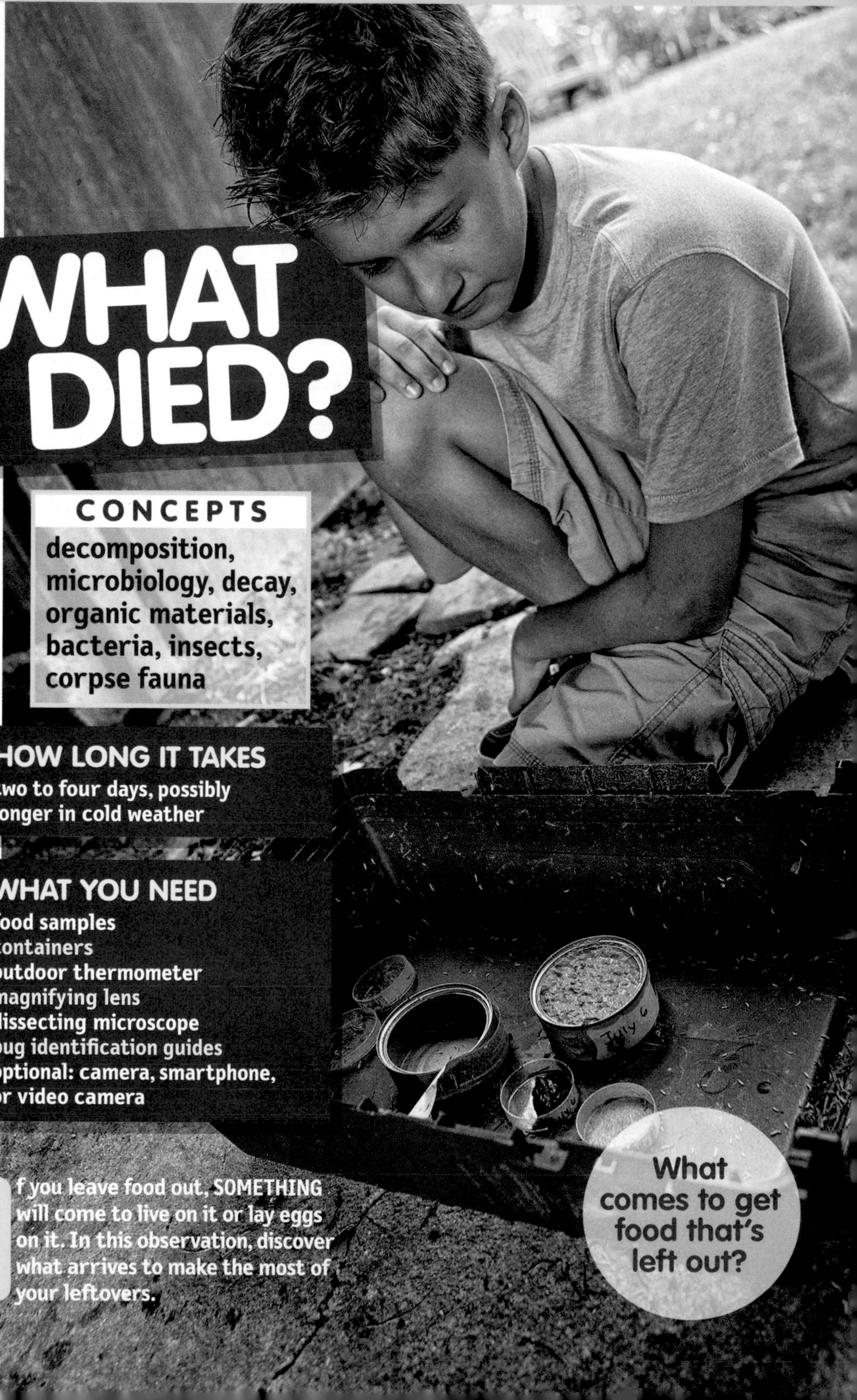

# WHAT DIED?

## CONCEPTS

decomposition, microbiology, decay, organic materials, bacteria, insects, corpse fauna

## HOW LONG IT TAKES

two to four days, possibly longer in cold weather

## WHAT YOU NEED

food samples
containers
outdoor thermometer
magnifying lens
dissecting microscope
bug identification guides
optional: camera, smartphone, or video camera

If you leave food out, SOMETHING will come to live on it or lay eggs on it. In this observation, discover what arrives to make the most of your leftovers.

What comes to get food that's left out?

176

## WHAT TO DO

### DAY ONE:

**1 WORK IN AN OPEN-AIR** area, compost heap, or compost bin—a place that is open to bugs but not birds or other animals. Ask an adult to help you choose a location.

**2 SET UP FOUR** containers with a small sample of food inside each. If you want, these samples can represent the four food groups: vegetable/fruit, meat/fish, bread/grains, and milk/dairy.

### DAYS TWO TO FOUR:

**3 KEEP A CAREFUL** record of what you observe through your senses. Each day, record the temperature in the area where your samples are. Note whether you can see signs that bugs or other creatures have been attracted to your samples, including any film or mold that forms. You may want to photograph the samples every day to compare them.

**4 EVERY ONE OR TWO** days (decide which interval you want to study), remove the samples from the containers to examine them with a magnifying lens and microscope. Count, try to identify, and sketch the bugs and other life-forms that colonize each sample. Add descriptions to your notes, including sensory observations: texture, color, and smell—but not taste!

**WHAT TO EXPECT?**
You may see mold, biofilm or scum, bugs, worms, flies, and so on.

**WHAT'S GOING ON?**
Nature abhors a vacuum. If there is food, something will come to eat it.

## OUR TRY

We put out duplicate food—chicken broth, blackberry jam, and cat food—every other day for six days. We set out the food in the yard, in a cat carrier with a brick on top, but that didn't stop coyotes from pulling it apart and getting the food on the second night. After that we replaced the food and kept the cat carrier in the garage, where flies could still get to it. After we opened it to see what we had and examine it with the microscope, we dumped the cat carrier near the compost heap—and later, we had a glorious infestation of beetles.

### QUESTION THIS!

- What would happen to this food if nothing were able to reach it?

- What would happen to this food if you let more time pass?

# QUIZ WHIZ

**Test your science and technology smarts by taking this quiz!**

Write your answers on a piece of paper. Then check them below.

**1** What did explorers recently discover in the Guatemalan rainforest?

**a.** an ancient city
**b.** a new species of bird
**c.** a crater the size of the Grand Canyon
**d.** a mysterious spaceship

**2** **True or false?** Butterflies are pollinators, like bees.

**3** Scientists have created robots that can _____.

**a.** identify different types of cheese
**b.** help humans with daily tasks
**c.** play Ping-Pong
**d.** all of the above

**4** How many species are in the kingdom Animalia?

**a.** 10
**b.** 1,000
**c.** 10,000
**d.** 1,000,000

**5** **True or false?** Your brain weighs about 13 pounds (6 kg).

Not **STUMPED** yet? Check out the *NATIONAL GEOGRAPHIC KIDS QUIZ WHIZ* collection for more crazy **SCIENCE AND TECHNOLOGY** questions!

**ANSWERS:**
1. a; 2. True; 3. d; 4. d; 5. False. It weighs about 3 pounds (1.3 kg).

# This Is How It's Done!

Sometimes, the most complicated problems are solved with step-by-step directions. These "how-to" instructions are also known as a process analysis essay. While scientists and engineers use this tool to program robots and write computer code, you also use process analysis every day, from following a recipe to putting together a new toy or gadget. Here's how to write a basic process analysis essay.

## Step 1: Choose Your Topic Sentence

Pick a clear and concise topic sentence that describes what you're writing about. Be sure to explain to the reader why the task is important—and how many steps there are to complete it.

## Step 2: List Materials

Do you need specific ingredients or equipment to complete your process? Mention these right away so the readers will have all they need to do this activity.

## Step 3: Write Your Directions

Your directions should be clear and easy to follow. Assume that you are explaining the process for the first time, and define any unfamiliar terms. List your steps in the exact order the reader will need to follow to complete the activity. Try to keep your essay limited to no more than six steps.

## Step 4: Restate Your Main Idea

Your closing idea should revisit your topic sentence, drawing a conclusion relating to the importance of the subject.

## EXAMPLE OF A PROCESS ANALYSIS ESSAY

Downloading an app is a simple way to enhance your tablet. Today, I'd like to show you how to search for and add an app to your tablet. First, you will need a tablet with the ability to access the internet. You'll also want to ask a parent for permission before you download anything onto your tablet. Next, select the specific app you're seeking by going to the app store on your tablet and entering the app's name into the search bar. Once you find the app you're seeking, select "download" and wait for the app to load. When you see that the app has fully loaded, tap on the icon and you will be able to access it. Now you can enjoy your app and have more fun with your tablet.

With a population of more than five million, Abidjan, Côte d'Ivoire (Ivory Coast), in Africa, is one of the largest French-speaking cities in the world.

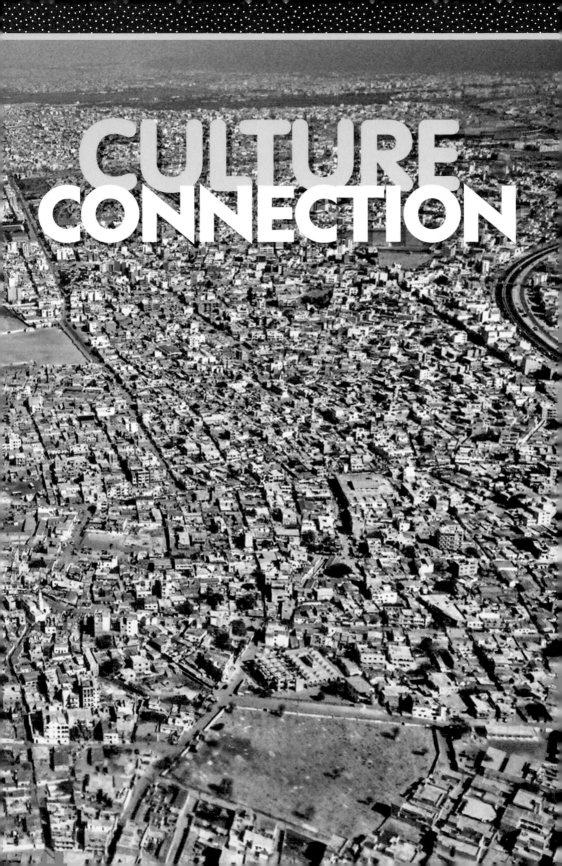

# CULTURE
# CONNECTION

# EIGHT
# Works of Mind-Bending
# STREET ART

**YOUR EYES DON'T DECEIVE YOU!
THESE OPEN-AIR WORKS OF ART
WILL MAKE YOU STOP IN YOUR TRACKS.**

**1**

## RUNAWAY RAILCAR
This 3D painting depicting a soon-to-be precarious predicament was part of a "Magic Art" special exhibition in the city of Hangzhou, China.

**2**

## ABOUT FACE
Toronto, Canada–based visual artist Dan Bergeron created this amazing illusion as part of his "Face of the City" series, which incorporates the surfaces of urban walls into his works of art.

**3**

## HOLE-Y MOLEY!
Whoa—that's a bad one. Actually, it's a really great illusion by artists 3D Joe and Max displayed in Trafalgar Square, London, U.K., calling attention to the pitfalls of potholes.

**4**

## NOAH'S ARK
This sprawling three-dimensional reimagining of the flood story was painted on Valois Square in Wilhelmshaven, Germany.

**5**

## HANGING AROUND

Created outside the main entrance to the Corinthia Hotel in London, U.K., this incredible 3D depiction features the likeness of a crystal chandelier in the hotel's Lobby Lounge.

**6**

## WHERE'S WALDO?

French street artist Oakoak's illusion references the children's book series that challenges readers to find the hidden main character among large groups of people in different locations.

**7**

## LONG JUMP

Can you make it across the abyss? This amazing 3D scene is painted on the dam on Dunajec River in Niedzica, Poland.

**8**

## DIVE IN!

Artists 3D Joe and Max created this work to commemorate the two-year anniversary of the London 2012 Olympics. It features iconic scenery as well as athletes from the games.

**183**

# Bet You Didn't Know!

# 10 edible facts about food

**1** Haggis, a meal of simmered sheep heart, liver, and lungs, is served alongside mashed potatoes in Scotland.

**2** In Poland, stuffed cabbage rolls are called gołąbki—which means "little pigeons."

**3** Food trucks at the Texas, U.S.A., State Fair serve a dish of pickles fried in red Kool-Aid.

**4** Fish-shaped marshmallows covered in chocolate are a favorite candy in New Zealand.

**5** Because of its strong smell, durian fruit is banned in some trains, buses, and hotels in Asia.

Durian

# from around the world

**6** Bunny chow— curry served in hollow bread— is popular in **South Africa.**

**7** In **Thailand, crickets** are farmed for **food.**

**8** Traditional Mongolian cuisine includes food made from the **"five snouts"**— goats, cows, horses, yaks, and camels.

**9** **Natto,** a blend of **fermented soybeans** popular in Japan, is said to **smell like sweaty socks.**

**10** **Ant eggs** are a high-end food in Mexico, where they're known as *escamoles.*

# CELEBRATIONS

## 1 CHINESE NEW YEAR

**February 12**
Also called Lunar New Year, this holiday marks the new year according to the lunar calendar. Families celebrate with parades, feasts, and fireworks. Young people may receive gifts of money in red envelopes.

## 2 NYEPI
**March 14**
A national day of silence, this Hindu holiday marks Lunar New Year in Bali, Indonesia, and encourages meditation and reflection. Those who follow traditional customs do not talk, use electricity, travel, or eat for 24 hours.

## 3 ST. PATRICK'S DAY
**March 17**
This celebration sparks parties across the planet. Major monuments like the Christ the Redeemer statue in Rio de Janeiro, Brazil, and the London Eye in England are cast in green light to celebrate Irish culture and honor Ireland's patron saint.

## 4 QINGMING FESTIVAL
**April 4**
Also known as Grave Sweeping Day, this Chinese celebration calls on people to return to the graves of their deceased loved ones. There, they tidy up the graves, as well as light firecrackers, burn fake money, and leave food as an offering to the spirits.

## 5 EASTER
**April 4**
A Christian holiday that honors the resurrection of Jesus Christ, Easter is celebrated by giving baskets filled with gifts, decorated eggs, or candy to children.

## 6 VESAK DAY
**April or May, date varies by country**
Buddhists around the world observe Buddha's birthday with rituals including chanting and prayer, candlelight processions, and meditation.

## 7 RAMADAN AND EID AL-FITR
**April 12\*–May 13\*\***
A Muslim holiday, Ramadan is a month long, ending in the Eid al-Fitr celebration. Observers fast during this month—eating only after sunset. People pray for forgiveness and hope to purify themselves through observance.

## 8 BERMUDA DAY
**May 28**
The first day of the year that Bermudians take a dip in the ocean. It is also traditionally the first day on which Bermuda shorts are worn as business attire. To celebrate the holiday, there is a parade in Hamilton, and a road race from the west end of the island into Hamilton.

## 9 ST. JOHN'S NIGHT
**June 23**
In Poland, people celebrate the longest day of the year—also known as the summer solstice—with rituals that include lighting bonfires, floating flower wreaths down a stream, and releasing thousands of paper lanterns into the night sky.

## 10 BORYEONG MUD FESTIVAL
**July**
During the Boryeong Mud Festival in South Korea, people swim, slide, and wrestle in the mud, then kick back and relax to music and fireworks.

\*Begins at sundown.
\*\*Dates may vary slightly by location.

# Around the World

## 11 ROSH HASHANAH
**September 6*–8**
A Jewish holiday marking the beginning of a new year on the Hebrew calendar. Celebrations include prayer, ritual foods, and a day of rest.

## 12 DÍA DE LOS MUERTOS
**October 31–November 2**
There's nothing scary about Día de los Muertos ("Day of the Dead"), a Mexican holiday that celebrates and honors the deceased. The three-day festival involves family gatherings, street fairs, and visits to graveyards to leave gifts for loved ones who have passed away.

## 13 DIWALI
**November 4**
India's largest and most important holiday. People light their homes with clay lamps to symbolize the inner light that protects against spiritual darkness.

## 14 HANUKKAH
**November 28*–December 6**
This Jewish holiday is eight days long. It commemorates the rededication of the Temple in Jerusalem. Hanukkah celebrations include the lighting of menorah candles for eight days and the exchange of gifts.

## 15 CHRISTMAS DAY
**December 25**

A Christian holiday marking the birth of Jesus Christ, Christmas is usually celebrated by decorating trees, exchanging presents, and having festive gatherings.

# 2021 CALENDAR

### JANUARY
| S | M | T | W | T | F | S |
|---|---|---|---|---|---|---|
|   |   |   |   |   | 1 | 2 |
| 3 | 4 | 5 | 6 | 7 | 8 | 9 |
| 10 | 11 | 12 | 13 | 14 | 15 | 16 |
| 17 | 18 | 19 | 20 | 21 | 22 | 23 |
| 24 | 25 | 26 | 27 | 28 | 29 | 30 |
| 31 |   |   |   |   |   |   |

### FEBRUARY
| S | M | T | W | T | F | S |
|---|---|---|---|---|---|---|
|   | 1 | 2 | 3 | 4 | 5 | 6 |
| 7 | 8 | 9 | 10 | 11 | 12 | 13 |
| 14 | 15 | 16 | 17 | 18 | 19 | 20 |
| 21 | 22 | 23 | 24 | 25 | 26 | 27 |
| 28 |   |   |   |   |   |   |

### MARCH
| S | M | T | W | T | F | S |
|---|---|---|---|---|---|---|
|   | 1 | 2 | 3 | 4 | 5 | 6 |
| 7 | 8 | 9 | 10 | 11 | 12 | 13 |
| 14 | 15 | 16 | 17 | 18 | 19 | 20 |
| 21 | 22 | 23 | 24 | 25 | 26 | 27 |
| 28 | 29 | 30 | 31 |   |   |   |

### APRIL
| S | M | T | W | T | F | S |
|---|---|---|---|---|---|---|
|   |   |   |   | 1 | 2 | 3 |
| 4 | 5 | 6 | 7 | 8 | 9 | 10 |
| 11 | 12 | 13 | 14 | 15 | 16 | 17 |
| 18 | 19 | 20 | 21 | 22 | 23 | 24 |
| 25 | 26 | 27 | 28 | 29 | 30 |   |

### MAY
| S | M | T | W | T | F | S |
|---|---|---|---|---|---|---|
|   |   |   |   |   |   | 1 |
| 2 | 3 | 4 | 5 | 6 | 7 | 8 |
| 9 | 10 | 11 | 12 | 13 | 14 | 15 |
| 16 | 17 | 18 | 19 | 20 | 21 | 22 |
| 23 | 24 | 25 | 26 | 27 | 28 | 29 |
| 30 | 31 |   |   |   |   |   |

### JUNE
| S | M | T | W | T | F | S |
|---|---|---|---|---|---|---|
|   |   | 1 | 2 | 3 | 4 | 5 |
| 6 | 7 | 8 | 9 | 10 | 11 | 12 |
| 13 | 14 | 15 | 16 | 17 | 18 | 19 |
| 20 | 21 | 22 | 23 | 24 | 25 | 26 |
| 27 | 28 | 29 | 30 |   |   |   |

### JULY
| S | M | T | W | T | F | S |
|---|---|---|---|---|---|---|
|   |   |   |   | 1 | 2 | 3 |
| 4 | 5 | 6 | 7 | 8 | 9 | 10 |
| 11 | 12 | 13 | 14 | 15 | 16 | 17 |
| 18 | 19 | 20 | 21 | 22 | 23 | 24 |
| 25 | 26 | 27 | 28 | 29 | 30 | 31 |

### AUGUST
| S | M | T | W | T | F | S |
|---|---|---|---|---|---|---|
| 1 | 2 | 3 | 4 | 5 | 6 | 7 |
| 8 | 9 | 10 | 11 | 12 | 13 | 14 |
| 15 | 16 | 17 | 18 | 19 | 20 | 21 |
| 22 | 23 | 24 | 25 | 26 | 27 | 28 |
| 29 | 30 | 31 |   |   |   |   |

### SEPTEMBER
| S | M | T | W | T | F | S |
|---|---|---|---|---|---|---|
|   |   |   | 1 | 2 | 3 | 4 |
| 5 | 6 | 7 | 8 | 9 | 10 | 11 |
| 12 | 13 | 14 | 15 | 16 | 17 | 18 |
| 19 | 20 | 21 | 22 | 23 | 24 | 25 |
| 26 | 27 | 28 | 29 | 30 |   |   |

### OCTOBER
| S | M | T | W | T | F | S |
|---|---|---|---|---|---|---|
|   |   |   |   |   | 1 | 2 |
| 3 | 4 | 5 | 6 | 7 | 8 | 9 |
| 10 | 11 | 12 | 13 | 14 | 15 | 16 |
| 17 | 18 | 19 | 20 | 21 | 22 | 23 |
| 24 | 25 | 26 | 27 | 28 | 29 | 30 |
| 31 |   |   |   |   |   |   |

### NOVEMBER
| S | M | T | W | T | F | S |
|---|---|---|---|---|---|---|
|   | 1 | 2 | 3 | 4 | 5 | 6 |
| 7 | 8 | 9 | 10 | 11 | 12 | 13 |
| 14 | 15 | 16 | 17 | 18 | 19 | 20 |
| 21 | 22 | 23 | 24 | 25 | 26 | 27 |
| 28 | 29 | 30 |   |   |   |   |

### DECEMBER
| S | M | T | W | T | F | S |
|---|---|---|---|---|---|---|
|   |   |   | 1 | 2 | 3 | 4 |
| 5 | 6 | 7 | 8 | 9 | 10 | 11 |
| 12 | 13 | 14 | 15 | 16 | 17 | 18 |
| 19 | 20 | 21 | 22 | 23 | 24 | 25 |
| 26 | 27 | 28 | 29 | 30 | 31 |   |

# HALLOWEEN PET PARADE

Forget sweets— these trick-or-treaters want belly scratches! Millions of pets will don a disguise for Halloween. Check out a few of the craziest getups.

What spell can I cast to get some oats and hay?

DISGUISED AS HARRY POTTER, RAMSEY THE HORSE MAKES MAGIC.

Stop in the name of the paw, er, law!

COREY THE DACHSHUND IS ARRESTING IN HIS WILD WEST SHERIFF GARB.

If you dress up your pet, check that the outfit is comfortable and allows the animal to breathe and walk safely.

I am one classy kitty.

ELROY THE CAT SHOWS SOME STYLE DRESSED AS THE MAD HATTER FROM *ALICE'S ADVENTURES IN WONDERLAND.*

I'm ready to say "I do" to a chew toy and a belly rub.

TANK THE ENGLISH BULLDOG ROCKS A BRIDAL COSTUME.

# What's Your Chinese Horoscope?
## Locate your birth year to find out.

In Chinese astrology the zodiac runs on a 12-year cycle, based on the lunar calendar. Each year corresponds to one of 12 animals, each representing one of 12 personality types. Read on to find out which animal year you were born in and what that might say about you.

### RAT
**1972, '84, '96, 2008, '20**
Say cheese! You're attractive, charming, and creative. When you get mad, you can have really sharp teeth!

### HORSE
**1966, '78, '90, 2002, '14**
Being happy is your "mane" goal. And while you're smart and hardworking, your teacher may ride you for talking too much.

### OX
**1973, '85, '97, 2009, '21**
You're smart, patient, and as strong as an ... well, you know what. Though you're a leader, you never brag.

### SHEEP
**1967, '79, '91, 2003, '15**
Gentle as a lamb, you're also artistic, compassionate, and wise. You're often shy.

### TIGER
**1974, '86, '98, 2010, '22**
You may be a nice person, but no one should ever enter your room without asking—you might attack!

### MONKEY
**1968, '80, '92, 2004, '16**
No "monkey see, monkey do" for you. You're a clever problem-solver with an excellent memory.

### RABBIT
**1975, '87, '99, 2011**
Your ambition and talent make you jump at opportunity. You also keep your ears open for gossip.

### ROOSTER
**1969, '81, '93, 2005, '17**
You crow about your adventures, but inside you're really shy. You're thoughtful, capable, brave, and talented.

### DRAGON
**1976, '88, 2000, '12**
You're on fire! Health, energy, honesty, and bravery make you a living legend.

### DOG
**1970, '82, '94, 2006, '18**
Often the leader of the pack, you're loyal and honest. You can also keep a secret.

### SNAKE
**1977, '89, 2001, '13**
You may not speak often, but you're very smart. You always seem to have a stash of cash.

### PIG
**1971, '83, '95, 2007, '19**
Even though you're courageous, honest, and kind, you never hog all the attention.

189

# GINGERBREAD HOUSES

## YOU WILL NEED

- VANILLA FROSTING
- CREAM OF TARTAR
- CARDBOARD
- GRAHAM CRACKERS (OR GINGERBREAD)
- SERRATED KNIFE (ASK FOR A PARENT'S HELP)
- ASSORTED CANDY, PRETZELS, AND COOKIES, INCLUDING SQUARE CARAMELS (NOT SHOWN)
- SHREDDED COCONUT

## WHAT TO DO

**MIX THE "GLUE":** Frosting will hold each graham cracker building together. Combine a can of ready-made vanilla frosting with 1/4 teaspoon cream of tartar. To apply the frosting, squeeze it out of a sealed freezer bag with a hole cut in one corner.

### BUILD THE HOUSE:

**BASE** Cut a piece of cardboard that's big enough to hold the scene.

**WALLS** The front and back walls are each made of a whole graham cracker turned horizontally. Ask a parent to create the two remaining sides. For each, use a serrated knife to gently saw the top of a whole graham cracker into a peak (inset, above). Run a bead of icing along the bottom edge and sides of the crackers. "Glue" them together in a rectangle on top of the cardboard. Prop up the walls while you work.

**PEAKED ROOF** Run icing along the tops of the walls. Place two whole graham crackers—turned horizontally—on top of the sides, using icing to hold them in place. Let the icing set overnight.

**WAGON** USE QUARTER CRACKERS FOR THE BOTTOM AND SIDES. USE HALF OF A QUARTER CRACKER FOR THE BACK. "GLUE" THE PIECES IN PLACE. ADD PRETZEL WHEELS AND A CARAMEL UNDER THE WAGON FOR SUPPORT.

**SILO** CUT OFF THE TOPS OF TWO CAKE CONES, THEN FROST THE OPEN ENDS TOGETHER. STICK ON COLORFUL LICORICE AND TOP WITH A FOIL BAKING CUP.

**SNOWMAN** SKEWER TWO MARSHMALLOWS ONTO A PRETZEL STICK. USE GUM-DROPS FOR THE HAT, EYES, AND NOSE; PRETZELS FOR THE ARMS; AND STRING LICORICE FOR A SCARF.

# Fun Winter Gift Idea

## Snow Globes

**YOU WILL NEED**
- SMALL JAR WITH A LID (A BABY FOOD JAR WORKS WELL.)
- SANDPAPER
- INSTANT-BONDING GLUE (FOLLOW DIRECTIONS ON THE TUBE AND USE WITH ADULT SUPERVISION.)
- PLASTIC ANIMAL OR FIGURINE THAT FITS IN THE JAR
- NAIL POLISH REMOVER
- BABY OIL
- 1/2 TEASPOON WHITE GLITTER

**WHAT TO DO**
Turn the jar's lid upside down. Use sandpaper to scuff the inside of the lid. Glue the bottom of the figurine to the center of the lid. (Nail polish remover cleans glue off skin and surfaces.) Dry for four hours. Fill the jar with baby oil. Add glitter. To seal, put glue around the rim of the jar. Close the lid tightly and dry for four hours. Turn the jar over, and let it snow!

**DOGHOUSE** Follow the steps at left, but use quarter crackers for all sides and the roof.

**BARN** Use graham cracker halves for the barn's roof and sides. For the front and back, cut a peak in a whole graham cracker (inset, above left).

**DECORATIONS** "Glue" on your favorite treats to create doors, rooftops, trees, and anything else you can imagine. Let everything set overnight. Cover the cardboard base with shredded coconut to finish your snowy scene.

**DOG** "GLUE" TWO GUMDROPS TOGETHER TO FORM THE BODY. STICK ON PIECES OF GUMDROPS FOR THE EARS, NOSE, AND TAIL.

# MONEY AROUND THE WORLD!

**Jordan's HALF-DINAR COIN** has seven sides.

ACCORDING to some **PEOPLE, CANADA'S $100 BANKNOTE** gives off the scent of **MAPLE SYRUP.**

A British businessman created his own currency —named the **PUFFIN**— for an island he owned off of England.

**IN FEBRUARY 2015,** SCUBA DIVERS OFF ISRAEL FOUND OVER **2,600 GOLD COINS** DATING BACK AS FAR AS THE NINTH CENTURY.

A **20,000**-PESO BANKNOTE FROM CHILE CONTAINS INK THAT CHANGES **COLOR** WHEN **TILTED.**

The INCA called gold "THE SWEAT OF THE SUN" and silver "THE TEARS OF THE MOON."

**3-CENT COINS** CIRCULATED IN THE **UNITED STATES** FROM **1851** TO **1889.**

*I knew I should've tried a fake ATM instead.*

IN 2002, A MAN OPENED A FAKE BANK AND TOOK IN **$650,000** BEFORE HE WAS CAUGHT.

COINS CREATED IN **1616** FOR WHAT IS NOW **BERMUDA** WERE NICKNAMED **"HOGGIES"** BECAUSE THEY PICTURED **HOGS.**

A 1913 U.S. LIBERTY HEAD NICKEL—ONE OF ONLY FIVE IN EXISTENCE— **SOLD AT** AUCTION FOR MORE THAN **$3.1 MILLION.**

THE PHRASE **"BRING HOME THE BACON"** STARTED AFTER A 12TH-CENTURY PRIEST REWARDED A MARRIED COUPLE WITH A SIDE OF BACON.

**A BRITISH ARTIST** MADE A DRESS OUT OF USED **BANKNOTES** FROM AROUND THE **WORLD.**

**MONEY TIP!** WHEN YOU GET YOUR ALLOWANCE OR A CASH GIFT, BREAK IT INTO **SMALLER BILLS.** SPEND ONLY HALF AND STASH THE REST IN YOUR **PIGGY BANK.**

# 15 Ways to Say Hello

1. ARMENIAN: Barev
2. DUTCH: Goedendag
3. FINNISH: Hei
4. FRENCH: Bonjour
5. GREEK: Yia sou
6. HEBREW: Shalom
7. HINDI: Namaste
8. ICELANDIC: Halló
9. ITALIAN: Ciao
10. MANDARIN: Ni hao
11. RUSSIAN: Privyet
12. SPANISH: Hola
13. SWAHILI: Jambo
14. TURKISH: Merhaba
15. WELSH: Helô

# LANGUAGES IN PERIL

**TODAY,** there are more than 7,000 languages spoken on Earth. But by 2100, more than half of those may disappear. In fact, experts say one language dies every two weeks, due to the increasing dominance of larger languages, such as English, Spanish, and Mandarin. So what can be done to keep dialects from disappearing? Efforts like National Geographic's Enduring Voices Project have been created to track and document the world's most threatened indigenous languages, such as Tofa, spoken only by people in Siberia, and Magati Ke, from Aboriginal Australia. The hope is to preserve these languages—and the cultures they belong to.

# 10 LEADING LANGUAGES

Approximate population of first-language speakers (in millions)

1. Chinese* 1,311
2. Spanish 460
3. English 379
4. Arabic 341
5. Hindi 319
6. Bengali 228
7. Portuguese 221
8. Russian 154
9. Japanese 128
10. Punjabi 93

Some languages have only a few hundred speakers, while Chinese has about 1.3 billion native speakers worldwide. That's nearly triple the next largest group of language speakers. Colonial expansion, trade, and migration account for the spread of the other most widely spoken languages. With growing use of the internet, English is becoming the language of the technology age.

*Includes all forms of the language.

# By the NumBers
# HIT THE BOOKS

## Got a minute?
If you spend a little time reading each day, by the time you reach high school you'll be a reading wizard. Check out how many times you can read *Harry Potter and the Sorcerer's Stone* if you read a little—or a lot—every day.

 IF YOU READ **1 HOUR** EVERY DAY

EVERY YEAR, A SIXTH GRADER WILL HAVE READ: **3,285,000 words**

THAT'S THE SAME AS READING *HARRY POTTER AND THE SORCERER'S STONE:* **42 times**

FROM KINDERGARTEN THROUGH HIGH SCHOOL GRADUATION, YOU'LL HAVE READ FOR NEARLY: **198 days**

 IF YOU READ **20 MINUTES** EVERY DAY

EVERY YEAR, A SIXTH GRADER WILL HAVE READ: **1,095,000 words**

THAT'S THE SAME AS READING *HARRY POTTER AND THE SORCERER'S STONE:* **14 times**

FROM KINDERGARTEN THROUGH HIGH SCHOOL GRADUATION, YOU'LL HAVE READ FOR NEARLY: **66 days**

 IF YOU READ **5 MINUTES** EVERY DAY

EVERY YEAR, A SIXTH GRADER WILL HAVE READ: **273,750 words**

THAT'S THE SAME AS READING *HARRY POTTER AND THE SORCERER'S STONE:* **3.5 times**

FROM KINDERGARTEN THROUGH HIGH SCHOOL GRADUATION, YOU'LL HAVE READ FOR NEARLY: **14 days**

# MYTHOLOGY

## GREEK

## EGYPTIAN

The ancient Greeks believed that many gods and goddesses ruled the universe. According to this mythology, the Olympians lived high atop Greece's Mount Olympus. Each of these 12 principal gods and goddesses had a unique personality that corresponded to particular aspects of life, such as love or death.

Egyptian mythology is based on a creation myth that tells of an egg that appeared on the ocean. When the egg hatched, out came Ra, the sun god. As a result, ancient Egyptians became worshippers of the sun and of the nine original deities, most of whom were the children and grandchildren of Ra.

### THE OLYMPIANS

**Aphrodite** was the goddess of love and beauty.

**Apollo,** Zeus's son, was the god of the sun, music, and healing. Artemis was his twin.

**Ares,** Zeus's son, was the god of war.

**Artemis,** Zeus's daughter and Apollo's twin, was the goddess of the hunt and of childbirth.

**Athena,** born from the forehead of Zeus, was the goddess of wisdom and crafts.

**Demeter** was the goddess of fertility and nature.

**Hades,** Zeus's brother, was the god of the underworld and the dead.

**Hephaestus,** the son of Hera, was the god of fire.

**Hera,** the wife and older sister of Zeus, was the goddess of women and marriage.

**Hermes,** Zeus's son, was the messenger of the gods.

**Poseidon,** the brother of Zeus, was the god of the seas and earthquakes.

**Zeus** was the most powerful of the gods and the top Olympian. He wielded a thunderbolt and was the god of the sky and thunder.

### THE NINE DEITIES

**Geb,** son of Shu and Tefnut, was the god of the earth.

**Isis (Ast),** daughter of Geb and Nut, was the goddess of fertility and motherhood.

**Nephthys (Nebet-Hut),** daughter of Geb and Nut, was protector of the dead.

**Nut,** daughter of Shu and Tefnut, was the goddess of the sky.

**Osiris (Usir),** son of Geb and Nut, was the god of the afterlife.

**Ra (Re),** the sun god, is generally viewed as the creator. He represents life and health.

**Seth (Set),** son of Geb and Nut, was the god of the desert and chaos.

**Shu,** son of Ra, was the god of air.

**Tefnut,** daughter of Ra, was the goddess of rain.

**A**ll cultures around the world have unique legends and traditions that have been passed down over generations. Many myths refer to gods or supernatural heroes who are responsible for occurrences in the world. For example, Norse mythology tells of the red-bearded Thor, the god of thunder, who is responsible for creating lightning and thunderstorms. And many creation myths, especially those from some of North America's native cultures, tell of an earth-diver represented as an animal that brings a piece of sand or mud up from the deep sea. From this tiny piece of earth, the entire world takes shape.

# NORSE

Norse mythology originated in Scandinavia, in northern Europe. It was complete with gods and goddesses who lived in a heavenly place called Asgard that could be reached only by crossing a rainbow bridge.

While Norse mythology is lesser known, we use it every day. Most days of the week are named after Norse gods, including some of these major deities.

## NORSE GODS

**Balder** was the god of light and beauty.

**Freya** was the goddess of love, beauty, and fertility.

**Frigg,** for whom Friday was named, was the queen of Asgard. She was the goddess of marriage, motherhood, and the home.

**Heimdall** was the watchman of the rainbow bridge and the guardian of the gods.

**Hel,** the daughter of Loki, was the goddess of death.

**Loki,** a shape-shifter, was a trickster who helped the gods—and caused them problems.

**Skadi** was the goddess of winter and of the hunt. She is often represented as "The Snow Queen."

**Thor,** for whom Thursday was named, was the god of thunder and lightning.

**Tyr,** for whom Tuesday was named, was the god of the sky and war.

**Wodan,** for whom Wednesday was named, was the god of war, wisdom, death, and magic.

# ROMAN

Much of Roman mythology was adopted from Greek mythology, but the Romans also developed a lot of original myths as well. The gods of Roman mythology lived everywhere, and each had a role to play. There were thousands of Roman gods, but here are a few of the stars of Roman myths.

## ANCIENT ROMAN GODS

**Ceres** was the goddess of the harvest and motherly love.

**Diana,** daughter of Jupiter, was the goddess of hunting and the moon.

**Juno,** Jupiter's wife, was the goddess of women and fertility.

**Jupiter,** the patron of Rome and master of the gods, was the god of the sky.

**Mars,** the son of Jupiter and Juno, was the god of war.

**Mercury,** the son of Jupiter, was the messenger of the gods and the god of travelers.

**Minerva** was the goddess of wisdom, learning, and the arts and crafts.

**Neptune,** the brother of Jupiter, was the god of the sea.

**Venus** was the goddess of love and beauty.

**Vesta** was the goddess of fire and the hearth. She was one of the most important of the Roman deities.

# GREEK MYTHS

## POSEIDON: GOD OF THE SEAS

Poseidon—along with his brother Hades and his sisters, Hestia, Demeter, and Hera—was swallowed at birth by his father, Cronus. Then a sixth child, Zeus, who was never swallowed, and thus had never known humiliation, freed them. Poseidon sized things up: Zeus was a force to be reckoned with—he was the guy to follow.

For 10 long years, the six brothers and sisters fought their father and aunts and uncles—the mighty Titans. It was a nasty war, but what war isn't? Poseidon gritted his teeth and did his part. He was no coward, after all. But now and then there was a lull in the battle, perhaps because Zeus got distracted or because the Titans needed a rest. Who knew? Whatever the case, Poseidon was grateful, and in those moments he took refuge in visiting Pontus, the ancient god of all the waters, the partner to his grandmother Gaia, Mother Earth, and his grandfather Uranus, Father Heaven. He swam in Pontus's waters, and despite how badly his life had gone so far, despite all the long years of savage war, he was happy.

Best of all, Poseidon found a friend in Nereus. He loved the watery depths as much as Poseidon did. Together they plunged to the corals and sponges that lived along the seabed. They rode on the backs of turtles. They flapped their arms like the rays they followed, then let their arms hang in the water, moving at the whim of the currents.

But then it was back to war ... until the glorious moment when the hundred-handed sons of Gaia joined the battle on Zeus's side, and then the Cyclopes gave Zeus the thunderbolt and Hades the helmet that made him invisible and Poseidon the trident. It worked, that

POSEIDON, GOD OF THE SEAS, WITH HIS TRIDENT

**CHECK OUT THIS BOOK!**

THE MORTAL MEDUSA EMBRACES HER HUSBAND, POSEIDON.

With his hair flying out behind him, he swam the seas in search of those who might need help. And when he wasn't patrolling, he let himself be absorbed in the watery mysteries.

That's when he discovered the finest mystery ever. She was the daughter of the sea god Phorcys and the sea goddess Ceto. That heritage made her the perfect wife in Poseidon's eyes. She was one of three sisters, called the Gorgons. The other two sisters were immortal, like the gods. But Medusa, as she was called, was mortal.

Poseidon found her mortality that much more alluring. How amazing to know someone vulnerable. He put his arms out and let the serpents of her hair swarm around them. Good! Those serpents could bite and poison—good protection. He gingerly touched the wings that jutted from her shoulder blades. Good! Those wings could carry her far from an attacker. He stroked her scales. Very good! They were harder than armor. And most assuring of all, she had a special power: Anything mortal that looked directly at her face would turn instantly to stone.

And so Poseidon felt almost safe in loving Medusa. They reveled together comfortably in his sea kingdom. At least for a while ...

trident. Poseidon struck it on the ground and the entire Earth shook. The Olympian gods won.

Zeus appointed Poseidon ruler of the seas. Poseidon knew his brother felt the seas were an inferior realm. Ha! Nothing could've pleased Poseidon more.

# World Religions

Around the world, religion takes many forms. Some belief systems, such as Christianity, Islam, and Judaism, are monotheistic, meaning that followers believe in just one supreme being. Others, like Hinduism, Shintoism, and most native belief systems, are polytheistic, meaning that many of their followers believe in multiple gods.

All of the major religions have their origins in Asia, but they have spread around the world. Christianity, with the largest number of followers, has three divisions—Roman Catholic, Eastern Orthodox, and Protestant. Islam, with about one-fifth of all believers, has two main divisions—Sunni and Shiite. Hinduism and Buddhism account for almost another one-fifth of believers. Judaism, dating back some 4,000 years, has more than 13 million followers, less than one percent of all believers.

## CHRISTIANITY

Based on the teachings of Jesus Christ, a Jew born some 2,000 years ago in the area of modern-day Israel, Christianity has spread worldwide and actively seeks converts. Followers in Switzerland (above) participate in an Easter season procession with lanterns and crosses.

## BUDDHISM

Founded about 2,400 years ago in northern India by the Hindu prince Gautama Buddha, Buddhism spread throughout East and Southeast Asia. Buddhist temples have statues, such as the Mihintale Buddha (above) in Sri Lanka.

## HINDUISM

Dating back more than 4,000 years, Hinduism is practiced mainly in India. Hindus follow sacred texts known as the Vedas and believe in reincarnation. During the festival of Navratri, which honors the goddess Durga, the Garba dance is performed (above).

# Novice Monks

**M**embers of the Wild Boars youth soccer team were rescued from a flooded Thai cave in July 2018. A few weeks later, 11 of the boys were ordained as novice Buddhist monks and spent nine days in a monastery. This act honored Saman Gunan, a Thai Navy SEAL who died while rescuing them.

## ISLAM

Muslims believe that the Quran, Islam's sacred book, records the words of Allah (God) as revealed to the Prophet Muhammad beginning around A.D. 610. Believers (above) circle the Kaaba in the Haram Mosque in Mecca, Saudi Arabia, the spiritual center of the faith.

## JUDAISM

The traditions, laws, and beliefs of Judaism date back to Abraham (the Patriarch) and the Torah (the first five books of the Old Testament). Followers pray before the Western Wall (above), which stands below Islam's Dome of the Rock in Jerusalem.

# QUIZ WHIZ

**How vast is your knowledge about the world around you? Quiz yourself!**

Write your answers on a piece of paper. Then check them below.

**1** Chinese astrology uses _____ to represent personality traits.
a. mythical characters
b. animals
c. numbers
d. letters

**2** Natto, a delicacy popular in Japan, is said to smell like _____.
a. vinegar
b. marshmallows
c. peanut butter
d. sweaty socks

**3** A rare U.S. nickel from 1913 sold at auction for more than _____.
a. $3,000,000
b. $300,000
c. $30,000
d. $3,000

**4** _____ is a holiday honoring the patron saint of Ireland.

**5** True or false? In Greek mythology, the snake-headed Medusa was immortal.

Not **STUMPED** yet? Check out the *NATIONAL GEOGRAPHIC KIDS QUIZ WHIZ* collection for more crazy **CULTURE** questions!

**ANSWERS: 1. b; 2. d; 3. a; 4. St. Patrick's Day; 5. False. She was mortal.**

## HOMEWORK HELP

# Explore a New Culture

STAMPS OF BRAZIL

Brasil 93   CR$ 22,00

BRASIL-CORREIO

AMÉRICA

ARARAS AZUIS

CURRENCY AND COINS OF BRAZIL

FLAG OF BRAZIL

**YOU'RE A STUDENT,** but you're also a citizen of the world. Writing a report on a foreign nation or your own country is a great way to better understand and appreciate how different people live. Pick the country of your ancestors, one that's been in the news, or one that you'd like to visit someday.

## Passport to Success

A country report follows the format of an expository essay because you're "exposing" information about the country you choose.

**The following step-by-step tips will help you with this monumental task.**

**1** **RESEARCH.** Gathering information is the most important step in writing a good country report. Look to internet sources, encyclopedias, books, magazine and newspaper articles, and other sources to find important and interesting details about your subject.

**2** **ORGANIZE YOUR NOTES.** Put the information you gathered into a rough outline. For example, sort everything you found about the country's system of government, climate, etc.

**3** **WRITE IT UP.** Follow the basic structure of good writing: introduction, body, and conclusion. Remember that each paragraph should have a topic sentence that is then supported by facts and details. Incorporate the information from your notes, but make sure it's in your own words. And make your writing flow with good transitions and descriptive language.

**4** **ADD VISUALS.** Include maps, diagrams, photos, and other visual aids.

**5** **PROOFREAD AND REVISE.** Correct any mistakes, and polish your language. Do your best!

**6** **CITE YOUR SOURCES.** Be sure to keep a record of your sources.

Students in Lahore, Pakistan, hit the runway to model recycled waste clothing in the Roots Ivy Recycling Fashion Fiesta to urge environmental support through education.

GOING GREEN

**Bet You Didn't Know!**

# 10 recyclable facts

**1** Nearly **half of all fruits and vegetables** grown are **wasted.**

**2** It can take up to **200 years** for an **aluminum can** to decompose.

**3** More than **95 percent** of food waste could have been **composted.**

**4** **Glass** is 100 percent **recyclable** and can be used again and again.

**5** The average American **throws away** almost **a pound** (.45 kg) **of food a day.**

**6** A mall in **Sweden** sells only recycled, reused, and sustainably produced goods.

# about trash

**7** One million plastic drink bottles are sold every minute around the world.

**8** Single-use plastic makes up about **40 percent** of all plastic produced.

**9** In terms of weight, it's estimated that the ocean will contain **more plastic than fish** by 2050.

Mount Everest **has banned** single-use plastics **to reduce trash** left by trekkers and climbers. **10**

Plastic bags floating in the ocean

# Save the Ocean!

# DUCK RESCUE

## A CARING HUMAN RESCUES AN INJURED BIRD FROM A PLASTIC RING.

A white-faced whistling duck walks backward with its head between its feet. It shakes its beak, stops to rest, and shakes again. The duck's odd movements catch the attention of Glenda Maguire, who's been watching the visiting animal from her patio in South Africa. Using her camera to zoom in for a closer look, she sees a ring of white plastic—likely from a milk bottle—wrapped around the duck's mouth and neck. She wants to help, but she knows if she tries to catch it, the wild duck will fly away and not come back to the lake.

Maguire sets out an animal trap with food pellets near the water. But the duck seems scared of the trap and later flies away. Maguire hopes that someone will save the duck before it's too late.

### RIVER TO SEA

Freshwater streams, lakes, and rivers are often the starting point for plastic that ends up in the ocean. "On a windy day you can see plastic bags and bottles tumbling around on the ground," says Carlie Herring, a research analyst with the National Oceanic and Atmospheric Administration in the U.S. "Those items might end up in a stream, then a river, and eventually the ocean."

One group of researchers found hundreds of thousands of pieces of plastic in just one square mile of North America's Great Lakes, one of the world's largest freshwater systems. That includes microplastic—supersmall plastic pieces about the size of the period at the end of this sentence. According to Herring, microplastics have been found in drinking water and may hurt wildlife like the white-faced whistling duck, which could mistake the plastic for food.

### TAKING FLIGHT

After two days, the little duck returns to the lake. But it's clearly in trouble. "It was just hanging its head, as if it had given up," Maguire says. But finally, three days later, the duck eventually walks into Maguire's cage and—snap!—she pulls a string to close the door. After retrieving the bird, she wraps a towel around it and carefully cuts the plastic loop off before releasing the duck back into the wild.

The exhausted duck spends two days resting and eating nearby as its flock comes and goes. Eventually the duck is ready to fly away and return to its family.

# Save the Ocean!

# SEAL RESCUE

## FISHERMEN SCOOP UP A HARBOR SEAL TRAPPED IN PLASTIC NETS.

Harbor seals can't rotate their hind flippers forward to walk on land—they can only scoot forward on their bellies.

Experts think just one fishing net can entangle up to 40 animals.

In the northeastern United States, about 880 seals were accidentally caught in fishing nets over a seven-year period.

A harbor seal pup floats in the water off the coast of Maine, U.S.A. The young seal has recently left its mother's care—and it's already in trouble. The little seal has a massive tangle of fishing nets wrapped around its body. Without help, the pup will not escape. Luckily a fishing boat passes by, and the people on board prepare to rescue the helpless animal.

## POLAR PROBLEMS

Harbor seals live in coastal waters in the Northern Hemisphere, which includes polar habitats in the Arctic. It might seem like this region— and southern polar habitats around Antarctica—would be plastic free because few people live there. But ocean currents carry the trash to these regions, where it has nowhere to go.

"The ocean is the ultimate transporter on our planet," environmental engineer Jenna Jambeck says. "Once plastic that floats enters the ocean, the currents can take it all over the world, including to the Arctic." In fact, one study of the Svalbard Islands near the North Pole found polar bears and reindeer entangled in plastic.

Scientists have also discovered microplastics frozen in Arctic sea ice: One study shows 12,000 particles of microplastic in one liter—or about four cups—of sea ice. "When even the sea ice has microplastic—well, then pollution is everywhere," says Carlie Herring, a research analyst with the National Oceanic and Atmospheric Administration in the U.S. Experts worry that as the ice caps melt, they'll release these microplastics into the seas, putting more animals like the harbor seal pup in danger.

## SAVED SEAL

The fishermen quickly scoop the seal out of the water and onto their boat. One of the fishermen holds the seal in place, using a knife to slowly cut the thick netting off the animal, one rope at a time. The seal is still at first but tries to wiggle away as it feels the net loosen. The fishermen keep the marine mammal calm for just a few more minutes until all the rope is off.

Finally the animal is no longer trapped in plastic. A fisherman gently lowers the pup into the water. The uninjured seal floats for a few seconds as it gets used to its surroundings. Then it gracefully swims away.

209

# Pollution
## Cleaning Up Our Act

**So what's the big deal** about a little dirt on the planet? Pollution can affect animals, plants, and people. In fact, some studies show that more people die every year from diseases linked to air pollution than from car accidents. And right now nearly one billion of the world's people don't have access to clean drinking water.

### A LITTLE POLLUTION = BIG PROBLEMS

You can probably clean your room in a couple of hours. (At least we hope you can!) But you can't shove air and water pollution under your bed or cram them into the closet. Once released into the environment, pollution—whether it's oil leaking from a boat or chemicals spewing from a factory's smokestack—can have a lasting environmental impact.

### KEEP IT CLEAN

It's easy to blame things like big factories for pollution problems. But some of the mess comes from everyday activities. Exhaust fumes from cars and garbage in landfills can seriously trash Earth's health. We all need to pitch in and do some housecleaning. It may mean bicycling more and riding in cars less. Or not dumping water-polluting oil or household cleaners down the drain. Look at it this way: Just as with your room, it's always better not to let Earth get messed up in the first place.

# kids vs. PLASTIC

A straw stuck in a sea turtle's nostril. A seahorse swimming along with its tail curled around a cotton swab. Seabirds washing up on sandy shores, entangled in plastic bags. Sadly, we do not have to look too far to see how animals are directly impacted by the staggering amount of plastic piling up on our planet. We've created more than 6.9 billion tons (6.3 billion t) of plastic waste, with only a small percentage landing in recycling bins. The rest of it lingers in landfills and winds up in our oceans. In fact, 700 species of animals are threatened because of ocean waste—and among seabirds, a whopping 90 percent eat plastic trash, according to a study. But as scary as these stats are, we can do something about them. Experts say it all starts with reducing the amount of plastic we use, including options for reusable containers or those materials that can't fully break down in the ocean. You can also pledge to do your part to reduce the plastic problem by visiting natgeokids.com/plastic. Together, we can work to cut back on plastic and protect our planet—and everything on it.

# Declining Biodiversity

## Saving All Creatures, Great and Small

Green sea turtle

Earth is home to a huge mix of plants and animals—millions and possibly billions of species—and scientists have officially identified and named only about 1.9 million so far! Scientists call this healthy mix biodiversity.

### THE BALANCING ACT

The bad news is that half of the planet's plant and animal species may be on the path to extinction, mainly because of human activity. People cut down trees, build roads and houses, pollute rivers, overfish, and overhunt. The good news is that many people care. Scientists and volunteers race against the clock every day, working to save wildlife before time runs out. By building birdhouses, planting trees, and following the rules for hunting and fishing, you can be a positive force for preserving biodiversity, too. Every time you do something to help a species survive, you help our planet to thrive.

# Habitats Threatened

## Living on the Edge

Jaguar

Even though tropical rainforests cover only about 7 percent of the planet's total land surface, they are home to half of all known species of plants and animals. Because people cut down so many trees for lumber and firewood and clear so much land for farms, hundreds of thousands of acres of rainforest disappear every year.

### SHARING THE LAND

Wetlands are also important feeding and breeding grounds. People have drained many wetlands, turning them into farm fields or sites for other industries. More than half the world's wetlands have disappeared within the past century, squeezing wildlife out. Balancing the needs of humans and animals is the key to lessening habitat destruction.

# kids vs. PLASTIC

**MAKE THIS** ▸ POM-POM DECORATIONS

**TO AVOID THAT** ▸ PLASTIC BALLOONS

## POM-POM PUFFS

Help keep Earth healthy by ditching single-use plastic items. Decorate your next party with paper pom-pom balls instead of balloons.

Why? Balloons released into the air or left outside can end up in the ocean, where they might entangle animals or be mistaken for food.

### ❯ MATERIALS

- 8 sheets of equal-size tissue paper (Bigger tissue paper will make bigger pom-poms.)
- 1 craft pipe cleaner
- Scissors
- String (optional)

NOTE: Please look for recycled tissue paper when possible.

### ❯ STEPS

**1** Stack 8 sheets of tissue paper together. (You can use the same color or mix it up.)

**2** Fold the tissue paper back and forth in 1-inch (2.5-cm) sections like an accordion. Press each fold firmly.

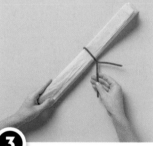

**3** Wrap the pipe cleaner around the center of the folded tissue-paper stack, then twist the pipe cleaner to secure it.

**4** Trim the pipe cleaner with scissors, then wrap the end of the pipe cleaner around itself so the wire doesn't poke out.

**5** Cut both ends of the tissue-paper stack into rounded, pointed, or frilly shapes.

**6** Flip the tissue-paper stack on its side.

**7** Separate each layer of tissue paper one at a time.

Pull the layers up and toward the center.

To hang your pom-pom, tie a piece of string to the center of the pipe cleaner.

# 10 WAYS YOU CAN SAVE THE OCEAN FROM PLASTIC

**1** Opt for reusable containers and bottles for your food and drinks.

**2** Stock up on metal or paper straws—and stop using plastic straws altogether.

**3** Encourage restaurants in your community to stop offering plastic utensils. Find tips for talking to restaurants at natgeokids.com/KidsVsPlastic.

**4** Convince your family to switch over to tote bags instead of plastic bags when you go grocery shopping.

**5** Always be sure to recycle as many plastic items as you can.

**6** Don't be a litterbug! Any trash left in the environment may blow into creeks or rivers and eventually make its way into the ocean.

**7** Instead of tossing plastic junk away, try to see if you can repurpose or "upcycle" any of it to create something new.

**8** Hungry? Reach for fruits like apples, bananas, and oranges over snack packs, which use extra packaging.

**9** Organize a local beach, lake, or creek cleanup with your friends and family.

**10** Reduce your plastic waste at school: Use pencils made of wood instead of plastic mechanical pencils.

# A GLOBAL RACE TO ZERO WASTE

BOTH SWEDEN (MAIN PHOTO) AND SINGAPORE (INSET) ARE WORLDWIDE LEADERS IN RECYCLING AND WASTE REDUCTION.

It's an ambitious goal, but one that some countries hope to achieve in less than 10 years. The aim? Zero waste, meaning every single piece of trash will be reused or composted. The idea may seem impossible, but several spots are coming close.

Take Sweden, for example. Less than one percent of the country's household garbage ends up in landfills. Rather, the Swedes recycle nearly everything—some 1.5 billion bottles and cans annually—and the rest winds up at waste-to-energy plants to produce electricity. The program is so successful that Sweden actually imports trash from other places, such as the United Kingdom, Norway, and Ireland, to keep up the rapid pace of its incinerators.

Other places narrowing in on zero waste? The Himalayan country of Bhutan is shooting for that status by 2030, while Singapore and Dubai have announced similar timelines. In the United States, individual cities like San Francisco and New York have also declared their dedication to going zero waste. The U.S. National Park Service, as well as major corporations like Lego and Nike, are also making big moves toward creating zero waste—all in an effort to make this world a cleaner place.

So what's the secret to zero waste? It's all about enforcing the rules of reducing, reusing, and recycling. In Sweden, for example, recycling stations must be no more than 984 feet (300 m) from any residential area. And in Bhutan—which is aspiring to become the world's first nation to have an all-organic farming system—composting from food scraps is the norm. Simple practices like these, as well as educating the public on the problems stemming from too much trash, can lead to major changes. And, perhaps, zero waste around the world one day.

DUBAI—HOME TO THE FAMOUS PALM JUMEIRAH ISLAND—IS AIMING TO GO WASTE FREE BY 2030.

# FROM FILTH **TO** FASHION

**Order up!** One creative company called Garbage Gone Glam made this dress out of diner menus. Other things they've made? A cocktail dress out of playing cards and a ball gown out of old magazines!

## HOW SOME TRASH TRAVELS FROM THE RECYCLING CENTER TO THE RUNWAYS—AND EVEN TO YOUR CLOSET

A hat made out of an old soccer ball brings new meaning to the term "header."

This eco-friendly bag is made from 365 recycled computer keyboard keys.

This head-piece, made from recycled corrugated cardboard, is hard to top!

LEVI STRAUSS & CO. MAKES JEANS OUT OF OLD COTTON T-SHIRTS.

This bow tie made out of an old aluminum can is both fashion-forward and eco-friendly.

# WORLD ENERGY & MINERALS

**A**lmost everything people do—from cooking to powering the International Space Station—requires energy. But energy comes in different forms. Traditional energy sources, still used by many people in the developing world, include burning dried animal dung and wood. Industrialized countries and urban centers around the world rely on coal, oil, and natural gas—called fossil fuels because they formed from decayed plant and animal material accumulated from long ago. Fossil fuel deposits, either in the ground or under the ocean floor, are unevenly distributed on Earth, and only some countries can afford to buy them. Fossil fuels are also not renewable, meaning they will run out one day. And unless we find other ways to create energy, we'll be stuck. Without energy we won't be able to drive cars, use lights, or send emails to friends.

## TAKING A TOLL

Environmentally speaking, burning fossil fuels isn't necessarily the best choice, either: Carbon dioxide from the burning of fossil fuels, as well as other emissions, are contributing to global warming. Concerned scientists are looking at new ways to harness renewable, alternative sources of energy, such as water, wind, and sun.

## HIGH VOLTAGE

**It seems like we use electricity for everything**—from TVs and cell phones to air conditioners and computers. In fact, power plants generate 3.7 times more electrical power than they did just 40 years ago. How they do this can differ around the world. Is it from burning coal or from taming the energy in moving water? Here's the global breakdown.

**5%** OTHER, SUCH AS GEOTHERMAL, SOLAR, WIND, HEAT, ETC.

**5%** OIL

**10.9%** NUCLEAR

**16.2%** HYDROPOWER

**40.4%** COAL

**22.5%** NATURAL GAS

Electricity travels at the speed of light—about 186,000 miles a second (299,340 km/s).

# Climate CHANGE

POLAR BEAR ON A PIECE OF MELTING ICEBERG

SCIENTISTS ARE CONCERNED THAT GREENLAND'S ICE SHEET HAS BEGUN TO MELT IN SUMMER. BIRTHDAY CANYON, SHOWN HERE, WAS CARVED BY MELTWATER.

## Rising Temperatures, Explained

### Fact: The world is getting warmer.

Earth's surface temperature has been increasing. In the past 50 years, our planet has warmed twice as fast as in the 50 years before that. This is the direct effect of climate change, which refers not only to the increase in Earth's average temperature (known as global warming), but also to the long-term effects on winds, rain, and ocean currents. Global warming is the reason glaciers and polar ice sheets are melting—resulting in rising sea levels and shrinking habitats. This makes survival for some animals a big challenge. Warming also means more flooding along the coasts and drought for inland areas.

### Why are temperatures climbing?

Some of the recent climate changes can be tied to natural causes—such as changes in the sun's intensity, the unusually warm ocean currents of El Niño, and volcanic activity—but human activities are a major factor as well.

Everyday activities that require burning fossil fuels, such as driving gasoline-powered cars, contribute to global warming. These activities produce greenhouse gases, which enter the atmosphere and trap heat. At the current rate, Earth's global average temperature is projected to rise between 1.8 and 11.5°F (1 and 6.4°C) by the year 2100, and it will get even warmer after that. And as the climate continues to warm, it will unfortunately continue to affect the environment and our society in many ways.

# QUIZ WHIZ

**What's your eco-friendly IQ? Find out with this quiz!**

Write your answers on a piece of paper. Then check them below.

**1** **True or false?** Sweden imports waste from other countries to recycle.

**2** Researchers found hundreds of thousands of _____ in just one square mile of North America's Great Lakes.
**a.** pieces of plastic
**b.** fish
**c.** boats
**d.** snakes

**3** What's considered a major threat to harbor seals?
**a.** pollution
**b.** fishing nets
**c.** microplastics
**d.** all of the above

**4** Some 700 species of animals are severely threatened because of _____ waste.
**a.** ocean
**b.** food
**c.** electronic
**d.** paper

**5** **True or false?** In the past 50 years, Earth has warmed twice as fast as in the 50 years before that.

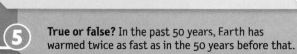

Not **STUMPED** yet? Check out the *NATIONAL GEOGRAPHIC KIDS QUIZ WHIZ* collection for more crazy **ENVIRONMENT** questions!

**ANSWERS: 1. True; 2. a; 3. d; 4. a; 5. True**

# Write a Letter That Gets Results

**Knowing how to write** a good letter is a useful skill. It will come in handy when you want to persuade someone to understand your point of view. Whether you're emailing your congressperson or writing a letter for a school project or to your grandma, a great letter will help you get your message across. Most important, a well-written letter leaves a good impression.

## CHECK OUT THE EXAMPLE BELOW FOR THE ELEMENTS OF A GOOD LETTER.

**Your address**

**Date**

**Salutation**
Always use "Dear" followed by the person's name; use Mr., Mrs., Ms., or Dr. as appropriate.

**Introductory paragraph**
Give the reason you're writing the letter.

**Body**
The longest part of the letter, which provides evidence that supports your position. Be persuasive!

**Closing paragraph**
Sum up your argument.

**Complimentary closing**
Sign off with "Sincerely" or "Thank you."

**Your signature**

Abby Jones
1204 Green Street
Los Angeles, CA 90045

April 22, 2021

Dear Ms. School Superintendent,

I am writing to you about how much excess energy our school uses and to offer a solution.

Every day, we leave the computers on in the classroom. The TVs are plugged in all the time, and the lights are on all day. All of this adds up to a lot of wasted energy, which is not only harmful for the Earth, as it increases the amount of harmful greenhouse gas emissions into the environment, but is also costly to the school. In fact, I read that schools spend more on energy bills than on computers and textbooks combined!

I am suggesting that we start an Energy Patrol to monitor the use of lighting, air-conditioning, heating, and other energy systems within our school. My idea is to have a group of students dedicated to figuring out ways we can cut back on our energy use in the school. We can do room checks, provide reminders to students and teachers to turn off lights and computers, replace old lightbulbs with energy-efficient products, and even reward the classrooms that do the most to save energy.

Above all, I think our school could help the environment tremendously by cutting back on how much energy we use. Let's see an Energy Patrol at our school soon. Thank you.

Sincerely,

*Abby Jones*

Abby Jones

### COMPLIMENTARY CLOSINGS
**Sincerely, Sincerely yours, Thank you, Regards, Best wishes, Respectfully,**

# HISTORY
## HAPPENS

Petra, an ancient city carved into the cliffs of southern Jordan, was voted one of the New Seven Wonders of the World.

**Bet You Didn't Know!**

# 10 awesome facts about the

**1** Egypt's **Lighthouse** of **Alexandria**, the world's first lighthouse, used **mirrors** to **reflect sunlight** for miles out to sea.

**2** **Australian Aboriginals**, people from the world's oldest living culture, have **existed** for at least **50,000 years.**

**3** The ancient **Celts** believed the **head** was the **seat of the soul.**

**4** An ancient **"snack bar"** was recently **unearthed** in the **ruins** of the **city** of **Pompeii,** in Italy.

**5** In **China**, the earliest **writing** dates to around **1200** B.C. and was **inscribed on the bones of animals.**

Ancient Aboriginal rock art, Australian outback

# ancient world

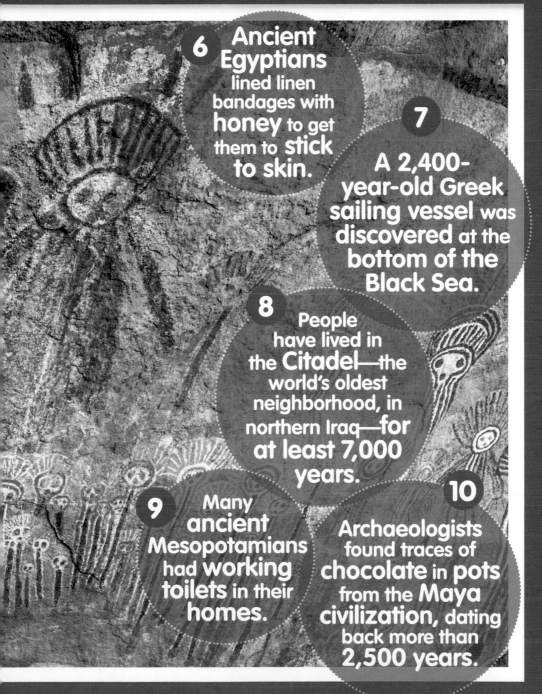

**6** Ancient Egyptians lined linen bandages with **honey** to get them to **stick** to skin.

**7** A 2,400-year-old Greek **sailing vessel** was **discovered** at the bottom of the **Black Sea.**

**8** People have lived in the **Citadel**—the world's oldest neighborhood, in northern Iraq—**for at least 7,000 years.**

**9** Many **ancient** Mesopotamians had **working toilets** in their **homes.**

**10** Archaeologists found traces of **chocolate** in **pots** from the **Maya** civilization, dating back more than **2,500 years.**

# The Search for Alexander the Great's
# Lost Tomb

ARCHAEOLOGIST CALLIOPE LIMNEOS-PAPAKOSTA

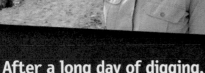

A PAINTING OF ALEXANDER ON HORSEBACK AT THE BATTLE WITH PORUS IN 326 B.C.

## After a long day of digging,

Greek archaeologist Calliope Limneos-Papakosta was ready to go home. She had spent many years of her career scouring the grounds of Alexandria, Egypt, in the hopes of finding Alexander the Great's tomb. But upon coming up empty-handed once again, Papakosta was just about to conclude her latest dig.

Until, that is, one of her assistants called her over. A flash of white poking out of the dirt caught her eye. She began to dig. Turns out that white object was part of a remarkably intact statue of Alexander the Great—and just the sign Papakosta needed to continue her search for the ancient conqueror-turned-pharaoh's tomb.

### CAPITAL GAINS

How did the ancient city of Alexandria come to be? In 332 B.C., Alexander the Great, a king from ancient Greece, defeated the Persians to take over Egypt as the new leader of the land. He went to work quickly, establishing a new capital at the mouth of the Nile River. It soon became one of the most powerful cities in the world— and an education epicenter that included one of the most famous libraries ever built.

By the time of his death, Alexander the Great had amassed the largest empire in the entire ancient world, spanning some 3,000 miles (4,828 km). It's said that when he died in 323 B.C. at the age of just 32, his body was embalmed in honey and buried in a tomb in Alexandria.

### SUNKEN CITY

The actual location of Alexander's final resting spot is a mystery that has baffled experts for decades. After a tsunami tore through the city in A.D. 356, many devastating earthquakes followed. This led to rising sea levels, causing the ancient part of the city to sink. As time

PAPAKOSTA AND HER TEAM HAVE UNCOVERED THE FOUNDATION WALLS OF A MONUMENTAL BUILDING IN ALEXANDRIA DATING TO THE ERA OF ALEXANDER THE GREAT.

ARTIST'S RENDERING OF ANCIENT ALEXANDRIA

passed and new portions of the city were built on top of the ancient section, Alexander's tomb went way underground.

## NEW DISCOVERIES

So while experts know Alexander's tomb was buried somewhere, its location is still unclear. For several years following the discovery of that one statue, Papakosta continued her search, relying on a combination of ancient accounts, old maps, and modern technology to determine where to dig. With the help of a tool called electrical resistivity tomography (ERT), which shoots electrical current into the soil to detect any objects buried below, her team has

been able to uncover more parts of the city's ancient royal quarter—including a Roman road and the remnants of a large public building that may be linked to the tomb.

## THE SEARCH CONTINUES

As for the tomb itself? Its location remains unknown. But as experts like Papakosta keep searching, the hope is that this long-standing mystery will soon be solved.

225

# GUARDIANS
# OF THE TOMB

**B**ack in 1974, Chinese farmers who were digging for water got a shock. Staring up from the soil was a face, eyes wide open, with features that looked almost human. But this was not a skeleton: It was one of thousands of life-size soldiers made of baked clay called terra-cotta—and they had been buried for 2,200 years.

## BURIED TREASURE

Row upon row of the soldiers—each face as different and as realistic as the next—were hidden in a pit the size of two football fields near Xi'an, which was China's capital city for nearly 2,000 years. Archaeologists eventually found four pits, some containing statues of horse-drawn chariots, cavalry (soldiers on horseback), and high-ranking officers.

## BODYGUARDS

Who could have built this huge underground army? Experts assume it was China's first emperor, Qin Shihuangdi (Chin She-hwong-dee). The brilliant but brutal ruler, who created the first unified China, was known for his big ideas and even bigger ego. It's believed that because Qin Shihuangdi had killed so many people during his reign, he may have wanted a large army to protect him from his victims' ghosts once he died. He probably had the clay soldiers created to guard his tomb, which was just one mile (1.6 km) away from where the pits were discovered.

## FINAL REWARDS

As it turned out, the emperor's living enemies—not the dead ones—took revenge. In 206 B.C., a few years after Qin Shihuangdi's death, invading armies destroyed the pits, burying the warriors and cracking every figure. The pits caved in more as time went on, and the soldiers were lost to the ages.

Experts have since pieced a thousand soldiers back together. But some 6,000 figures are still buried. As work continues, who knows what secrets these soldiers have yet to tell?

STATUES OF ARCHERS, LIKE THE ONE ABOVE, WERE BURIED HOLDING REAL CROSSBOWS.

**ANCIENT CRAFTSMEN MADE THOUSANDS OF LIFE-SIZE TERRA-COTTA WARRIORS, EACH WITH A UNIQUE FACE.**

# UNDER
## RECONSTRUCTION

Experts have painstakingly rebuilt and restored a thousand terra-cotta warriors found in underground pits near the emperor's tomb. The complex is so vast that excavations may continue for generations.

A warrior's head poking out of the dirt still has traces of red paint. Originally all of the warriors were painted bright colors.

Workers brush dirt away from the collapsed roof that sheltered the terra-cotta warriors.

A toppled terra-cotta warrior lies in its 2,200-year-old underground tomb.

ASIA

CHINA

PACIFIC OCEAN

TERRA-COTTA WARRIORS

CHINA

HORSE-DRAWN CHARIOT

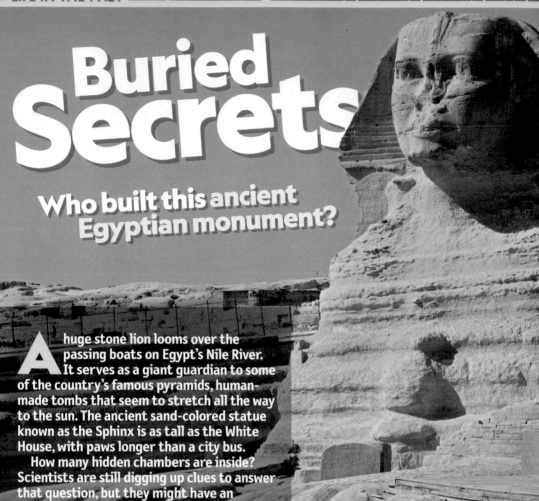

# Buried Secrets

## Who built this ancient Egyptian monument?

**A** huge stone lion looms over the passing boats on Egypt's Nile River. It serves as a giant guardian to some of the country's famous pyramids, human-made tombs that seem to stretch all the way to the sun. The ancient sand-colored statue known as the Sphinx is as tall as the White House, with paws longer than a city bus.

How many hidden chambers are inside? Scientists are still digging up clues to answer that question, but they might have an answer for one of the monument's biggest mysteries: Who built it?

## SET IN STONE

In ancient Egypt, people worshipped sphinxes as mythical creatures with the power to ward off evil. Some think the Sphinx was built as a protector of the pyramids, which were once used as burial places for Egyptian kings. Nobody's sure when the Sphinx was built, but experts believe it was already ancient when Egyptian queen Cleopatra saw it around 47 B.C. Since then, many other historical figures have visited the monument. But which historical figure *built* the monument?

## FACE OFF

Historians' two top suspects are Pharaoh Khufu, who ruled Egypt from 2589 B.C. to 2566 B.C., and his son, Pharaoh Khafre, who reigned from 2558 to 2532 B.C. Most experts agree that one of these rulers oversaw the construction of the statue and had his own face carved atop the giant lion. But which one was it—Khufu or Khafre?

Some think the Sphinx is the work of Khufu. They say the statue's face matches a sculpture of the king discovered in A.D. 1903.

But most experts, including Egyptologist Mark Lehner, think Khufu's son, Khafre, built the Sphinx. As father and son, the pair shared a resemblance.

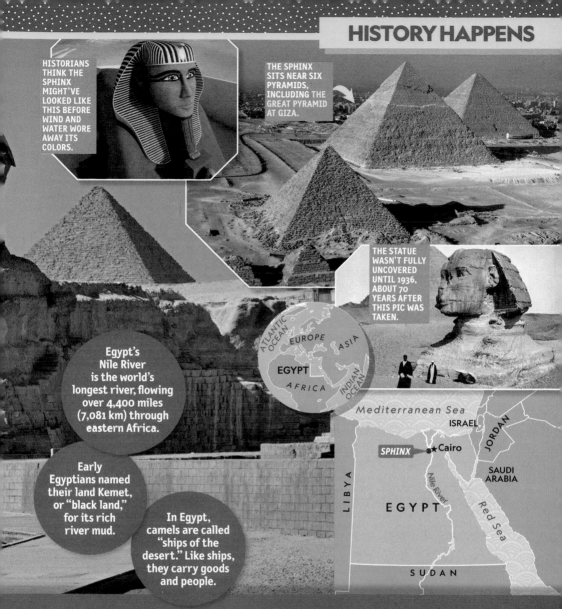

HISTORIANS THINK THE SPHINX MIGHT'VE LOOKED LIKE THIS BEFORE WIND AND WATER WORE AWAY ITS COLORS.

THE SPHINX SITS NEAR SIX PYRAMIDS, INCLUDING THE GREAT PYRAMID AT GIZA.

THE STATUE WASN'T FULLY UNCOVERED UNTIL 1936, ABOUT 70 YEARS AFTER THIS PIC WAS TAKEN.

Egypt's Nile River is the world's longest river, flowing over 4,400 miles (7,081 km) through eastern Africa.

Early Egyptians named their land Kemet, or "black land," for its rich river mud.

In Egypt, camels are called "ships of the desert." Like ships, they carry goods and people.

But Lehner says the most convincing evidence lies in a temple that was built in front of the statue. Lehner believes that the temple and the Sphinx are part of the same master building plan overseen by one person. Ancient workers built the temple on top of part of another structure that's been proven to be the work of Khafre. Lehner believes that this means the Sphinx and its temple must have been constructed after Khafre's first structure was built—Khufu wouldn't have been around to build on top of Khafre's lower structure. "To me, that's strong evidence that the Sphinx couldn't have been Khufu's," Lehner says.

## DISAPPEARING ACT

Today the ancient Egyptians' work is crumbling. Centuries of wind and water have ground away at the Sphinx's limestone, and shifting sands have threatened to cover much of it. Archaeologists work tirelessly to repair the structure to keep it from completely disappearing.

By preserving the Sphinx, experts are also protecting clues that might still be hidden in the statue's stone. Someday, these could be the keys that unlock even more of the Sphinx's secrets.

# HISTORY'S MYSTERIES

## CURIOUS CLUES, COLD CASES, AND UNSOLVED PUZZLES FROM THE PAST

## THE MYSTERY

### DOES THE YETI EXIST?

POSSIBLE YETI FOOTPRINTS

HIKERS COULD BE MISTAKING A TIBETAN BLUE BEAR FOR A YETI.

The yeti is also known as the Abominable Snowman.

### THE BACKGROUND

The word "yeti" means "little manlike animal" in the Tibetan language. According to legend, yetis are hairy (and not so little) ogres that look like a cross between a human and a bear. People today still report seeing the mysterious creatures roaming Asia's Himalayan mountains. The fur-covered monster reportedly stands eight feet (2.4 m) tall, weighs some 400 pounds (181 kg), and snacks on goats. Debate has raged for centuries about whether this creature is man, bear, or myth.

### THE CLUES

In 1986, a man hiking in the Himalaya photographed what he thought was a yeti in the snow.

Other believers have tried testing furry scalps and hair samples, hoping they belonged to an unknown animal. One man even collected what he said was a yeti finger!

### WHAT THE YETI COULD BE

So far, nothing proves that the yeti exists. Test results showed that the scalp belonged to a goat, and the hair samples were from a bear. That 1986 photograph turned out to be a weird rock shape. And the "yeti finger"? Tests revealed it was actually from a human. (That's a whole other mystery!) Some scientists believe that the Tibetan blue bear, a rare type of brown bear that walks upright, is being mistaken for a yeti.

## THE MYSTERY

### WHY IS THIS ANCIENT MUMMY MOANING?

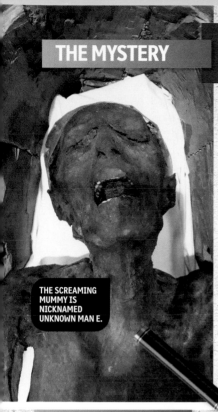

THE SCREAMING MUMMY IS NICKNAMED UNKNOWN MAN E.

Sheepskin and a strange dried-out paste covered Unknown Man E.

#### THE BACKGROUND

Back in 1886, the director of the Egyptian Antiquities Service was removing the wrappings of a mummy that had been discovered in Egypt's Valley of the Kings when he got a scary surprise. The mummy's mouth was open, its eyes were shut, and its nostrils were flared, as though he was in pain.

#### WHAT COULD'VE HAPPENED

Experts guessed that Unknown Man E, as the mummy came to be known, may have been poisoned—a punishment for a crime. In 2008, a team of scientists used CT scans, DNA evidence, and x-rays to figure out who the mummy was. By comparing the high-tech results with descriptions from ancient Egyptian scrolls, experts think it might be Prince Pentewere. He was suspected of plotting the murder of his father, Pharaoh Ramses III in 1155 B.C. As a member of the royal family, he might have been killed by being forced to drink poison rather than face execution. Researchers are still trying to unravel the clues on this mummy mystery.

## THE MYSTERY

### WHY DID PEOPLE VANISH FROM THE LOST COLONY OF ROANOKE?

The lost colonists of Roanoke included entire families—90 men, 17 women, and 11 children.

A REPLICA OF A 16TH-CENTURY SHIP

#### THE BACKGROUND

About a hundred English colonists arrived in 1587 to Roanoke Island, a spot near modern-day Manteo, North Carolina, U.S.A. Not long after, the colony's governor, John White, traveled back to England for more supplies. When White returned in 1590, he found an empty village. What happened?

#### THE CLUES

Archaeologists found artifacts like broken bowls that likely belonged to the colonists on Mettaquem, a nearby Native American settlement. They also found buried cannons and coffins that might date back to when the colonists lived in the area where the Mettaquem would've been.

One theory to what happened to the colonists is that they faced some kind of threat, so they split into smaller groups and fled. The artifacts found at Mettaquem may mean some of them sought shelter there, but to this day, the disappearance of the colonists remains a mystery.

ROANOKE GOVERNOR JOHN WHITE (POINTING) FOUND THE WORD "CROATOAN" ON A TREE. EXPERTS WONDER IF THE COLONISTS FLED TO THIS NEARBY ISLAND (NOW CALLED HATTERAS ISLAND).

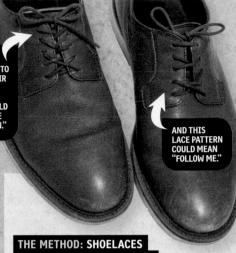

SPIES ARE ENCOURAGED TO MAKE UP THEIR OWN CODES. SO THIS LACE PATTERN COULD MEAN "I HAVE INFORMATION."

AND THIS LACE PATTERN COULD MEAN "FOLLOW ME."

# SUPER SNEAKY CODE BREAKERS

## ›› CHECK OUT SNEAKY WAYS PEOPLE HAVE SENT MESSAGES.

You need to tell your best friend a secret. But if anyone else reads your note, you're busted. Get the sneaky scoop on ways other people have delivered secret messages. You just might find a new way to get that info to your BFF!

**THE METHOD: SHOELACES**
**THE MESSENGER: U.S. SPIES**
**THE STORY:** Yeah, you learned how to tie your shoes years ago. But do you know how to send a message with your sneakers? In the 1950s, the U.S. Central Intelligence Agency created a book of tips to teach spies ways to communicate in public in case they were being watched. One tip: Lace up your sneakers. Tied one way, the laces might mean "I have information"; tied another, "Follow me." The spies could communicate while everyone else probably just thought: That guy can't tie his shoes correctly!

THE HISTORIAN HERODOTUS

**THE METHOD: TATTOOED HEAD**
**THE MESSENGER: HISTIAEUS OF MILETUS**
**THE STORY:** Around 513 B.C., Histiaeus was forced out as the ruler of an ancient city in what's now Turkey. So he wanted to send a message to his supporters: to revolt against the king who took away his power. According to the Greek historian Herodotus (who lived around the same time), Histiaeus summoned a slave, shaved his head, and tattooed the message onto the man's scalp. After the slave's hair grew back, he traveled to Greece with instructions to shave his head again. Message received!

**THE METHOD: SECRET SCARVES**
**THE MESSENGER: BELGIAN SPIES**
**THE STORY:** "An old lady knitting doesn't look like a threat," says Vince Houghton, the historian and curator at the International Spy Museum in Washington, D.C. That's why during World War I (in the 1910s), Belgian resistance fighters asked women who lived near railways to keep track of the types of trains passing by, which gave the fighters information about the German invaders' movements. The women would knit a bumpy stitch for one type of train, and knit a small hole in the fabric for another. Then they'd pass the cozy scarf to a soldier so the cloth could be decoded.

## Make Invisible Ink

You'll need:
- baking soda
- water
- small cup
- paper
- paintbrush
- sponge
- grape juice

**THE METHOD: SONGS**
**THE MESSENGER: SLAVES IN THE UNITED STATES**
**THE STORY:** African-American slaves in the 1800s couldn't talk openly about their plans to escape to freedom—so they secretly sang about it. For instance, "Swing Low, Sweet Chariot" might sound like a religious song. But for slaves, the "sweet chariot" was code for the Underground Railroad, the network of people who helped slaves head to northern states and Canada, where slavery was illegal. The song "Wade in the Water" warned escaped slaves to get in the water so dogs would lose their scent trail. With these methods, hundreds of people escaped slavery.

**Step one**
Mix equal amounts of baking soda and water in a small cup.

**Step two** Write your message on paper using the mixture and the paintbrush.

**Step three** Wait for the paper to dry, then pass the note to your friend.

**THE METHOD: ORANGE JUICE**
**THE MESSENGER: JOHN GERARD**
**THE STORY:** In 1597, a priest named John Gerard was imprisoned in the Tower of London in England by Queen Elizabeth I. He asked the warden to let him send letters written in charcoal. But then he scrawled another message on top using the juice from an orange—which was only visible when the juice was dry and the page heated. With his invisible ink, he coordinated an escape out of a window and into a boat rowed by his supporters.

**Step four** To reveal the message, use a sponge or brush to paint the paper with grape juice.

The slight acidity of the juice reacts with the baking soda to reveal your message.

# GOING TO WAR

Since the beginning of time, different countries, territories, and cultures have feuded with each other over land, power, and politics. Major military conflicts include the following wars:

## 1095–1291 THE CRUSADES
Starting late in the 11th century, these wars over religion were fought in the Middle East for nearly 200 years.

## 1337–1453 HUNDRED YEARS' WAR
France and England battled over rights to land for more than a century before the French eventually drove the English out in 1453.

## 1754–1763 FRENCH AND INDIAN WAR (part of Europe's Seven Years' War)
A nine-year war between the British and French for control of North America.

## 1775–1783 AMERICAN REVOLUTION
Thirteen British colonies in America united to reject the rule of the British government and to form the United States of America.

## 1861–1865 AMERICAN CIVIL WAR
This war occurred when the northern states (the Union) went to war with the southern states, which had seceded, or withdrawn, to form the Confederate States of America. Slavery was one of the key issues in the Civil War.

## 1910–1920 MEXICAN REVOLUTION
The people of Mexico revolted against the rule of dictator President Porfirio Díaz, leading to his eventual defeat and to a democratic government.

## 1914–1918 WORLD WAR I
The assassination of Austria's Archduke Ferdinand by a Serbian nationalist sparked this wide-spreading war. The U.S. entered after Germany sank the British ship *Lusitania*, killing more than 120 Americans.

## 1918–1920 RUSSIAN CIVIL WAR
Following the 1917 Russian Revolution, this conflict pitted the Communist Red Army against the foreign-backed White Army. The Red Army won, leading to the establishment of the Union of Soviet Socialist Republics (U.S.S.R.) in 1922.

## 1936–1939 SPANISH CIVIL WAR
Aid from Italy and Germany helped Spain's Nationalists gain victory over the Communist-supported Republicans. The war resulted in the loss of more than 300,000 lives and increased tension in Europe leading up to World War II.

## 1939–1945 WORLD WAR II
This massive conflict in Europe, Asia, and North Africa involved many countries that aligned with the two sides: the Allies and the Axis. After the bombing of Pearl Harbor in Hawaii in 1941, the U.S. entered the war on the side of the Allies. More than 50 million people died during the war.

## 1946–1949 CHINESE CIVIL WAR

Also known as the "War of Liberation," this war pitted the Communist and Nationalist Parties in China against each other. The Communists won.

## 1950–1953 KOREAN WAR

Kicked off when the Communist forces of North Korea, with backing from the Soviet Union, invaded their democratic neighbor to the south. A coalition of 16 countries from the United Nations stepped in to support South Korea. An armistice, or temporary truce, ended active fighting in 1953.

## 1950s–1975 VIETNAM WAR

This war was fought between the Communist North, supported by allies including China, and the government of South Vietnam, supported by the United States and other anticommunist nations.

## 1967 SIX-DAY WAR

This was a battle for land between Israel and the states of Egypt, Jordan, and Syria. The outcome resulted in Israel's gaining control of coveted territory, including the Gaza Strip and the West Bank.

## 1991–PRESENT SOMALI CIVIL WAR

The war began when Somalia's last president, a dictator named Mohamed Siad Barre, was overthrown. It has led to years of fighting and anarchy.

## 2001–2014 WAR IN AFGHANISTAN

After attacks in the U.S. by the terrorist group al Qaeda, a coalition that eventually included more than 40 countries invaded Afghanistan to find Osama bin Laden and other al Qaeda members and to dismantle the Taliban. Bin Laden was killed in a U.S. covert operation in 2011. The North Atlantic Treaty Organization (NATO) took control of the coalition's combat mission in 2003. That combat mission officially ended in 2014.

## 2003–2011 WAR IN IRAQ

A coalition led by the U.S., and including Britain, Australia, and Spain, invaded Iraq over suspicions that Iraq had weapons of mass destruction.

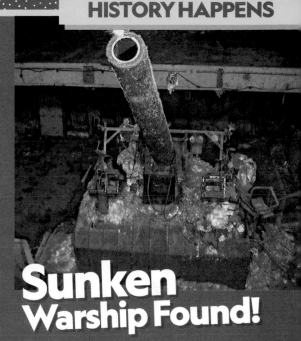

# Sunken Warship Found!

In October 1942, during one of the fiercest battles of World War II, the U.S. aircraft carrier U.S.S. *Hornet* plunged to the bottom of the South Pacific Ocean. After taking heavy fire from Japanese dive-bombers, torpedo planes, and destroyers, the *Hornet*—which played pivotal roles in several other World War II battles—eventually went down. It sank 17,500 feet (5,330 m) down to the ocean floor. Some 140 of the *Hornet*'s fallen crew went with the ship to its watery grave.

Now, nearly 80 years later, the *Hornet* has been found, thanks to a high-tech deep-sea drone that's part of the research vessel *Petrel*. After scanning the ocean floor near the Solomon Islands in the South Pacific, the drone sent images and video feed of the ship to a crew of experts above the surface. They were able to identify the *Hornet* by its naval designation—*CV 8*—on the side of the ship. Other striking images of the shipwreck include a gun stationed on the deck of the ship, a jacket still hanging on a hatch, and a sailor's toothbrush partially buried in the sand.

The *Hornet*'s exact location will not be released to the public in order to protect it. This way, it can forever serve as an untouched memorial to the brave soldiers who sacrificed their lives during World War II.

235

# THE CONSTITUTION & THE BILL OF RIGHTS

**The United States Constitution was written in 1787 by a group of political leaders from the 13 states that made up the U.S. at the time.** Thirty-nine men, including Benjamin Franklin and James Madison, signed the document to create a national government. While some feared the creation of a strong federal government, all 13 states eventually ratified, or approved, the Constitution, making it the law of the land. The Constitution has three major parts: the preamble, the articles, and the amendments.

**Here's a summary of what topics are covered in each part of the Constitution. Check out the Constitution online or at your local library for the full text.**

**THE PREAMBLE** outlines the basic purposes of the government: *We the People of the United States, in order to form a more perfect Union, establish justice, insure domestic tranquility, provide for the common defense, promote the general welfare, and secure the blessings of liberty to ourselves and our posterity, do ordain and establish this Constitution for the United States of America.*

**SEVEN ARTICLES** outline the powers of Congress, the president, and the court system:

Article I outlines the legislative branch—the Senate and the House of Representatives—and its powers and responsibilities.

Article II outlines the executive branch—the presidency—and its powers and responsibilities.

Article III outlines the judicial branch—the court system—and its powers and responsibilities.

Article IV describes the individual states' rights and powers.

Article V outlines the amendment process.

Article VI establishes the Constitution as the law of the land.

Article VII gives the requirements for the Constitution to be approved.

**THE AMENDMENTS,** or additions to the Constitution, were put in later as needed. In 1791, the first 10 amendments, known as the **Bill of Rights,** were added. Since then, another 17 amendments have been added. This is the Bill of Rights:

**1st Amendment:** guarantees freedom of religion, speech, and the press, and the right to assemble and petition. The U.S. may not have a national religion.

**2nd Amendment:** discusses the militia and the right of people to bear arms

**3rd Amendment:** prohibits the military or troops from using private homes without consent

**4th Amendment:** protects people and their homes from search, arrest, or seizure without probable cause or a warrant

**5th Amendment:** grants people the right to have a trial and prevents punishment before prosecution; protects private property from being taken without compensation

**6th Amendment:** guarantees the right to a speedy and public trial

**7th Amendment:** guarantees a trial by jury in certain cases

**8th Amendment:** forbids "cruel and unusual punishments"

**9th Amendment:** states that the Constitution is not all-encompassing and does not deny people other, unspecified rights

**10th Amendment:** grants the powers not covered by the Constitution to the states and the people

Read the full text version of the United States Constitution at constitutioncenter.org/constitution/full-text

White House

# BRANCHES OF GOVERNMENT

The **UNITED STATES GOVERNMENT** is divided into three branches: **executive**, **legislative**, and **judicial**. The system of checks and balances is a way to control power and to make sure one branch can't take the reins of government. For example, most of the president's actions require the approval of Congress. Likewise, the laws passed in Congress must be signed by the president before they can take effect.

## Executive Branch

**The Constitution lists the central powers of the president:** to serve as commander in chief of the armed forces; make treaties with other nations; grant pardons; inform Congress on the state of the union; and appoint ambassadors, officials, and judges. The executive branch includes the president and the 15 governmental departments.

## Legislative Branch

This branch is made up of Congress—the Senate and the House of Representatives. The Constitution grants Congress the power to make laws. Congress is made up of elected representatives from each state. Each state has two representatives in the Senate, while the number of representatives in the House is determined by the size of the state's population. Washington, D.C., and the territories elect nonvoting representatives to the House of Representatives. The Founding Fathers set up this system as a compromise between big states—which wanted representation based on population—and small states—which wanted all states to have equal representation rights.

The U.S. Capitol in Washington, D.C.

## Judicial Branch

The judicial branch is composed of the federal court system—the U.S. Supreme Court, the courts of appeals, and the district courts. The Supreme Court is the most powerful court. Its motto is "Equal Justice Under Law." This influential court is responsible for interpreting the Constitution and applying it to the cases that it hears. The decisions of the Supreme Court are absolute—they are the final word on any legal question.

The U.S. Supreme Court Building in Washington, D.C.

There are nine justices on the Supreme Court. They are appointed by the president of the United States and confirmed by the Senate.

# The Native American Experience

## Native Americans are indigenous

to North and South America—they are the people who were here before Columbus and other European explorers came to these lands. They lived in nations, tribes, and bands across both continents. For decades following the arrival of Europeans in 1492, Native Americans clashed with the newcomers who had ruptured the indigenous people's ways of living.

## Tribal Land

During the 19th century, both United States legislation and military action restricted the movement of Native Americans, forcing them to live on reservations and attempting to dismantle tribal structures. For centuries, Native Americans were displaced or killed, or became assimilated into the general U.S. population. In 1924 the Indian Citizenship Act granted citizenship to all Native Americans. Unfortunately, this was not enough to end the social discrimination and mistreatment that many indigenous people have faced. Today, Native Americans living in the U.S. still face many challenges.

## Healing the Past

Many members of the 560-plus recognized tribes in the United States live primarily on reservations. Some tribes have more than one reservation, while others have none. Together these reservations make up less than 3 percent of the nation's land area. The tribal governments on reservations have the right to form their own governments and to enforce laws, similar to individual states. Many feel that this sovereignty is still not enough to right the wrongs of the past: They hope for a change in the U.S. government's relationship with Native Americans.

An annual powwow in New Mexico features more than 3,000 dancers from more than 500 North American tribes.

Navajo is the most commonly spoken Native American language in the United States.

Top: A Cherokee and Catawba man dances at a powwow.
Middle: A Monacan girl dances in a traditional jingle dress.
Bottom: Little Shell men in traditional costume

**The president of the United States** is the chief of the executive branch, the commander in chief of the U.S. armed forces, and head of the federal government. Elected every four years, the president is the highest policy-maker in the nation. The 22nd Amendment (1951) says that no person may be elected to the office of president more than twice. There have been 45 presidencies and 44 presidents.

## GEORGE WASHINGTON
*1st President of the United States ★ 1789–1797*

BORN Feb. 22, 1732, in Pope's Creek, Westmoreland County, VA
POLITICAL PARTY Federalist
NO. OF TERMS two
VICE PRESIDENT John Adams
DIED Dec. 14, 1799, at Mount Vernon, VA

## JOHN ADAMS
*2nd President of the United States ★ 1797–1801*

BORN Oct. 30, 1735, in Braintree (now Quincy), MA
POLITICAL PARTY Federalist
NO. OF TERMS one
VICE PRESIDENT Thomas Jefferson
DIED July 4, 1826, in Quincy, MA

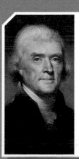

## THOMAS JEFFERSON
*3rd President of the United States ★ 1801–1809*

BORN April 13, 1743, at Shadwell, Goochland (now Albemarle) County, VA
POLITICAL PARTY Democratic-Republican
NO. OF TERMS two
VICE PRESIDENTS 1st term: Aaron Burr
2nd term: George Clinton
DIED July 4, 1826, at Monticello, Charlottesville, VA

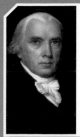

## JAMES MADISON
*4th President of the United States ★ 1809–1817*

BORN March 16, 1751, at Belle Grove, Port Conway, VA
POLITICAL PARTY Democratic-Republican
NO. OF TERMS two
VICE PRESIDENTS 1st term: George Clinton
2nd term: Elbridge Gerry
DIED June 28, 1836, at Montpelier, Orange County, VA

## JAMES MONROE
*5th President of the United States ★ 1817–1825*

BORN April 28, 1758, in Westmoreland County, VA
POLITICAL PARTY Democratic-Republican
NO. OF TERMS two
VICE PRESIDENT Daniel D. Tompkins
DIED July 4, 1831, in New York, NY

## JOHN QUINCY ADAMS
*6th President of the United States ★ 1825–1829*

BORN July 11, 1767, in Braintree (now Quincy), MA
POLITICAL PARTY Democratic-Republican
NO. OF TERMS one
VICE PRESIDENT John Caldwell Calhoun
DIED Feb. 23, 1848, at the U.S. Capitol, Washington, D.C.

## JOHN QUINCY ADAMS ONCE RECEIVED AN ALLIGATOR AS A GIFT.

## ANDREW JACKSON
*7th President of the United States ★ 1829–1837*

BORN March 15, 1767, in the Waxhaw region, NC and SC
POLITICAL PARTY Democrat
NO. OF TERMS two
VICE PRESIDENTS 1st term: John Caldwell Calhoun
2nd term: Martin Van Buren
DIED June 8, 1845, in Nashville, TN

## MARTIN VAN BUREN
*8th President of the United States ★ 1837–1841*

BORN Dec. 5, 1782, in Kinderhook, NY
POLITICAL PARTY Democrat
NO. OF TERMS one
VICE PRESIDENT Richard M. Johnson
DIED July 24, 1862, in Kinderhook, NY

## WILLIAM HENRY HARRISON

*9th President of the United States ★ 1841*

BORN Feb. 9, 1773, in Charles City County, VA

POLITICAL PARTY Whig

NO. OF TERMS one (died while in office)

VICE PRESIDENT John Tyler

DIED April 4, 1841, in the White House, Washington, D.C.

## JOHN TYLER

*10th President of the United States ★ 1841–1845*

BORN March 29, 1790, in Charles City County, VA

POLITICAL PARTY Whig

NO. OF TERMS one (partial)

VICE PRESIDENT none

DIED Jan. 18, 1862, in Richmond, VA

## JAMES K. POLK

*11th President of the United States ★ 1845–1849*

BORN Nov. 2, 1795, near Pineville, Mecklenburg County, NC

POLITICAL PARTY Democrat

NO. OF TERMS one

VICE PRESIDENT George Mifflin Dallas

DIED June 15, 1849, in Nashville, TN

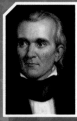

## ZACHARY TAYLOR

*12th President of the United States ★ 1849–1850*

BORN Nov. 24, 1784, in Orange County, VA

POLITICAL PARTY Whig

NO. OF TERMS one (died while in office)

VICE PRESIDENT Millard Fillmore

DIED July 9, 1850, in the White House, Washington, D.C.

## MILLARD FILLMORE

*13th President of the United States ★ 1850–1853*

BORN Jan. 7, 1800, in Cayuga County, NY

POLITICAL PARTY Whig

NO. OF TERMS one (partial)

VICE PRESIDENT none

DIED March 8, 1874, in Buffalo, NY

## FRANKLIN PIERCE

*14th President of the United States ★ 1853–1857*

BORN Nov. 23, 1804, in Hillsborough (now Hillsboro), NH

POLITICAL PARTY Democrat

NO. OF TERMS one

VICE PRESIDENT William Rufus De Vane King

DIED Oct. 8, 1869, in Concord, NH

## JAMES BUCHANAN

*15th President of the United States ★ 1857–1861*

BORN April 23, 1791, in Cove Gap, PA

POLITICAL PARTY Democrat

NO. OF TERMS one

VICE PRESIDENT John Cabell Breckinridge

DIED June 1, 1868, in Lancaster, PA

## ABRAHAM LINCOLN

*16th President of the United States ★ 1861–1865*

BORN Feb. 12, 1809, near Hodgenville, KY

POLITICAL PARTY Republican (formerly Whig)

NO. OF TERMS two (assassinated)

VICE PRESIDENTS 1st term: Hannibal Hamlin
2nd term: Andrew Johnson

DIED April 15, 1865, in Washington, D.C.

## ABRAHAM LINCOLN received an award from the NATIONAL WRESTLING HALL OF FAME.

## ANDREW JOHNSON

*17th President of the United States ★ 1865–1869*

BORN Dec. 29, 1808, in Raleigh, NC

POLITICAL PARTY Democrat

NO. OF TERMS one (partial)

VICE PRESIDENT none

DIED July 31, 1875, in Carter's Station, TN

## ULYSSES S. GRANT
*18th President of the United States* ★ *1869–1877*

BORN April 27, 1822,
in Point Pleasant, OH
POLITICAL PARTY Republican
NO. OF TERMS two
VICE PRESIDENTS 1st term: Schuyler Colfax
2nd term: Henry Wilson
DIED July 23, 1885, in Mount
McGregor, NY

## GROVER CLEVELAND
*22nd and 24th President of the United States*
*1885–1889* ★ *1893–1897*

BORN March 18, 1837, in Caldwell, NJ
POLITICAL PARTY Democrat
NO. OF TERMS two (nonconsecutive)
VICE PRESIDENTS 1st administration:
Thomas Andrews Hendricks
2nd administration:
Adlai Ewing Stevenson
DIED June 24, 1908, in Princeton, NJ

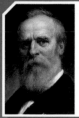

## RUTHERFORD B. HAYES
*19th President of the United States* ★ *1877–1881*

BORN Oct. 4, 1822,
in Delaware, OH
POLITICAL PARTY Republican
NO. OF TERMS one
VICE PRESIDENT William Almon Wheeler
DIED Jan. 17, 1893, in Fremont, OH

## BENJAMIN HARRISON
*23rd President of the United States* ★ *1889–1893*

BORN Aug. 20, 1833, in North Bend, OH
POLITICAL PARTY Republican
NO. OF TERMS one
VICE PRESIDENT Levi Parsons Morton
DIED March 13, 1901, in Indianapolis, IN

## JAMES A. GARFIELD
*20th President of the United States* ★ *1881*

BORN Nov. 19, 1831, near
Orange, OH
POLITICAL PARTY Republican
NO. OF TERMS one (assassinated)
VICE PRESIDENT Chester A. Arthur
DIED Sept. 19, 1881, in Elberon, NJ

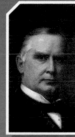

## WILLIAM MCKINLEY
*25th President of the United States* ★ *1897–1901*

BORN Jan. 29, 1843, in Niles, OH
POLITICAL PARTY Republican
NO. OF TERMS two (assassinated)
VICE PRESIDENTS 1st term:
Garret Augustus Hobart
2nd term:
Theodore Roosevelt
DIED Sept. 14, 1901, in Buffalo, NY

**JAMES A. GARFIELD
was AMBIDEXTROUS—
able to write well with both
hands—and would reportedly
WRITE WITH BOTH HANDS
SIMULTANEOUSLY.**

## THEODORE ROOSEVELT
*26th President of the United States* ★ *1901–1909*

BORN Oct. 27, 1858, in New York, NY
POLITICAL PARTY Republican
NO. OF TERMS one, plus balance of
McKinley's term
VICE PRESIDENTS 1st term: none
2nd term: Charles
Warren Fairbanks
DIED Jan. 6, 1919, in Oyster Bay, NY

## CHESTER A. ARTHUR
*21st President of the United States* ★ *1881–1885*

BORN Oct. 5, 1829, in Fairfield, VT
POLITICAL PARTY Republican
NO. OF TERMS one (partial)
VICE PRESIDENT none
DIED Nov. 18, 1886, in New York, NY

## WILLIAM HOWARD TAFT
*27th President of the United States* ★ *1909–1913*

BORN Sept. 15, 1857, in Cincinnati, OH
POLITICAL PARTY Republican
NO. OF TERMS one
VICE PRESIDENT James Schoolcraft
Sherman
DIED March 8, 1930, in Washington, D.C.

## WOODROW WILSON
*28th President of the United States ★ 1913–1921*
BORN Dec. 29, 1856, in Staunton, VA
POLITICAL PARTY Democrat
NO. OF TERMS two
VICE PRESIDENT Thomas Riley Marshall
DIED Feb. 3, 1924, in Washington, D.C.

## WARREN G. HARDING
*29th President of the United States ★ 1921–1923*
BORN Nov. 2, 1865, in Caledonia
(now Blooming Grove), OH
POLITICAL PARTY Republican
NO. OF TERMS one (died while in office)
VICE PRESIDENT Calvin Coolidge
DIED Aug. 2, 1923, in San Francisco, CA

## CALVIN COOLIDGE
*30th President of the United States ★ 1923–1929*
BORN July 4, 1872, in Plymouth, VT
POLITICAL PARTY Republican
NO. OF TERMS one, plus balance of
Harding's term
VICE PRESIDENTS 1st term: none
2nd term:
Charles Gates Dawes
DIED Jan. 5, 1933, in Northampton, MA

## HERBERT HOOVER
*31st President of the United States ★ 1929–1933*
BORN Aug. 10, 1874,
in West Branch, IA
POLITICAL PARTY Republican
NO. OF TERMS one
VICE PRESIDENT Charles Curtis
DIED Oct. 20, 1964, in New York, NY

## FRANKLIN D. ROOSEVELT
*32nd President of the United States ★ 1933–1945*
BORN Jan. 30, 1882, in Hyde Park, NY
POLITICAL PARTY Democrat
NO. OF TERMS four (died while in office)
VICE PRESIDENTS 1st & 2nd terms: John
Nance Garner; 3rd term:
Henry Agard Wallace;
4th term: Harry S. Truman
DIED April 12, 1945,
in Warm Springs, GA

## HARRY S. TRUMAN
*33rd President of the United States ★ 1945–1953*
BORN May 8, 1884, in Lamar, MO
POLITICAL PARTY Democrat
NO. OF TERMS one, plus balance of
Franklin D. Roosevelt's term
VICE PRESIDENTS 1st term: none
2nd term:
Alben William Barkley
DIED Dec. 26, 1972, in Independence, MO

## DWIGHT D. EISENHOWER
*34th President of the United States ★ 1953–1961*
BORN Oct. 14, 1890, in Denison, TX
POLITICAL PARTY Republican
NO. OF TERMS two
VICE PRESIDENT Richard Nixon
DIED March 28, 1969,
in Washington, D.C.

## JOHN F. KENNEDY
*35th President of the United States ★ 1961–1963*
BORN May 29, 1917, in Brookline, MA
POLITICAL PARTY Democrat
NO. OF TERMS one (assassinated)
VICE PRESIDENT Lyndon B. Johnson
DIED Nov. 22, 1963, in Dallas, TX

## LYNDON B. JOHNSON
*36th President of the United States ★ 1963–1969*
BORN Aug. 27, 1908, near Stonewall, TX
POLITICAL PARTY Democrat
NO. OF TERMS one, plus balance of
Kennedy's term
VICE PRESIDENTS 1st term: none
2nd term: Hubert
Horatio Humphrey
DIED Jan. 22, 1973, near San Antonio, TX

# Franklin D. Roosevelt DISLIKED the NUMBER 13.

### RICHARD NIXON
*37th President of the United States* ★ *1969–1974*
BORN Jan. 9, 1913, in Yorba Linda, CA
POLITICAL PARTY Republican
NO. OF TERMS two (resigned)
VICE PRESIDENTS 1st term & 2nd term (partial): Spiro Theodore Agnew; 2nd term (balance): Gerald R. Ford
DIED April 22, 1994, in New York, NY

### GERALD R. FORD
*38th President of the United States* ★ *1974–1977*
BORN July 14, 1913, in Omaha, NE
POLITICAL PARTY Republican
NO. OF TERMS one (partial)
VICE PRESIDENT Nelson Aldrich Rockefeller
DIED Dec. 26, 2006, in Rancho Mirage, CA

### JIMMY CARTER
*39th President of the United States* ★ *1977–1981*
BORN Oct. 1, 1924, in Plains, GA
POLITICAL PARTY Democrat
NO. OF TERMS one
VICE PRESIDENT Walter Frederick (Fritz) Mondale

### RONALD REAGAN
*40th President of the United States* ★ *1981–1989*
BORN Feb. 6, 1911, in Tampico, IL
POLITICAL PARTY Republican
NO. OF TERMS two
VICE PRESIDENT George H. W. Bush
DIED June 5, 2004, in Los Angeles, CA

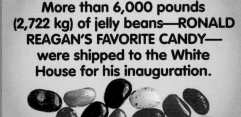

**More than 6,000 pounds (2,722 kg) of jelly beans—RONALD REAGAN'S FAVORITE CANDY—were shipped to the White House for his inauguration.**

### GEORGE H. W. BUSH
*41st President of the United States* ★ *1989–1993*
BORN June 12, 1924, in Milton, MA
POLITICAL PARTY Republican
NO. OF TERMS one
VICE PRESIDENT James Danforth (Dan) Quayle III
DIED November 30, 2018, in Houston, TX

### BILL CLINTON
*42nd President of the United States* ★ *1993–2001*
BORN Aug. 19, 1946, in Hope, AR
POLITICAL PARTY Democrat
NO. OF TERMS two
VICE PRESIDENT Albert Arnold Gore, Jr.

### GEORGE W. BUSH
*43rd President of the United States* ★ *2001–2009*
BORN July 6, 1946, in New Haven, CT
POLITICAL PARTY Republican
NO. OF TERMS two
VICE PRESIDENT Richard Bruce Cheney

### BARACK OBAMA
*44th President of the United States* ★ *2009–2017*
BORN Aug. 4, 1961, in Honolulu, HI
POLITICAL PARTY Democrat
NO. OF TERMS two
VICE PRESIDENT Joseph R. Biden, Jr.

### DONALD TRUMP
*45th President of the United States* ★ *2017–present*
BORN June 14, 1946, in Queens, NY
POLITICAL PARTY Republican
VICE PRESIDENT Mike Pence

# PRANKSTERS IN CHIEF

## Real-life practical jokes played by U.S. presidents

The job of president of the United States is a stressful one. But even the most serious commanders in chief had fun while working in the White House. Check out seven of the best pranks ever pulled by U.S. presidents.

### BARRY FUNNY

Barack Obama is best known as the 44th president of the United States—not as "Barry," a childhood nickname. But the former president dusted off his old title in 2009 to prank call then Virginia governor Tim Kaine. Kaine was being interviewed on a radio show when Obama dialed in to pose as a regular local citizen, Barry in D.C. The in-disguise president quickly revealed his true identity, then thanked the good-natured Kaine for his service to the state of Virginia.

### LOST LETTERS

In 2001, incoming president George W. Bush's staff faced an unexpected problem: They couldn't type Bush's full name! That's because pranksters working for the previous president, Bill Clinton, had pried the W's from dozens of keyboards across the White House complex.

### COPYCAT IN CHIEF

Before President Abraham Lincoln was known as the "Great Emancipator" for freeing the slaves during the Civil War of 1861 to 1865, he earned a reputation as a great imitator. In 1840, Lincoln mimicked the mannerisms of political rival Jesse Thomas so well that he had the audience cracking up. His impersonation was talked about for years afterward.

## HIDE AND SNEAK

The job of president comes with many perks—including the ability to summon Secret Service agents at the push of a button. President Calvin Coolidge reportedly liked this power a little too much when he was in office from 1923 to 1929. He would supposedly call his security detail into the Oval Office, then hide under his desk as his employees searched the office for the man they were sworn to protect.

## BIG SHOT

When reporter Tony Vaccaro was told he might need an immunization shot to travel with President Harry S. Truman to South America in 1947, he wasn't happy—especially when Vaccaro saw the giant needle. That's when a man burst into the room and said, "This won't hurt a bit, Tony." It was President Truman, who had learned of Vaccaro's fear of needles and decided to make the reporter sweat.

## WATER LANDING

President Lyndon B. Johnson, who served from 1963 to 1969, loved to collect vehicles. One of his favorites was a blue convertible that he kept at his Texas ranch. But disaster always seemed to strike as he and his guests sped down a hill toward a lake. "The brakes don't work—we're going in!" he'd yell as the car hit the water. But just as his passengers tried to escape, President Johnson would laugh. The convertible was actually an Amphicar, a vehicle that looked like a car ... but could float like a boat!

## UP AND AWAY

President Franklin D. Roosevelt, who was in office from 1933 to 1945, once told a Secret Service agent to climb on the roof of a farm building to fetch something. But Roosevelt didn't stick around for the agent to climb down. The president had the ladder removed and drove away, leaving the agent (temporarily) stranded.

# CIVIL RIGHTS

Although the Constitution protects the civil rights of American citizens, it has not always been able to protect all Americans from persecution or discrimination. During the first half of the 20th century, many Americans, particularly African Americans, were subjected to widespread discrimination and racism. By the mid-1950s, many people were eager to end the bonds of racism and bring freedom to all men and women.

The civil rights movement of the 1950s and 1960s sought to end racial discrimination against African Americans, especially in the southern states. The movement wanted to restore the fundamentals of economic and social equality to those who had been oppressed.

## Woolworth Counter Sit-in

On February 1, 1960, four African-American college students strolled into a Woolworth's "five-and-dime" store in Greensboro, North Carolina. They planned to have lunch there, but were refused service as soon as they sat down at the counter. In a time of heightened racial tension, the Woolworth's manager had a strict whites-only policy. But the students wouldn't take no for an answer. The men—later dubbed the "Greensboro Four"—stayed seated, peacefully and quietly, at the lunch counter until closing. The next day, they returned with 15 additional college students. The following day, even more. By February 5, some 300 students gathered at Woolworth's, forming one of the most famous sit-ins of the civil rights movement. The protest—which sparked similar sit-ins throughout the country—worked: Just six months later, restaurants across the south began to integrate.

## Key Events in the Civil Rights Movement

| | |
|---|---|
| 1954 | The Supreme Court case *Brown* v. *Board of Education* declares school segregation illegal. |
| 1955 | Rosa Parks refuses to give up her bus seat to a white passenger and spurs a bus boycott. |
| 1957 | The Little Rock Nine help to integrate schools. |
| 1960 | Four black college students begin sit-ins at a restaurant in Greensboro, North Carolina. |
| 1961 | Freedom Rides to southern states begin as a way to protest segregation in transportation. |
| 1963 | Martin Luther King, Jr., leads the famous March on Washington. |
| 1964 | The Civil Rights Act, signed by President Lyndon B. Johnson, prohibits discrimination based on race, color, religion, sex, and national origin. |
| 1967 | Thurgood Marshall becomes the first African American to be named to the Supreme Court. |
| 1968 | President Lyndon B. Johnson signs the Civil Rights Act of 1968, which prohibits discrimination in the sale, rental, and financing of housing. |

# STONE OF HOPE:
## THE LEGACY OF MARTIN LUTHER KING, JR.

On April 4, 1968, Dr. Martin Luther King, Jr., was shot by James Earl Ray while standing on a hotel balcony in Memphis, Tennessee. The news of his death sent shock waves throughout the world: Dr. King, a Baptist minister and founder of the Southern Christian Leadership Conference (SCLC), was the most prominent civil rights leader of his time. His nonviolent protests and marches against segregation, as well as his powerful speeches—including his famous "I Have a Dream" speech—motivated people to fight for justice for all.

More than 50 years after his death, Dr. King's dream lives on through a memorial on the National Mall in Washington, D.C. Built in 2011, the memorial features a 30-foot (9-m) statue of Dr. King carved into a granite boulder named the "Stone of Hope."

Today, Dr. King continues to inspire people around the world with his words and his vision for a peaceful world without racism. He will forever be remembered as one of the most prominent leaders of the civil rights movement.

"The time is always right to do what is right."

Martin Luther King, Jr. Memorial in Washington, D.C.

The Smithsonian's National Museum of African American History and Culture in Washington, D.C., is filled with powerful artifacts, including stools from the Woolworth's lunch counter in Greensboro, North Carolina, and a dress Rosa Parks was making the day she was famously arrested for refusing to give up her bus seat for a white person.

The Museum of African American History displays a segregated railcar that is so big, the museum was built around it.

# WOMEN

## FIGHTING FOR EQUALITY

Women in New York City cast their votes for the first time in November 1920.

Today, women make up about half of the workforce in the United States. But a little over a century ago, less than 20 percent worked outside the home. In fact, they didn't even have the right to vote!

That began to change in the mid-1800s when women, led by pioneers like Elizabeth Cady Stanton and Susan B. Anthony, started speaking up about inequality. They organized public demonstrations, gave speeches, published documents, and wrote newspaper articles to express their ideas. In 1848, about 300 people attended the Seneca Falls Convention in New York State to address the need for equal rights. By the late 1800s, the National American Woman Suffrage Association had made great strides toward giving women the freedom to vote. One by one, states began allowing women to vote. By 1920, the U.S. Constitution was amended, giving women across the country the ability to cast a vote during any election.

But the fight for equality did not end there. In the 1960s and 1970s, the women's rights movement experienced a rebirth, as feminists protested against injustices in areas such as the workplace and in education.

While these efforts enabled women to make great strides in our society, the efforts to even the playing field among men and women continue today.

New Zealand gave women the right to vote in 1893, becoming the world's first country to do so.

In 2018, Saudi Arabia allowed women to drive for the first time.

**Women's March in Boston, Massachusetts, on January 21, 2017**

# Key Events in U.S. Women's History

**1848:** Elizabeth Cady Stanton and Lucretia Mott organize the Seneca Falls Convention in New York. Attendees rally for equitable laws, equal educational and job opportunities, and the right to vote.

**1920: The 19th Amendment,** guaranteeing women the right to vote, is ratified.

**1964: Title VII of the Civil Rights Act of 1964,** which prohibits employment discrimination on the basis of sex, is successfully amended.

**1971:** Gloria Steinem heads up the National Women's Political Caucus, which encourages women to be active in government. She also launches *Ms.*, a magazine about women's issues.

**1972:** Congress approves **the Equal Rights Amendment** (ERA), proposing that women and men have equal rights under the law. It is ratified by 35 of the necessary 38 states, and is still not part of the U.S. Constitution.

**1981:** President Ronald Reagan appoints **Sandra Day O'Connor** as the first female Supreme Court justice.

**2009:** President Obama signs **the Lilly Ledbetter Fair Pay Act** to protect against pay discrimination among men and women.

**2013:** The **ban against women in military combat positions** is removed, overturning a 1994 Pentagon decision restricting women from combat roles.

**2016:** Democratic presidential nominee **Hillary Rodham Clinton** becomes the first woman to lead the ticket of a major U.S. party.

**2017:** A crowd of some four million people turned out for the first ever **Women's March,** a protest advocating women's rights. Events were held in locations throughout the country.

## Harriet Tubman
### Making Freedom Her Mission

Harriet Tubman wasn't afraid to take chances. As a "conductor" on the Underground Railroad, which helped escaped slaves flee to freedom in the U.S. north, Tubman risked her life for the sake of others. Aside from her work with the Underground Railroad, Tubman was also essential in planning a military mission to free slaves from South Carolina, U.S.A., plantations. Her mission was remarkably successful, helping to free more than 700 slaves without losing a single soldier during the raid. It was the first time in American history a woman helped lead a military expedition. This selfless move, as well as Tubman's other efforts to create equality for all, landed her as the face of the newly designed $20 bill, which is set to debut in 2028.

## Peggy Whitson
### The Sky's the Limit

In a field dominated by men, Peggy Whitson is a game changer. The astronaut sparked headlines when she spent 665 consecutive days in space, more than any other American astronaut, male or female. She is also the first woman to command the International Space Station (ISS), and was part of NASA's first women-led mission to space. Prior to her retirement in 2018, Whitson went up once more, when, at the age of 56, she became the oldest woman in space. On the ground, Whitson's work was equally impressive, as she became the first woman to hold the position of chief of the astronaut corps, from 2009 to 2012. Whitson's groundbreaking career has forever etched her name among the most accomplished astronauts in the history of the space program.

# QUIZ WHIZ

## Go back in time to seek the answers to this history quiz!

Write your answers on a piece of paper. Then check them below.

**1** **True or false?** Ancient Egyptians lined linen bandages with honey to get them to stick to skin.

**2** The city of _____ was part of the largest empire in the ancient world.
a. Timbuktu
b. Cairo
c. Alexandria
d. Troy

**3** Farmers in China once discovered thousands of _____ buried in a field.
a. clay soldiers
b. diamonds
c. dinosaur bones
d. diamonds

**4** **True or false?** The yeti is also known as Bigfoot.

**5** What did Belgian resistance fighters use as a sneaky way to relay messages about the Germans during World War I?
a. secret scarves
b. hidden messages in songs
c. Morse code
d. carrier pigeons

Not **STUMPED** yet? Check out the *NATIONAL GEOGRAPHIC KIDS QUIZ WHIZ* collection for more crazy **HISTORY** questions!

**ANSWERS: 1.** True; **2.** c; **3.** a; **4.** False. It's known as the Abominable Snowman; **5.** a

## HOMEWORK HELP

# Brilliant Biographies

Malala Yousafzai

**A biography is the story of a person's life.** It can be a brief summary or a long book. Biographers—those who write biographies—use many different sources to learn about their subjects. You can write your own biography of a famous person you find inspiring.

## How to Get Started

Choose a subject you find interesting. If you think Cleopatra is cool, you have a good chance of getting your reader interested, too. If you're bored by ancient Egypt, your reader will be snoring after your first paragraph.

Your subject can be almost anyone: an author, an inventor, a celebrity, a politician, or a member of your family. To find someone to write about, ask yourself these simple questions:

1. Who do I want to know more about?
2. What did this person do that was special?
3. How did this person change the world?

## Do Your Research

• Find out as much about your subject as possible. Read books, news articles, and encyclopedia entries. Watch video clips and movies, and search the internet. Conduct interviews, if possible.

• Take notes, writing down important facts and interesting stories about your subject.

## Write the Biography

• Come up with a title. Include the person's name.
• Write an introduction. Consider asking a probing question about your subject.
• Include information about the person's childhood. When was this person born? Where did he or she grow up? Who did he or she admire?
• Highlight the person's talents, accomplishments, and personal attributes.
• Describe the specific events that helped to shape this person's life. Did this person ever have a problem and overcome it?
• Write a conclusion. Include your thoughts about why it is important to learn about this person.
• Once you have finished your first draft, revise and then proofread your work.

Here's a SAMPLE BIOGRAPHY of Malala Yousafzai, a human rights advocate and the youngest ever recipient of the Nobel Peace Prize. Of course, there is so much more for you to discover and write about on your own!

### Malala Yousafzai

Malala Yousafzai was born in Pakistan on July 12, 1997. Malala's father, Ziauddin, a teacher, made it his priority for his daughter to receive a proper education. Malala loved school. She learned to speak three languages and even wrote a blog about her experiences as a student.

Around the time Malala turned 10, the Taliban—a group of strict Muslims who believe women are to stay at home—took over the region where she lived. The Taliban did not approve of Malala's outspoken love of learning. One day, on her way home from school, Malala was shot in the head by a Taliban gunman. Very badly injured, she was sent to a hospital in England.

Not only did Malala survive the shooting—she thrived. She used her experience as a platform to fight for girls' education worldwide. She began speaking out about educational opportunities for all. Her efforts gained worldwide attention, and she was eventually awarded the Nobel Peace Prize in 2014 at the age of 17. She is the youngest person to earn the prestigious prize.

Each year on July 12, World Malala Day honors her heroic efforts to bring attention to human rights issues.

At Giant's Causeway in County Antrim, Northern Ireland, U.K., visitors climb the unique rock formations created millions of years ago by rapidly cooling lava.

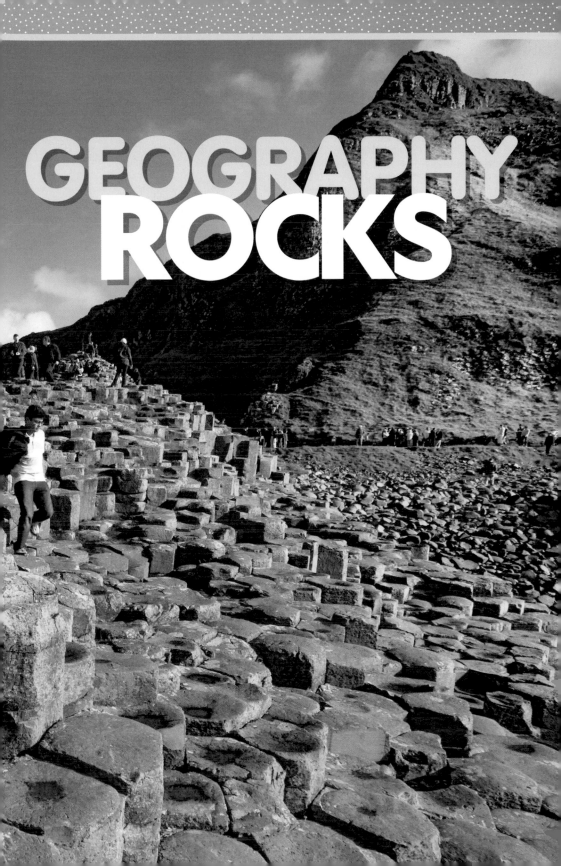

# GEOGRAPHY
# ROCKS

# THE POLITICAL WORLD

Earth's land area is made up of seven continents, but people have divided much of the land into smaller political units called countries. Australia is a continent made up of a single country, and Antarctica is used for scientific research. But the other five continents include almost 200 independent countries. The political map shown here depicts boundaries—imaginary lines created by treaties—that separate countries. Some boundaries, such as the one between the United States and Canada, are very stable and have been recognized for many years.

Other boundaries, such as the one between Sudan and South Sudan in northeast Africa, are relatively new and still disputed. Countries come in all shapes and sizes. Russia and Canada are giants; others, such as El Salvador and Qatar, are small. Some countries are long and skinny—look at Chile in South America! Still other countries—such as Indonesia and Japan in Asia—are made up of groups of islands. The political map is a clue to the diversity that makes Earth so fascinating.

OCEAN

North Land

New Siberian Islands

East Siberian Sea

Barents Sea

Kara Sea

Laptev Sea

Svalbard (Norway)

Novaya Zemlya

NORWAY

SWEDEN

FINLAND

DEN.
GERMANY

EST.
LATV.
LITH.

BELARUS

POLAND

UKRAINE
MOLD.

ROMANIA

GEORGIA

BULGARIA

ITALY

ALBANIA

GREECE

TURKEY

Mediterranean Sea

TUNISIA

CYPRUS SYRIA

LEBANON

ISRAEL

IRAQ

JORDAN

KUWAIT

ALGERIA

LIBYA

EGYPT

SAUDI ARABIA

BAHRAIN QATAR

U.A.E.

OMAN

Red Sea

NIGER

CHAD

SUDAN

ERITREA

YEMEN

Arabian Sea

DJIBOUTI

BENIN

NIGERIA

CAMEROON

C.A.R.

SOUTH SUDAN

ETHIOPIA

SOMALIA

TOGO

GABON

CONGO

DEM. REP. OF THE CONGO

RWANDA

BURUNDI

UGANDA

KENYA

Cabinda (Angola)

TANZANIA

SEYCHELLES

ANGOLA

ZAMBIA

MALAWI

COMOROS

NAMIBIA

ZIMBABWE

BOTSWANA

MOZAMBIQUE

MADAGASCAR

MAURITIUS

Réunion (France)

ESWATINI (SWAZILAND)

SOUTH AFRICA

LESOTHO

RUSSIA

Caspian Sea

KAZAKHSTAN

UZBEK.

ARM.
AZERB.

TURKMEN.

KYRGYZSTAN

TAJIKISTAN

IRAN

AFGHAN.

PAKISTAN

NEPAL

BHUTAN

INDIA

BANGLADESH

MYANMAR (BURMA)

Lake Baikal

MONGOLIA

CHINA

Sea of Okhotsk

Bering Sea

NORTH KOREA

SOUTH KOREA

JAPAN

TAIWAN
The People's Republic of China claims Taiwan as its 23rd province. Taiwan's government (Republic of China) maintains that there are two political entities.

Taiwan

South China Sea

Bay of Bengal

THAILAND

LAOS

VIETNAM

CAMBODIA

Philippine Sea

Northern Mariana Islands (U.S.)

PACIFIC

Guam (U.S.)

PHILIPPINES

MARSHALL ISLANDS

SRI LANKA

MALDIVES

BRUNEI

MALAYSIA

SINGAPORE

PALAU

FEDERATED STATES OF MICRONESIA

OCEAN

KIRIBATI

INDONESIA

New Guinea

PAPUA NEW GUINEA

SOLOMON ISLANDS

EQUATOR

NAURU

TUVALU

TIMOR-LESTE (EAST TIMOR)

INDIAN

OCEAN

Coral Sea

VANUATU

New Caledonia (France)

FIJI

AUSTRALIA

Great Australian Bight

Tasman Sea

North Island

Tasmania

NEW ZEALAND

South Island

Kerguelen Islands (France)

CIRCLE

Ross Sea

ARCTICA

60°

30°

60°

90°

150°

0°

30°

60°

60°

# THE PHYSICAL WORLD

Earth is dominated by large landmasses called continents—seven in all—and by an interconnected global ocean that is divided into four parts by the continents. More than 70 percent of Earth's surface is covered by oceans, and the rest is made up of land areas.

Different landforms give variety to the surface of the continents. The Rocky Mountains divide North America, the Andes mark the western edge of South America, and the Himalaya tower above South Asia. The Plateau of Tibet forms the rugged core of Asia,

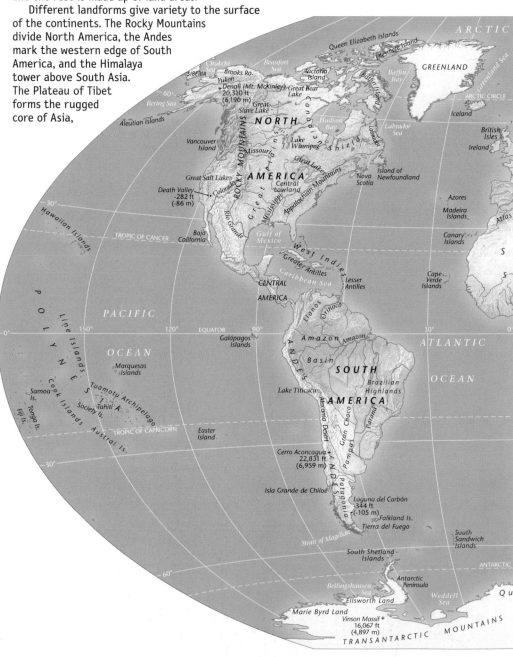

while the Northern European Plain extends from the North Sea to the Ural Mountains. Much of Africa is a plateau, and dry plains cover large areas of Australia. Mountains rise more than 16,000 feet (4,877 m) above Antarctica's massive ice sheets. Mountains and trenches make the ocean floors as varied as any continent. A mountain chain called the Mid-Atlantic Ridge runs the length of the Atlantic Ocean. In the western Pacific, trenches drop deep into the ocean floor.

OCEAN

North Land

New Siberian Islands

Laptev Sea

East Siberian Sea

Svalbard

Novaya Zemlya

Kara Sea

Yenisey

Lena

Barents Sea

Norwegian Sea

Scandinavia

West Siberian Plateau

Central Siberian Plateau

Sea of Okhotsk

Bering Sea

Kamchatka Peninsula

Aleutian Is.

Ural Mountains

Ob

Irtysh

Angara

Lena

Amur

Kuril Islands

North Sea

Volga

West Siberian Plain

Ob

Lake Baikal

Sea of Japan (East Sea)

Hokkaido

Northern European Plain

EUROPE

The Steppes

Altay Mountains

GOBI

JAPAN

Honshu

Alps

El'brus 18,510 ft (5,642 m)

Caucasus Mts.

Tian Shan

ASIA

North China Plain

Yellow

Korea

Nampo Shoto

Danube

Black Sea

Caspian Sea

Kunlun Mts.

Plateau of Tibet

East China Sea

Ryukyu Is.

Mediterranean Sea

Zagros Mts.

Dead Sea -1,401 ft (-427 m)

HIMALAYA

Brahmaputra

Yangtze

Mts.

Nile

Libyan Desert

ARABIAN PENINSULA

Indus

Mt. Everest 29,035 ft (8,850 m)

Ganges

INDIA

Salween

Mekong

Hainan

Taiwan

Luzon

PACIFIC

SAHARA

Niger

Lake Chad

Lake Assal -509 ft (-155 m)

Gulf of Aden

Arabian Sea

Bay of Bengal

Andaman Islands

Indochina Peninsula

South China Sea

Philippine Islands

Philippine Sea

Mariana Islands

OCEAN

SAHEL

Ethiopian Highlands

Somali Peninsula

Sri Lanka

Nicobar Is.

Andaman Sea

Malay Peninsula

MICRONESIA

Marshall Islands

AFRICA

Congo

Lake Victoria

Kilimanjaro +19,340 ft (5,895 m)

Maldive Islands

Borneo

Celebes

Moluccas

Gilbert Islands

EQUATOR

Congo Basin

Great Rift Valley

Seychelles

INDIAN

Sumatra

INDONESIA

Greater Sunda Islands

Java

New Guinea

MELANESIA

Bismarck Archipelago

Mt. Wilhelm 14,793 ft (4,509 m)

Solomon Islands

Lake Tanganyika

Comoros Is.

OCEAN

Timor

Arafura Sea

Vanuatu

Zambezi

Madagascar

Mascarene Is.

Coral Sea

Fiji Islands

Kalahari Desert

Great Sandy Desert

AUSTRALIA

Lake Eyre -49 ft (-15 m)

Great Victoria Desert

Great Dividing Range

Darling

Central Lowlands

New Caledonia

Tasman Sea

North Island

NEW ZEALAND

South Island

miles 2000

kilometers 3000

Winkel Tripel Projection

Kerguelen Islands

Tasmania

Auckland Islands

CIRCLE

een Maud Land

Transantarctic Mountains

Victoria Land

Byrd Glacier -9,416 ft (-2,870 m)

ANTARCTICA

**257**

# KINDS OF MAPS

Maps are special tools that geographers use to tell a story about Earth. Maps can be used to show just about anything related to places. Some maps show physical features, such as mountains or vegetation. Maps can also show climates or natural hazards and other things we cannot easily see. Other maps illustrate different features on Earth—political boundaries, urban centers, and economic systems.

## AN IMPERFECT TOOL

Maps are not perfect. A globe is a scale model of Earth with accurate relative sizes and locations. Because maps are flat, they involve distortions of size, shape, and direction. Also, cartographers—people who create maps—make choices about what information to include. Because of this, it is important to study many different types of maps to learn the complete story of Earth. Three commonly found kinds of maps are shown on this page.

**PHYSICAL MAPS.** Earth's natural features—landforms, water bodies, and vegetation—are shown on physical maps. The map above uses color and shading to illustrate mountains, lakes, rivers, and deserts of central South America. Country names and borders are added for reference, but they are not natural features.

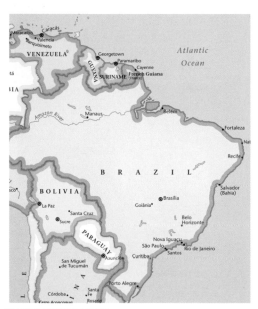

**POLITICAL MAPS.** These maps represent characteristics of the landscape created by humans, such as boundaries, cities, and place-names. Natural features are added only for reference. On the map above, capital cities are represented with a star inside a circle, while other cities are shown with black dots.

**THEMATIC MAPS.** Patterns related to a particular topic or theme, such as population distribution, appear on these maps. The map above displays the region's climate zones, which range from tropical wet (bright green) to tropical wet and dry (light green) to semiarid (dark yellow) to arid or desert (light yellow).

258

# MAKING MAPS

Long ago, cartographers worked with pen and ink, carefully handcrafting maps based on explorers' observations and diaries. Today, mapmaking is a high-tech business. Cartographers use Earth data stored in "layers" in a geographic information system (GIS) and special computer programs to create maps that can be easily updated as new information becomes available.

National Geographic staff cartographers Mike McNey and Rosemary Wardley review a map of Africa for the *National Geographic Kids World Atlas.*

Satellites in orbit around Earth act as eyes in the sky, recording data about the planet's land and ocean areas. The data is converted to numbers that are transmitted back to computers that are specially programmed to interpret the data. They record it in a form that cartographers can use to create maps.

# MAP PROJECTIONS

To create a map, cartographers transfer an image of the round Earth to a flat surface, a process called projection. All projections involve distortion. For example, an interrupted projection (bottom map) shows accurate shapes and relative sizes of land areas, but oceans have gaps. Other types of projections are cylindrical, conic, or azimuthal—each with certain advantages, but all with some distortion.

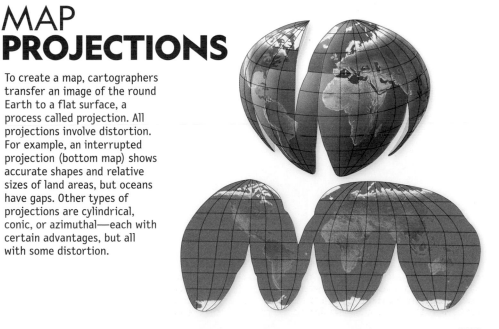

# GEOGRAPHIC FEATURES

From roaring rivers to parched deserts, from underwater canyons to jagged mountains, Earth is covered with beautiful and diverse environments. Here are examples of the most common types of geographic features found around the world.

## WATERFALL

Waterfalls form when a river reaches an abrupt change in elevation. At left, the Iguazú waterfall system—on the border of Brazil and Argentina—is made up of 275 falls.

### VALLEY

Valleys, cut by running water or moving ice, may be broad and flat or narrow and steep, such as the Indus River Valley (above) in Ladakh, India.

### RIVER

As a river moves through flatlands, it twists and turns. Above, the Rio Los Amigos winds through a rainforest in Peru.

### MOUNTAIN

Mountains are Earth's tallest landforms, and Mount Everest (above) rises highest of all, at 29,035 feet (8,850 m) above sea level.

### GLACIER

Glaciers—"rivers" of ice—such as Hubbard Glacier (above) in Alaska, U.S.A., move slowly from mountains to the sea. Global warming is shrinking them.

### CANYON

Steep-sided valleys called canyons are created mainly by running water. Buckskin Gulch (above) in Utah, U.S.A., is the deepest "slot" canyon in the American Southwest.

### DESERT

Deserts are land features created by climate, specifically by a lack of water. Here, a camel caravan crosses the Sahara in North Africa.

## THE TALLEST THING ON EARTH
# MAUNA LOA

**MAUNA LOA IS SO MASSIVE THAT IT ACTUALLY SUNK THE OCEAN FLOOR OVER 26,000 FEET (8,000 M) IN THE SHAPE OF AN INVERTED CONE.**

Think the tallest mountain on Earth is Everest? Surprise! It's Mauna Loa, an active volcano in Hawaii, U.S.A. Now, before you demand a re-measure, here's the scoop: At 56,000 feet (17,170 m) from its peak to its base, which is depressed 26,200 feet (7,990 m) below the ocean floor, Mauna Loa is almost twice as tall as Mount Everest's 29,035 feet (8,850 m). So why doesn't it look like it? Because only a quarter of Mauna Loa is above water! Although Everest's summit is the highest above sea level, Mauna Loa takes the prize from top to bottom. To further bruise Everest's ego, Mauna Loa's neighbor, Mauna Kea, also towers: From the ocean floor to its summit, Mauna Kea stands 32,000 feet (9,750 m).

**VOLCANO TYPE:**
SHIELD VOLCANO*

**HEIGHT BASE TO SUMMIT:**
56,000 FEET (17,170 M)

**HEIGHT ABOVE SEA LEVEL:**
13,680 FEET (4,170 M)

**ABOVE-WATER SURFACE AREA:**
HALF OF THE BIG ISLAND OF HAWAII

**ERUPTIONS SINCE 1843:**
33

**LAST ERUPTION:**
1984

**NAME'S MEANING:**
"LONG MOUNTAIN"

*For more about types of volcanoes, see page 121.

261

# AFRICA

Baobab trees from South Africa can live for 2,000 years.

Hippos show they claim a territory by yawning.

Hippopotamus

The massive continent of Africa, where humankind began millions of years ago, is second only to Asia in size. Stretching nearly as far from west to east as it does from north to south, Africa is home to both the longest river in the world (the Nile) and the largest hot desert on Earth (the Sahara).

Luanda, Angola

# SPEEDY SPECIES

Some of the world's fastest animals live in Africa, such as cheetahs, pronghorn antelopes, wildebeests, and lions. Each of these species can reach speeds topping 50 miles an hour (80 km/h).

# ON LOCATION

Nigeria's film industry—also known as "Nollywood"—produces nearly 1,500 movies every year. It's the world's second largest film producer, ahead of Hollywood and behind India's Bollywood.

## Great Pyramid, Great Numbers
### How do the numbers for Earth's biggest pyramid stack up?

Due to erosion the pyramid is **30 feet (9 m)** shorter than it was originally.

Weight of largest stone blocks: **15 tons (14 t)**

Number of stone blocks: **2.3 million**

Number of builders: **20,000**

Angle at which the sides rise: **51°52'**

Height: **451 Feet (138 M)**

Average length of each side: **756 feet (230 m)**

# HIDDEN GEM

High atop Mount Mabu in Mozambique is a hidden rainforest where new species of snakes, butterflies, chameleons, and other critters were recently found. Among the discoveries? The aptly named all-white ghost slug.

## PHYSICAL

**HIGHEST POINT**
Kilimanjaro, Tanzania
19,340 ft (5,895 m)

**LAND AREA**
11,608,000 sq mi
(30,065,000 sq km)

**LONGEST RIVER**
Nile / 4,400 mi
(7,081 km)

**LOWEST POINT**
Lake Assal, Djibouti
-509 ft (-155 m)

**LARGEST LAKE**
Victoria
26,800 sq mi
(69,500 sq km)

## POLITICAL

**LARGEST COUNTRY**
Algeria / 919,595 sq mi
(2,381,741 sq km)

**MOST DENSELY POPULATED COUNTRY**
Mauritius / 1,731 people
per sq mi (669 per sq km)

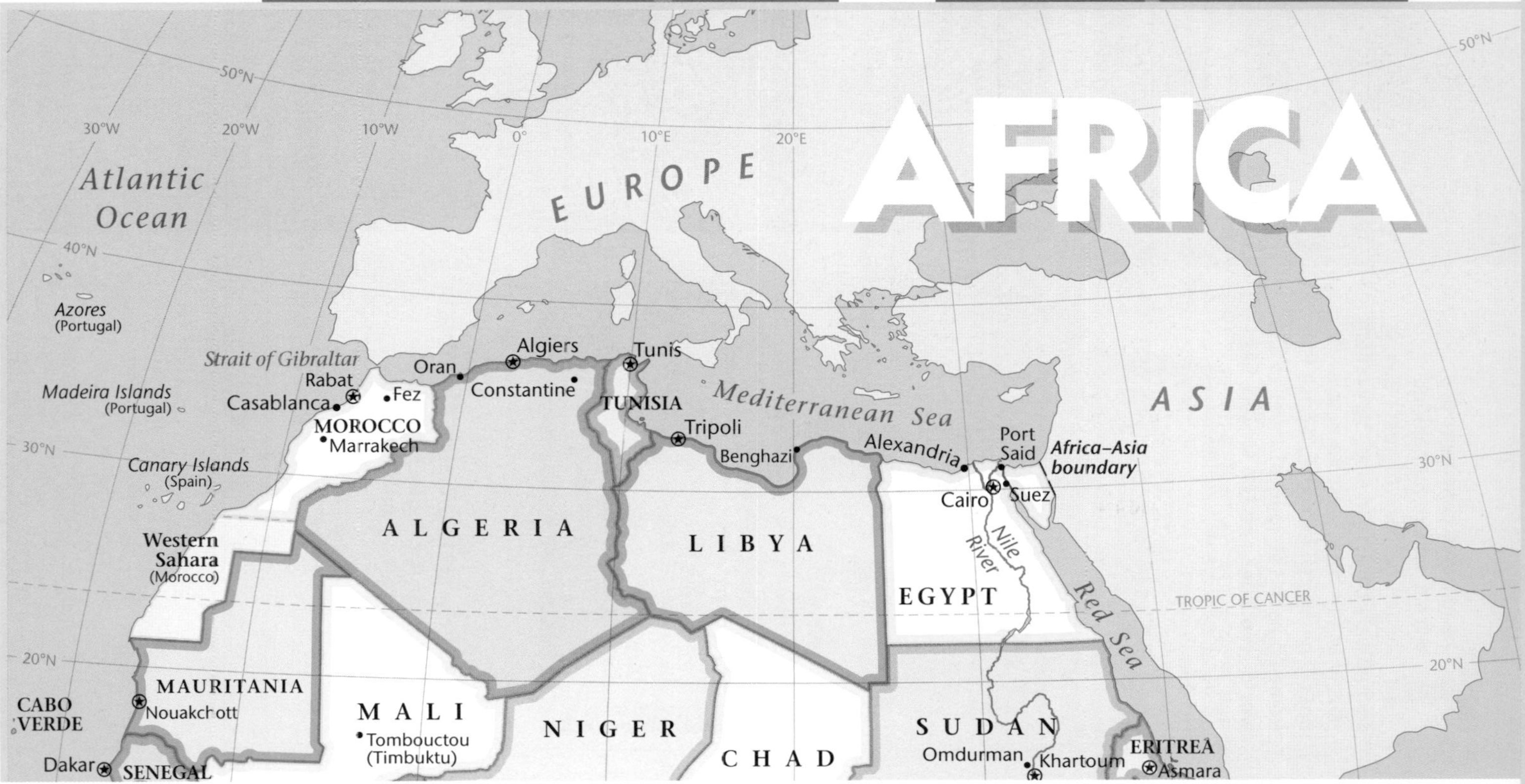

**POPULATION**
1,215,763,000

**LARGEST METROPOLITAN AREA**
Cairo, Egypt
Pop. 20,076,000

AFRICA

ASIA

EUROPE

Atlantic Ocean

Mediterranean Sea

Red Sea

Nile River

TROPIC OF CANCER

Africa–Asia boundary

Port Said
Suez
Cairo
Alexandria

EGYPT
LIBYA
ALGERIA
SUDAN
CHAD
NIGER
MALI
MAURITANIA
MOROCCO
TUNISIA
ERITREA

Khartoum
Omdurman
Asmara
Benghazi
Tripoli
Tunis
Algiers
Constantine
Oran
Fez
Rabat
Casablanca
Marrakech
Tombouctou (Timbuktu)
Nouakchott
Dakar
SENEGAL
CABO VERDE
Western Sahara (Morocco)
Canary Islands (Spain)
Madeira Islands (Portugal)
Azores (Portugal)
Strait of Gibraltar

264

10°N
0°
10°S
30°S
60°E

Victoria ⊛

SEYCHELLES

MAURITIUS ⊛
Port Louis ○
Réunion ○
(France)

SOMALIA

⊛ Mogadishu

Gulf of Aden

Lake Assal
(-155 m) -509 ft ▼
DJIBOUTI Djibouti

SOMALILAND

Addis
Ababa ⊛

ETHIOPIA

MADAGASCAR

Antananarivo ⊛

Indian
Ocean

50°E
40°E

COMOROS
Moroni ⊛

Mombasa

Kilimanjaro
19,340 ft ▲
(5,895 m)

Dar es Salaam ⊛

Mozambique Channel

Nairobi ⊛

KENYA

● Juba

UGANDA

Lake
Victoria

Kampala ⊛

SOUTH
SUDAN

DARFUR

RWANDA
Kigali ⊛
BURUNDI
Bujumbura ⊛

Dodoma ⊛

TANZANIA

MOZAMBIQUE

MALAWI
Lilongwe ⊛

Maputo ⊛
Lobamba ⊛
Mbabane ⊛

ESWATINI (SWAZILAND)

Durban ●

LESOTHO
Maseru ⊛

30°E

CENTRAL
AFRICAN REPUBLIC

Bangui ⊛

Kisangani ●

DEMOCRATIC
REPUBLIC
OF THE CONGO

Lubumbashi ●

Kananga ●
Mbuji-Mayi ●

ZAMBIA

Kolwezi ●
Kitwe ●
Kitwe ●
Lusaka ⊛

ZIMBABWE

Harare ⊛

Pretoria
(Tshwane) ⊛

Johannesburg ●
Bloemfontein ⊛

Port
Elizabeth ●

SOUTH
AFRICA

N'Djamena ⊛

CAMEROON

Yaoundé ⊛
Douala ●

Libreville ⊛

GABON

CONGO

Brazzaville ⊛

Pointe-Noire ●

Cabinda
(Angola)

Kinshasa ⊛

ANGOLA

Luanda ⊛

NAMIBIA

Windhoek ⊛

BOTSWANA

Gaborone ⊛

Cape Town ●

20°E

Kano ●
Abuja ⊛
Ogbomosho ●
Lagos ●
Porto-
Novo ⊛
Cotonou Malabo ⊛

NIGERIA

BENIN
TOGO
GHANA

EQUATORIAL GUINEA

SAO TOME & PRINCIPE

São Tomé ●

St. Helena
(U.K.)

Atlantic
Ocean

10°E

Ascension
(U.K.)

EQUATOR
0°
10°S
20°S
30°S

Banjul ⊛
GAMBIA
Bissau ⊛
GUINEA-
BISSAU
Conakry ⊛
GUINEA
Freetown ⊛
SIERRA
LEONE
Monrovia ⊛
LIBERIA

Bamako ⊛

BURKINA
FASO
Niamey ⊛
Ouagadougou ⊛

Yamoussoukro ⊛
Abidjan ●

CÔTE D'IVOIRE
(IVORY COAST)

Accra ⊛
Lomé ⊛

TROPIC OF CAPRICORN

0°
10°W
20°W

**Map Key**

⊛ National capital
● Other city
▲ Highest point
▼ Lowest point

800 Miles
0
800 Kilometers
0

Azimuthal Equal-Area Projection

# ANTARCTICA

Gentoo penguin

Scientists found stardust in a meteorite from Antarctica.

An adult gentoo penguin makes as many as 450 dives a day looking for food.

This frozen continent may be a cool place to visit, but unless you're a penguin, you probably wouldn't want to hang out in Antarctica for long. The fact that it's the coldest, windiest, and driest continent helps explain why humans never colonized this ice-covered land surrounding the South Pole.

Weddell seal

## GOING THE DISTANCE

Each year, a few hundred runners from around the world compete in the Antarctica Marathon and Half-Marathon, a hilly and twisty race along the continent's icy peninsula.

## A DAY TO CELEBRATE

DECEMBER

1

Signed in 1959, the Antarctic Treaty, which governs Antarctica, says that the continent should be used only for peaceful purposes. The treaty, which has now been signed by 54 countries, also established Antarctica as a scientific reserve and a place for scientific exploration. Any activities that may disrupt the natural environment are prohibited. Each year on December 1, World Antarctica Day marks the signing of the treaty and celebrates this unique and fascinating place on Earth.

## Annual Average Snowfall

17 feet (5 m)

8 feet (2 m)

0.7 foot (0.2 m)

| Sapporo, Japan | Buffalo, New York, U.S.A. | South Pole, Antarctica |

## SEEING GREEN

Emerald icebergs? Only in Antarctica! Here you can spot these rare and beautiful bergs in a deep green hue. So how do these icebergs acquire their stunning shade? Experts say it could be a combo of the bluish tint of glacial ice and yellow-red glacial dust dredged up from deep below the surface.

# PHYSICAL

**LAND AREA**
5,100,000 sq mi
(13,209,000 sq km)

**HIGHEST POINT**
Vinson Massif
16,067 ft (4,897 m)

**LOWEST POINT**
Byrd Glacier
-9,416 ft (-2,870 m)

**COLDEST PLACE**
Ridge A, annual
average temperature
-94°F (-70°C)

**AVERAGE
PRECIPITATION ON
THE POLAR PLATEAU**
Less than 2 in (5 cm)

# POLITICAL

**POPULATION**
There are no
indigenous inhabitants,
but there are both
permanent and
summer-only staffed
research stations.

**NUMBER OF
INDEPENDENT
COUNTRIES** 0

**NUMBER OF
COUNTRIES
CLAIMING LAND** 7

**NUMBER OF
COUNTRIES
OPERATING YEAR-
ROUND RESEARCH
STATIONS** 21

**NUMBER OF YEAR-
ROUND RESEARCH
STATIONS** 40

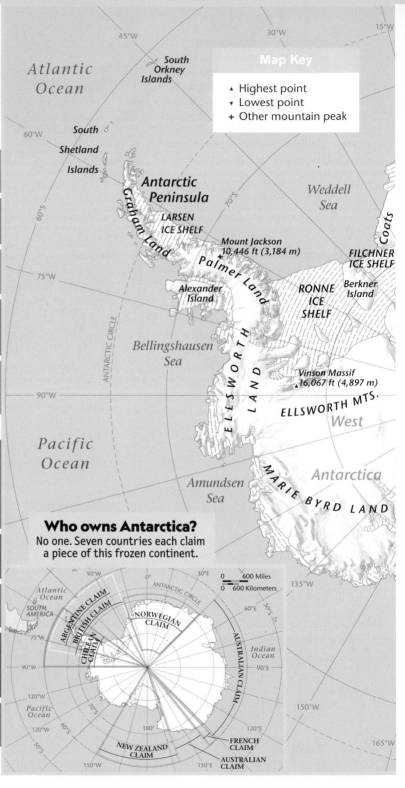

**Map Key**
- ▲ Highest point
- ▼ Lowest point
- + Other mountain peak

## Who owns Antarctica?
No one. Seven countries each claim
a piece of this frozen continent.

# ANTARCTICA

0°

FIMBUL
ICE SHELF

RIISER-LARSEN
ICE SHELF

Land

QUEEN MAUD LAND

ENDERBY
LAND

60°E

Indian
Ocean

Valkyrie
Dome

MacKenzie Bay  75°E

Lambert
Glacier

AMERY ICE SHELF

AMERICAN
HIGHLAND

WEST
ICE SHELF

Ridge A ✛

POLAR PLATEAU

East

90°E

SHACKLETON
ICE SHELF

★ South Pole

Antarctica

TRANSANTARCTIC MOUNTAINS

80°S

105°E

WILKES LAND

ROSS
ICE
SHELF

Byrd Glacier
-9,416 ft (-2,870 m)

Roosevelt
Island

Taylor
Glacier

Ross Island

70°S

Mount Erebus
12,448 ft
(3,794 m)

VICTORIA LAND

120°E

Ross
Sea

Talos
Dome

180°

60°S

0                  600 Miles
0            600 Kilometers

150°E

135°E

Indian
Ocean

Azimuthal Equidistant Projection

# ASIA

Children with a water buffalo
in Sa Pa, Vietnam

A water buffalo's wide hooves keep it from sinking in mud.

The Bengal tiger is India's national animal.

Made up of 46 countries, Asia is the world's largest continent. Just how big is it? From western Turkey to the eastern tip of Russia, Asia spans nearly half the globe! Home to more than four billion citizens—that's three out of five people on the planet—Asia's population is bigger than that of all the other continents combined.

Kuala Lumpur, Malaysia

## ON THE MOVE

About a third of the population of Mongolia moves seasonally. They live in portable huts called *ger* while traveling up to 70 miles (112 km) on foot to find food sources for their livestock.

## FLYING HIGH

Native to Central Asia, the bar-headed goose can soar at altitudes higher than even helicopters can fly. Powerful lungs and strong wings allow these birds to cross over the Himalaya during their annual migration.

## GOING BATTY

From the giant golden-crowned flying fox to the itty-bitty bumblebee bat, Asia is home to at least 435 of the world's more than 1,300 species of bats. Indonesia has the world's largest number of species, with more than 175 different types of bats. And in Malaysia? Bats outnumber all other mammals in the country, including humans! The winged mammals help keep the ecosystem healthy, especially in Southeast Asia's forests, where the bats play a key role in spreading the seeds of trees and other plants.

## World's Deepest Lakes

| Lake Baikal (Russia) | Lake Tanganyika (eastern Africa) | Caspian Sea (Central Asia/Europe border) | Lake Malawi (eastern Africa) | Ysyk-Köl (Kyrgyzstan) |
|---|---|---|---|---|
| 5,369 ft (1,637 m) | 4,708 ft (1,435 m) | 3,104 ft (946 m) | 2,316 ft (706 m) | 2,297 ft (700 m) |

Most of Earth's surface water is stored in lakes. The deepest of all is Asia's Lake Baikal, which contains about 20 percent of Earth's total surface freshwater.

# PHYSICAL

**LAND AREA**
17,208,000 sq mi
(44,570,000 sq km)

**HIGHEST POINT**
Mount Everest,
China–Nepal
29,035 ft (8,850 m)

**LOWEST POINT**
Dead Sea,
Israel–Jordan
-1,401 ft (-427 m)

**LONGEST RIVER**
Yangtze, China
3,880 mi (6,244 km)

**LARGEST LAKE
ENTIRELY IN ASIA**
Lake Baikal, Russia
12,200 sq mi
(31,500 sq km)

# POLITICAL

**POPULATION**
4,402,007,000

**LARGEST
METROPOLITAN AREA**
Tokyo, Japan
Pop. 37,468,000

**LARGEST COUNTRY
ENTIRELY IN ASIA**
China
3,705,405 sq mi
(9,596,960 sq km)

**MOST DENSELY
POPULATED COUNTRY**
Singapore
22,290 people
per sq mi
(8,603 per sq km)

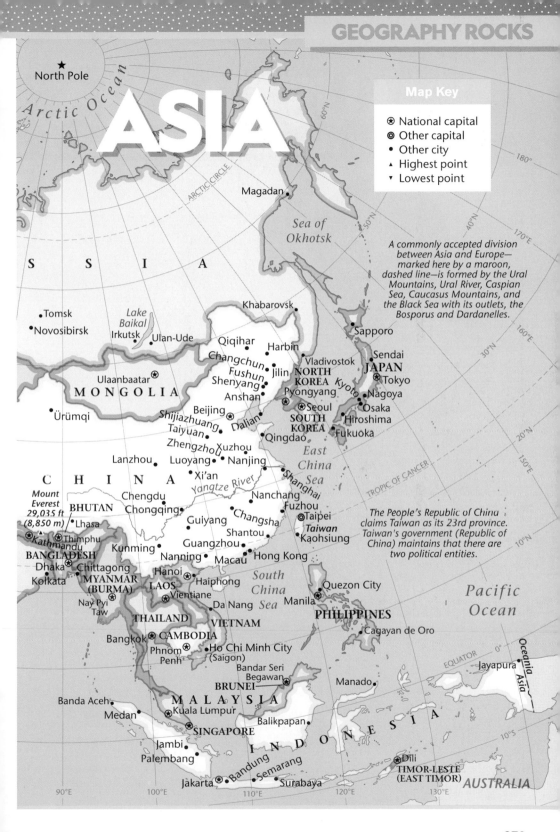

★ North Pole

Arctic Ocean

# ASIA

## Map Key
⊛ National capital
◎ Other capital
• Other city
▲ Highest point
▼ Lowest point

Magadan

Sea of Okhotsk

R U S S I A

*A commonly accepted division between Asia and Europe—marked here by a maroon, dashed line—is formed by the Ural Mountains, Ural River, Caspian Sea, Caucasus Mountains, and the Black Sea with its outlets, the Bosporus and Dardanelles.*

•Tomsk
•Novosibirsk
Lake Baikal
Irkutsk• •Ulan-Ude

Khabarovsk•

Sapporo

Qiqihar
Harbin
Changchun
Fushun
Jilin
Shenyang
Vladivostok
Sendai
JAPAN
⊛Tokyo
NORTH KOREA
Pyongyang⊛
Kyoto
Nagoya
Ulaanbaatar ⊛
M O N G O L I A
Anshan•
⊛Seoul
Osaka
•Ürümqi
Beijing ⊛
SOUTH KOREA
Hiroshima
Shijiazhuang•
•Dalian
Fukuoka
Taiyuan•
Qingdao•
Zhengzhou•
•Xuzhou
East China Sea
Lanzhou•
Luoyang• •Nanjing
C H I N A
•Xi'an
Yangtze River
•Shanghai
Mount Everest
29,035 ft
(8,850 m)
BHUTAN
Chengdu•
Chongqing•
Nanchang•
Fuzhou•
▲•Lhasa
Guiyang•
•Changsha
⊚Taipei
*Taiwan*
⊛Kathmandu ⊚Thimphu
Shantou•
Kaohsiung
BANGLADESH
Kunming•
Guangzhou•
Dhaka⊛ •Chittagong
Nanning• •Macau Hong Kong•
Kolkata•
MYANMAR
(BURMA)
Hanoi ⊛
LAOS
South China Sea
Nay Pyi Taw ⊛
•Haiphong
⊚Vientiane
•Quezon City
THAILAND
VIETNAM
Da Nang•
Manila⊛
PHILIPPINES
Bangkok ⊛ CAMBODIA
Phnom Penh ⊛
•Ho Chi Minh City (Saigon)
•Cagayan de Oro
Bandar Seri Begawan
•Manado
Banda Aceh•
BRUNEI ⊚
M A L A Y S I A
•Medan
⊛Kuala Lumpur
Balikpapan•
⊛SINGAPORE
I N D O N E S I A
•Jambi
Palembang•
•Bandung
⊛Jakarta• •Semarang
Surabaya
⊚Dili
TIMOR-LESTE
(EAST TIMOR)

*The People's Republic of China claims Taiwan as its 23rd province. Taiwan's government (Republic of China) maintains that there are two political entities.*

Pacific Ocean

Jayapura
Oceania
Asia

EQUATOR

AUSTRALIA

TROPIC OF CANCER

ARCTIC CIRCLE

90°E   100°E   110°E   120°E   130°E

# AUSTRALIA,
## NEW ZEALAND, AND OCEANIA

More than one-third of New Zealand's population lives in the city of Auckland.

Australia's last volcanic eruption was about 5,000 years ago.

Auckland Harbour in Auckland, New Zealand

G 'day, mate! This vast region, covering almost 3.3 million square miles (8.5 million sq km), includes Australia—the world's smallest and flattest continent—and New Zealand, as well as a fleet of mostly tiny islands scattered across the Pacific Ocean. Also known as "down under," most of the countries in this region are in the Southern Hemisphere, below the Equator.

Aboriginal children of Australia in ceremonial dress

## COLORFUL CRITTER

Almost half of known peacock spiders on the planet live in Western Australia. This eight-eyed spider, named for the bright blue markings on the males of the species, can jump a distance of more than 20 times its body length.

## FLAT LAND

Australia has mountain ranges with low elevations compared to the other continents of the world. This makes it the flattest continent on Earth. Its highest point? Mount Kosciuszko, which is only about one-quarter the height of Mount Everest.

## More Animals Than People

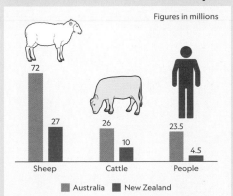

Figures in millions

72
27
26
10
23.5
4.5

Sheep    Cattle    People

■ Australia  ■ New Zealand

## GROW ON

About 80 percent of the plants in New Zealand are not found anywhere else in the world. And some of them doubled as dinosaur snacks! Plants like the kauri—a coniferous tree—have ancestors that date back to the Jurassic period. And New Zealand's magnificent lowland forests have been nicknamed "dinosaur forests" because of the prehistoric plants that grow there.

# PHYSICAL

**LAND AREA**
3,278,000 sq mi
(8,490,000 sq km)

**HIGHEST POINT***
Mount Wilhelm,
Papua New Guinea
14,793 ft (4,509 m)
*Includes Oceania

**LOWEST POINT**
Lake Eyre, Australia
-49 ft (-15 m)

**LONGEST RIVER**
Murray-Darling,
Australia
2,282 mi (3,672 km)

**LARGEST LAKE**
Lake Eyre, Australia
3,430 sq mi
(8,884 sq km)

# POLITICAL

**POPULATION**
38,004,000

**LARGEST
METROPOLITAN AREA**
Melbourne, Australia
Pop. 4,968,000

**LARGEST COUNTRY**
Australia
2,988,901 sq mi
(7,741,220 sq km)

**MOST DENSELY
POPULATED COUNTRY**
Nauru
1,250 people per sq mi
(476 per sq km)

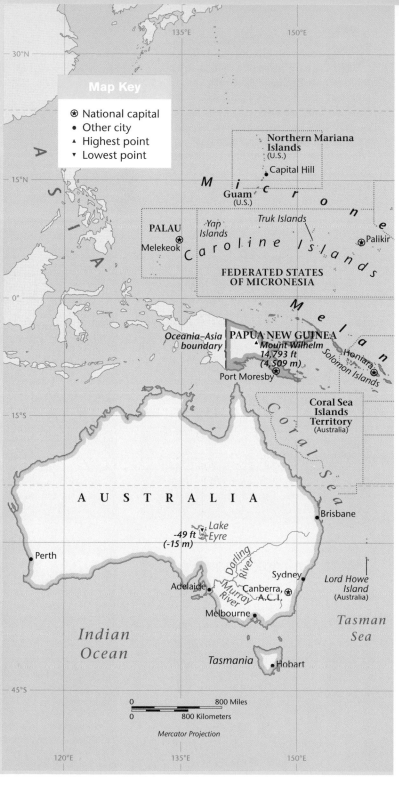

**Map Key**

⊛ National capital
• Other city
▲ Highest point
▼ Lowest point

ASIA

Micronesia

Northern Mariana
Islands
(U.S.)
• Capital Hill

Guam
(U.S.)

Truk Islands

PALAU ⊛
Melekeok

Yap
Islands

Caroline Islands

⊛ Palikir

FEDERATED STATES
OF MICRONESIA

Melanesia

Oceania–Asia
boundary

PAPUA NEW GUINEA
▲ Mount Wilhelm
14,793 ft
(4,509 m)

Honiara ⊛
Solomon Islands

• Port Moresby

Coral Sea
Islands
Territory
(Australia)

Coral Sea

AUSTRALIA

• Brisbane

Lake
Eyre
-49 ft ▼
(-15 m)

Darling
River

Murray
River

Sydney •
Adelaide •
Canberra, ⊛
A.C.T.

Perth •

Lord Howe
Island
(Australia)

Melbourne •

Tasman
Sea

Indian
Ocean

Tasmania
• Hobart

0    800 Miles
0    800 Kilometers

Mercator Projection

276

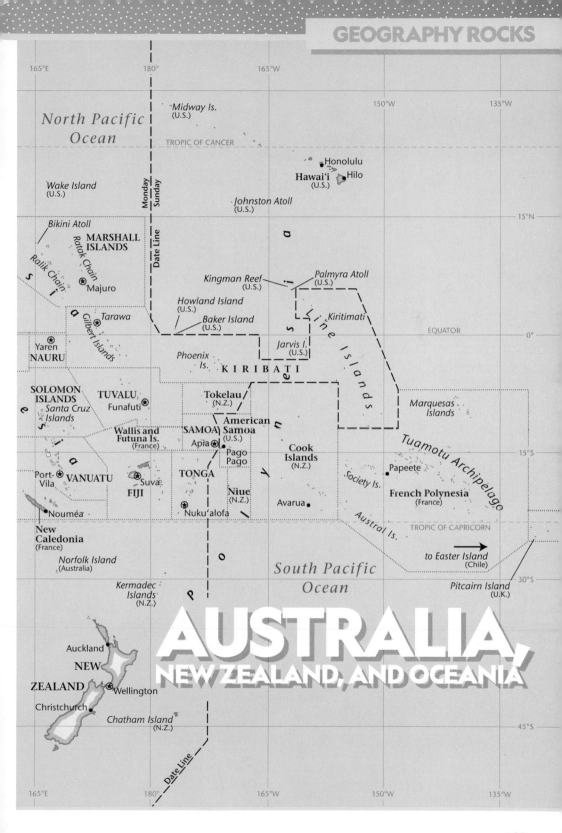

165°E    180°    165°W    150°W    135°W

*North Pacific Ocean*

Midway Is.
(U.S.)

TROPIC OF CANCER

Wake Island
(U.S.)

Monday | Sunday

Honolulu
**Hawai'i** • Hilo
(U.S.)

Johnston Atoll
(U.S.)

15°N

Bikini Atoll

**MARSHALL ISLANDS**

Ratak Chain

Ralik Chain

Date Line

Kingman Reef
(U.S.)

Palmyra Atoll
(U.S.)

Majuro

Howland Island
(U.S.)

Gilbert Islands

Tarawa

Baker Island
(U.S.)

Kiritimati

Line Islands

EQUATOR   0°

Yaren
**NAURU**

Jarvis I.
(U.S.)

Phoenix
Is.

**K I R I B A T I**

Marquesas
Islands

**SOLOMON ISLANDS**
Santa Cruz
Islands

**TUVALU**
Funafuti

Tokelau
(N.Z.)

Tuamotu Archipelago

Wallis and
Futuna Is.
(France)

**SAMOA** **American Samoa** (U.S.)

Apia
Pago
Pago

**Cook Islands**
(N.Z.)

15°S

Port-
Vila
**VANUATU**

Suva
**FIJI**

**TONGA**

Niue
(N.Z.)

Avarua

Papeete

Society Is.

**French Polynesia**
(France)

Nouméa

Nuku'alofa

**New Caledonia**
(France)

Norfolk Island
(Australia)

Austral Is.

TROPIC OF CAPRICORN

to Easter Island
(Chile)

Kermadec
Islands
(N.Z.)

*South Pacific Ocean*

Pitcairn Island
(U.K.)

30°S

# AUSTRALIA,
## NEW ZEALAND, AND OCEANIA

Auckland

**NEW ZEALAND**
Wellington

Christchurch

Chatham Island
(N.Z.)

Date Line

45°S

165°E    180°    165°W    150°W    135°W

# EUROPE

On sunny days, the Eiffel Tower in Paris, France, leans toward the shade.

You can cross the border between Spain and Portugal on a zip line.

Acrobats build human castles at the La Merce festival in Barcelona, Spain.

A cluster of islands and peninsulas jutting west from Asia, Europe is bordered by the Atlantic and Arctic Oceans and more than a dozen seas. Here you'll find a variety of scenery, from mountains to countryside to coastlines. Europe is also known for its rich culture and fascinating history, which make it one of the most visited continents on Earth.

Traditional dance performed in Greece

## SPOT IT

Dalmatians get their name from Dalmatia, a region of Croatia along the Adriatic Sea. The spotted canines have served as border guard dogs during conflicts in the region.

## LONG REIGN

The longest reign of any European monarch was that of Afonso Henriques, who served from 1112 to 1185, first as count, then as king of Portugal. Also known as Afonso the Conqueror, this leader is credited with securing Portugal's independence from the kingdom of Leon in 1139. A close runner-up? Louis XIV, who reigned as king of France for 72 years, from 1643 until 1715.

## Europe's Six Most Visited Cities

1. London, U.K.
🏴 †††††††††††††††††††††† 20.72 million

2. Paris, France
█ █ †††††††††††††††††† 16.84 million

3. Istanbul, Turkey
☪ ††††††††††† 12.12 million

4. Antalya, Turkey
☪ †††††††††† 10.73 million

5. Rome, Italy
█ █ †††††††††† 9.70 million

6. Prague, Czechia
█ †††††††† 9.04 million

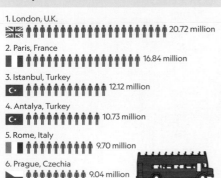

Estimated international visitors in 2018
Source: Euromonitor International

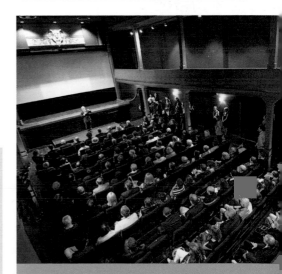

## OLD SHOW

Folks have been watching films at the Eden Theatre in La Ciotat, a seaside town in southern France, since 1899. The 166-seat theater is considered one of the oldest cinemas in the world.

# PHYSICAL

**LAND AREA**
3,841,000 sq mi
(9,947,000 sq km)

**HIGHEST POINT**
El'brus, Russia
18,510 ft (5,642 m)

**LOWEST POINT**
Caspian Sea
-92 ft (-28 m)

**LONGEST RIVER**
Volga, Russia
2,290 mi
(3,685 km)

**LARGEST LAKE
ENTIRELY IN EUROPE**
Ladoga, Russia
6,853 sq mi
(17,749 sq km)

# POLITICAL

**POPULATION**
751,632,000

**LARGEST
METROPOLITAN AREA**
Moscow, Russia
Pop. 12,410,000

**LARGEST COUNTRY
ENTIRELY IN EUROPE**
Ukraine
233,032 sq mi
(603,550 sq km)

**MOST DENSELY
POPULATED COUNTRY**
Monaco
38,000 people per sq
mi (19,000 per sq km)

**Map Key**

⊛ National capital
• Other city
▫ Small country
▲ Highest point
▼ Lowest point

0 — 400 Miles
0 — 400 Kilometers
Azimuthal Equidistant Projection

# EUROPE

10°E   20°E   30°E   40°E   50°E   60°E

*A commonly accepted division between Asia and Europe—marked here by a maroon, dashed line—is formed by the Ural Mountains, Ural River, Caspian Sea, Caucasus Mountains, and the Black Sea with its outlets, the Bosporus and Dardanelles.*

Barents Sea

Murmansk

Asia
Europe

Archangel

R   U   S   S   I   A

60°N

N   O   R   W   A   Y

S   W   E   D   E   N

F   I   N   L   A   N   D

Lake Ladoga

Helsinki

St. Petersburg

Tallinn
Stockholm
ESTONIA

Baltic Sea

Riga
LATVIA

LITHUANIA

Kaliningrad
(Russia)

Vitsyebsk
Vilnius

Kaunas

Gdańsk

Minsk

POLAND

Warsaw

BELARUS

Homyel'

Bydgoszcz
Łódź
Wrocław
Kraków

CZECHIA
(CZECH REP.)

Vienna
SLOVAKIA
Bratislava

Budapest

HUNGARY

Zagreb

CROATIA
BOSNIA &
HERZEGOVINA
Sarajevo

SERBIA

Belgrade

MONTENEGRO
Podgorica
Tirana
ALBANIA
N. MACED.

KOSOVO
Pristina

BULGARIA
Sofia

Skopje

Thessaloníki

GREECE

Athens

Sea

Crete

Yaroslavl'

Tver'

Moscow

Ryazan'

Smolensk

Bryansk

Kursk

Kiev

Poltava
L'viv   U K R A I N E   Donets'k
Vinnytsya

MOLDOVA
Chişinău

Odesa

Simferopol'

CRIMEA

Sevastopol'

Varna

Bucharest

ROMANIA

Bosporus

Dardanelles

T   U   R   K   E   Y

Istanbul

Black   Sea

Boundary claimed by Ukraine

Dnipropetrovs'k

Rostov

El'brus
(5,642 m) 18,510 ft

Sochi

GEORGIA

Volga River   Kazan'

Nizhniy
Novgorod

Penza

Saratov

Volgograd

Astrakhan'

Ufa

Samara   Orenburg

50°N

KAZAKHSTAN

-92 ft
(-28 m)

Groznyy

AZERBAIJAN

Caspian Sea

Baku

40°N

Kharkiv

NORTHERN CYPRUS
Nicosia
CYPRUS

20°E   30°E   40°E

# NORTH AMERICA

Grand Banks, Newfoundland, Canada, is the foggiest place on Earth.

Wolves howl more often in the winter.

A gray wolf running along a forest trail during autumn in Minnesota, U.S.A.

From the Great Plains of the United States and Canada to the rainforests of Panama, North America stretches 5,500 miles (8,850 km) from north to south. The third largest continent, North America can be divided into five regions: the mountainous west (including parts of Mexico and Central America's western coast), the Great Plains, the Canadian Shield, the varied eastern region (including Central America's lowlands and coastal plains), and the Caribbean.

Onlookers celebrate the opening of the Panama Canal expansion in 2016.

## BIG BONES

Canada was once a hotbed of activity for dinosaurs. In fact, the skeleton of the largest *Tyrannosaurus rex* to date was recently uncovered by researchers at a site in Saskatchewan, Canada. Estimated to weigh more than an elephant, the giant dino—nicknamed "Scotty"—stomped around some 68 million years ago.

## BERRY GOOD

The United States is the world's largest producer of strawberries, with some 90 percent of the crops grown in the coastal climates of California. That's about two billion pounds (907 million kg) of strawberries plucked from the state each year! Other top strawberry-producing states? Florida, Oregon, North Carolina, and Washington.

## International Tourist Arrivals

Cuba — 4,594,000

Puerto Rico — 3,797,000

Jamaica — 2,353,000

Bahamas — 1,439,000

International tourist arrivals, 2018 data

## TAKING FLIGHT

Millions of monarchs migrate up to 3,000 miles (4,828 km) to Mexico every year from the United States and Canada. They're the only butterflies to make such a massive journey.

283

## PHYSICAL

**LAND AREA**
9,449,000 sq mi
(24,474,000 sq km)

**LONGEST RIVER**
Mississippi–Missouri,
United States
3,710 mi (5,970 km)

**HIGHEST POINT**
Denali, Alaska, U.S.A.
20,310 ft (6,190 m)

**LOWEST POINT**
Death Valley,
California, U.S.A.
-282 ft (-86 m)

**LARGEST LAKE**
Lake Superior, U.S.–
Canada / 31,700 sq mi
(82,100 sq km)

## POLITICAL

**POPULATION**
569,914,000

**LARGEST COUNTRY**
Canada
3,855,101 sq mi
(9,984,670 sq km)

**LARGEST METROPOLITAN AREA**
Mexico City, Mexico
Pop. 21,581,000

**MOST DENSELY POPULATED
COUNTRY**
Barbados / 1,765 people
per sq mi (681 per sq km)

**Map Key**

⊛ National capital
• Other city
▲ Highest point
▼ Lowest point

EUROPE

Greenland
(Denmark)

ARCTIC
CIRCLE

Arctic Ocean

C A N A D A

Montreal

Thunder
Bay

Winnipeg

Edmonton

Calgary

Seattle

Vancouver
Victoria

ASIA

Alaska

(Mount McKinley) Denali
(6,190 m) 20,310 ft
(U.S.)
▲ Anchorage

800 Miles

8CO Kilometers

Azimuthal Equidistant Projection

160°W

180°

60°N

40°N

0

0

20°W

40°W

40°N

80°N

284

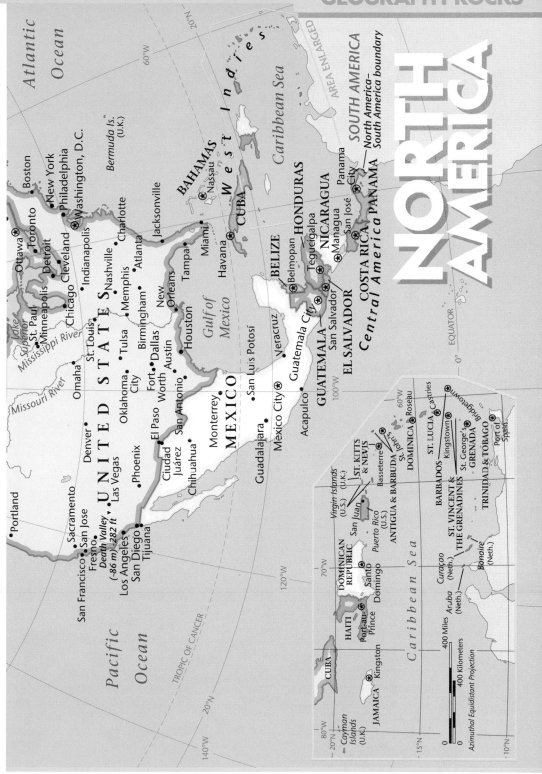

# NORTH AMERICA

SOUTH AMERICA
North America–
South America boundary

AREA ENLARGED

Atlantic
Ocean

Pacific
Ocean

Caribbean Sea

West Indies

BAHAMAS

CUBA

Gulf of
Mexico

UNITED STATES

MEXICO

BELIZE
GUATEMALA
HONDURAS
EL SALVADOR
NICARAGUA
COSTA RICA
PANAMA
Central America

Boston
New York
Philadelphia
Washington, D.C.
Bermuda Is.
(U.K.)
Ottawa
Toronto
Detroit
Cleveland
Indianapolis
Charlotte
Nashville
Atlanta
Jacksonville
Portland
Lake Superior
St. Paul
Minneapolis
Chicago
St. Louis
Memphis
Birmingham
New Orleans
Tampa
Miami
Nassau
Havana
Belmopan
Tegucigalpa
Managua
San José
Panama
City
San Salvador
Guatemala City
Veracruz
Acapulco
Mexico City
San Luis Potosí
Monterrey
Guadalajara
Houston
Austin
San Antonio
Dallas
Fort Worth
Oklahoma City
Tulsa
Omaha
Denver
Phoenix
Las Vegas
El Paso
Ciudad Juárez
Chihuahua
Sacramento
San Jose
Fresno
San Francisco
Los Angeles
San Diego
Tijuana
Death Valley
(–86 m, –282 ft) ▼

Mississippi River
Missouri River

TROPIC OF CANCER

EQUATOR

20°N
60°W
80°W
100°W
120°W
140°W
0°
20°N

## Inset Map (West Indies)

Caribbean Sea

CUBA
JAMAICA
Kingston
Cayman Islands
(U.K.)
HAITI
Port-au-Prince
DOMINICAN REPUBLIC
Santo Domingo
Puerto Rico
(U.S.)
San Juan
Virgin Islands
(U.S.)
ST. KITTS & NEVIS
Basseterre
ANTIGUA & BARBUDA
St. John's
DOMINICA
Roseau
ST. LUCIA
Castries
Bridgetown
BARBADOS
St. Vincent
Kingstown
ST. VINCENT & THE GRENADINES
GRENADA
St. George's
Aruba
(Neth.)
Curaçao
(Neth.)
Bonaire
(Neth.)
TRINIDAD & TOBAGO
Port of Spain

Azimuthal Equidistant Projection

0     400 Miles
0     400 Kilometers

70°W
60°W
20°N
15°N
10°N

285

# SOUTH AMERICA

Lasting about five minutes, Uruguay's national anthem is the world's longest in duration.

Brazil has participated in the FIFA World Cup 21 times— more than any other team.

A boy plays soccer in Manaus, Brazil.

S outh America is bordered by three major bodies of water—the Caribbean Sea, Atlantic Ocean, and Pacific Ocean. The world's fourth largest continent extends over a range of climates, from tropical in the north to subarctic in the south. South America produces a rich diversity of natural resources, including nuts, fruits, sugar, grains, coffee, and chocolate.

Santiago Cathedral in Santiago, Chile

## BIG BIRD

The Andean condor, which lives exclusively in the mountains and valleys of the Andes, is the largest raptor in the world and the largest flying bird in South America.

## OCEANS ALL AROUND

South America is surrounded by both the Pacific and Atlantic Oceans. Experts think that the two oceans used to be one massive body of water until North and South America joined together at the Isthmus of Panama some three million years ago. That move, scientists think, divided the original ocean into two. Today, Colombia and Chile are the only two countries in South America with a coastline on each ocean.

## Vast Watershed

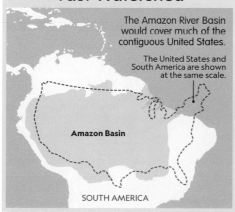

The Amazon River Basin would cover much of the contiguous United States.

The United States and South America are shown at the same scale.

Amazon Basin

SOUTH AMERICA

## ANCIENT BRIDGE

Deep in the Peruvian Andes, a suspension bridge made of handwoven grass stretches more than 100 feet (30 m) over a rushing river. Once used to connect two villages on either side of the river, the bridge, which dates back more than 500 years, is now more of a symbolic nod to the past. Each June, the suspension bridge is rebuilt and replaced by the local indigenous community.

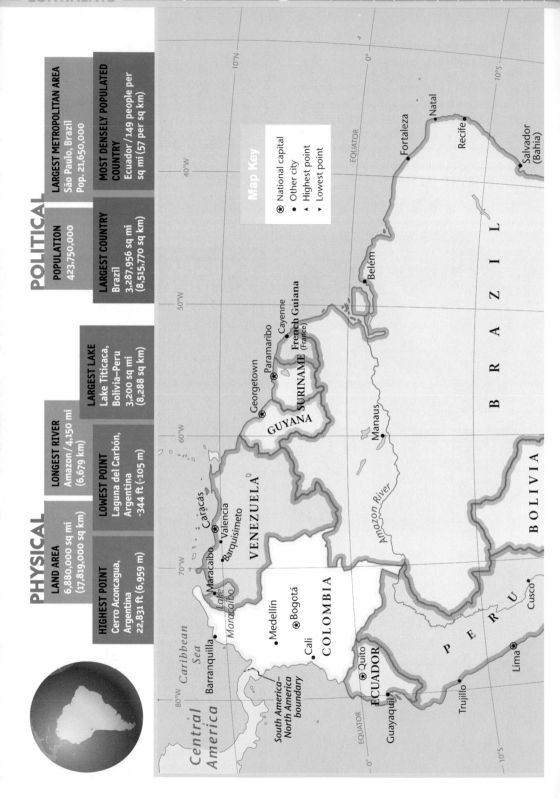

## PHYSICAL

**LAND AREA**
6,880,000 sq mi
(17,819,000 sq km)

**HIGHEST POINT**
Cerro Aconcagua,
Argentina
22,831 ft (6,959 m)

**LOWEST POINT**
Laguna del Carbón,
Argentina
-344 ft (-105 m)

**LONGEST RIVER**
Amazon / 4,150 mi
(6,679 km)

**LARGEST LAKE**
Lake Titicaca,
Bolivia–Peru
3,200 sq mi
(8,288 sq km)

## POLITICAL

**POPULATION**
423,750,000

**LARGEST COUNTRY**
Brazil
3,287,956 sq mi
(8,515,770 sq km)

**LARGEST METROPOLITAN AREA**
São Paulo, Brazil
Pop. 21,650,000

**MOST DENSELY POPULATED COUNTRY**
Ecuador / 149 people per
sq mi (57 per sq km)

**Map Key**
⊛ National capital
• Other city
▲ Highest point
▼ Lowest point

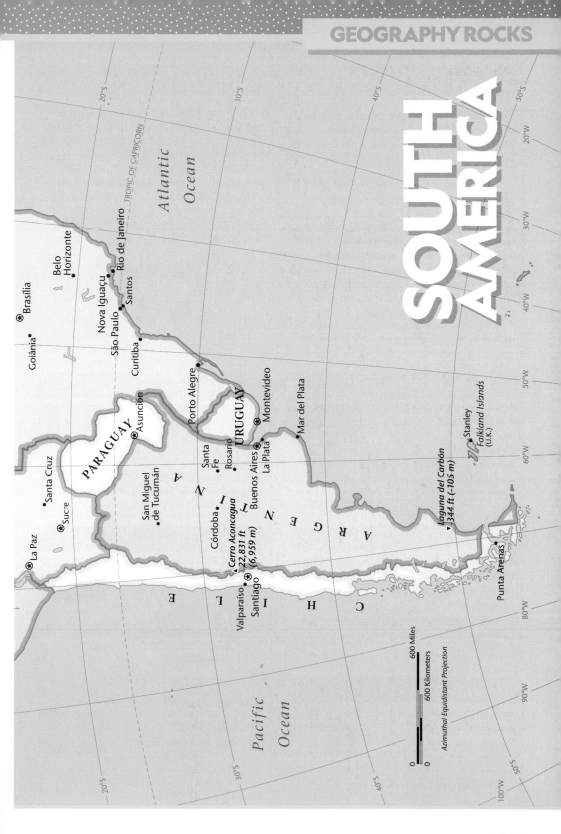

# SOUTH AMERICA

Atlantic Ocean

Pacific Ocean

20°S
30°S
40°S
50°S

20°W
30°W
40°W
50°W
60°W
70°W
80°W
90°W
100°W

TROPIC OF CAPRICORN

⊛ Brasília
Goiânia •
• Belo Horizonte
◉ Nova Iguaçu
Rio de Janeiro •
São Paulo •
• Santos
Curitiba •
Porto Alegre •

• Santa Cruz
• Suce
⊛ Sucre
⊛ La Paz

**PARAGUAY**
⊛ Asunción

**URUGUAY**
Montevideo ⊛

**A R G E N T I N A**

Santa Fe •
Rosario •
Buenos Aires ⊛
• La Plata
• Mar del Plata

San Miguel • de Tucumán
Córdoba •
▲ Cerro Aconcagua 22,831 ft (6,959 m)
Valparaíso •
Santiago ⊛

**C H I L E**

▼ Laguna del Carbón 344 ft (-105 m)

Punta Arenas •

🏳 Stanley
Falkland Islands (U.K.)

0        600 Miles
0        600 Kilometers
Azimuthal Equidistant Projection

**289**

# COUNTRIES OF THE WORLD

**The following pages** present a general overview of all 195 independent countries recognized by the National Geographic Society, including the newest nation, South Sudan, which gained independence in 2011.

The flags of each independent country symbolize diverse cultures and histories. The statistical data cover highlights of geography and demography and provide a brief overview of each country. They present general characteristics and are not intended to be comprehensive. For example, not every language spoken in a specific country can be listed. Thus, languages shown are the most representative of that area. This is also true of the religions mentioned.

A country is defined as a political body with its own independent government, geographical space, and, in most cases, laws, military, and taxes.

Disputed areas such as Northern Cyprus and Taiwan, and dependencies of independent nations, such as Bermuda and Puerto Rico, are not included in this listing.

Note the color key at the bottom of the pages and the locator map below, which assign a color to each country based on the continent on which it is located. Some capital city populations include that city's metro area. All information is accurate as of press time.

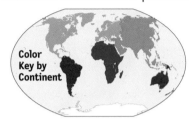

Color Key by Continent

## Afghanistan

**Area:** 251,827 sq mi (652,230 sq km)
**Population:** 34,941,000
**Capital:** Kabul, pop. 4,012,000
**Currency:** afghani
**Religions:** Sunni Muslim, Shia Muslim
**Languages:** Afghan Persian (Dari), Pashto, Uzbek, Turkmen

## Andorra

**Area:** 181 sq mi (468 sq km)
**Population:** 86,000
**Capital:** Andorra la Vella, pop. 23,000
**Currency:** euro
**Religion:** Roman Catholic
**Languages:** Catalan, French, Castilian, Portuguese

## Albania

**Area:** 11,100 sq mi (28,748 sq km)
**Population:** 3,057,000
**Capital:** Tirana, pop. 476,000
**Currency:** lek
**Religions:** Muslim, Roman Catholic, Orthodox
**Languages:** Albanian, Greek, Vlach, Romani, Slavic dialects

## Angola

**Area:** 481,353 sq mi (1,246,700 sq km)
**Population:** 30,356,000
**Capital:** Luanda, pop. 7,774,000
**Currency:** kwanza
**Religions:** Roman Catholic, Protestant, indigenous beliefs
**Languages:** Portuguese, Umbundu, other African languages

## Algeria

**Area:** 919,595 sq mi (2,381,741 sq km)
**Population:** 41,657,000
**Capital:** Algiers, pop. 2,694,000
**Currency:** Algerian dinar
**Religion:** Sunni Muslim
**Languages:** Arabic, French, Berber dialects

## Antigua and Barbuda

**Area:** 171 sq mi (443 sq km)
**Population:** 96,000
**Capital:** St. John's, pop. 21,000
**Currency:** East Caribbean dollar
**Religions:** Anglican, Methodist, other Protestant, Roman Catholic
**Languages:** English, Antiguan creole

## Argentina

**Area:** 1,073,518 sq mi (2,780,400 sq km)
**Population:** 44,694,000
**Capital:** Buenos Aires, pop. 14,967,000
**Currency:** Argentine peso
**Religion:** Roman Catholic
**Languages:** Spanish, Italian, English, German, French

## Armenia

**Area:** 11,484 sq mi (29,743 sq km)
**Population:** 3,038,000
**Capital:** Yerevan, pop. 1,080,000
**Currency:** Armenian dram
**Religions:** Armenian Apostolic, other Christian
**Languages:** Armenian, Russian

## Australia

**Area:** 2,988,901 sq mi (7,741,220 sq km)
**Population:** 23,470,000
**Capital:** Canberra, A.C.T., pop. 423,000
**Currency:** Australian dollar
**Religions:** Anglican, Roman Catholic, other Christian
**Language:** English

## Austria

**Area:** 32,383 sq mi (83,871 sq km)
**Population:** 8,793,000
**Capital:** Vienna, pop. 1,901,000
**Currency:** euro
**Religions:** Roman Catholic, Protestant, Muslim
**Languages:** German, Turkish, Serbian, Croatian, Slovene, Hungarian

## Azerbaijan

**Area:** 33,436 sq mi (86,600 sq km)
**Population:** 10,047,000
**Capital:** Baku, pop. 2,286,000
**Currency:** Azerbaijani manat
**Religions:** Muslim, Russian Orthodox
**Languages:** Azerbaijani (Azeri), Russian, Armenian

## Bahamas

**Area:** 5,359 sq mi (13,880 sq km)
**Population:** 333,000
**Capital:** Nassau, pop. 280,000
**Currency:** Bahamian dollar
**Religions:** Baptist, Anglican, Pentecostal, Roman Catholic
**Languages:** English, Creole

## Bahrain

**Area:** 293 sq mi (760 sq km)
**Population:** 1,443,000
**Capital:** Manama, pop. 565,000
**Currency:** Bahraini dinar
**Religions:** Muslim (Shia and Sunni), Christian
**Languages:** Arabic, English, Farsi, Urdu

## Bangladesh

**Area:** 57,321 sq mi (148,460 sq km)
**Population:** 159,453,000
**Capital:** Dhaka, pop. 19,578,000
**Currency:** taka
**Religions:** Muslim, Hindu
**Language:** Bangla (Bengali)

# 3 cool things about BANGLADESH

1. Hailstones the size of grapefruits once hammered the Gopalganj district of Bangladesh. Weighing two pounds (1 kg), they are the heaviest hailstones on record.

2. Bangladesh provides plenty of the world's fruit, including mangoes, guavas, papayas, lemons, pineapples, and watermelons. The jackfruit, which can weigh as much as a 12-year-old, also comes from the country.

3. Much of the remaining Bengal tiger population prowls around the area of Bangladesh known as the Sundarban. It's estimated that fewer than than 200 tigers roam the area, the world's only coastal habitat for the big cats.

● Asia ● Europe ● North America ● South America

## Barbados

**Area:** 166 sq mi (430 sq km)
**Population:** 293,000
**Capital:** Bridgetown, pop. 89,000
**Currency:** Barbadian dollar
**Religions:** Protestant, Roman Catholic
**Languages:** English, Bajan

## Belarus

**Area:** 80,155 sq mi
(207,600 sq km)
**Population:** 9,528,000
**Capital:** Minsk, pop. 2,005,000
**Currency:** Belarusian ruble
**Religions:** Eastern Orthodox, Roman Catholic
**Languages:** Russian, Belarusian

## Belgium

**Area:** 11,787 sq mi (30,528 sq km)
**Population:** 11,571,000
**Capital:** Brussels, pop. 2,050,000
**Currency:** euro
**Religions:** Roman Catholic, Muslim, Protestant
**Languages:** Dutch, French, German

## Belize

**Area:** 8,867 sq mi (22,966 sq km)
**Population:** 386,000
**Capital:** Belmopan, pop. 23,000
**Currency:** Belize dollar
**Religions:** Roman Catholic, Protestant
(includes Pentecostal, Seventh-Day Adventist,
Mennonite, Methodist)
**Languages:** English, Spanish, Creole, Maya

## Benin

**Area:** 43,484 sq mi (112,622 sq km)
**Population:** 11,341,000
**Capitals:** Porto-Novo, pop. 285,000;
Cotonou, pop. 685,000
**Currency:** Communauté Financière Africaine franc
**Religions:** Muslim, Roman Catholic, Protestant, Vodoun
**Languages:** French, Fon, Yoruba, tribal languages

## Bhutan

**Area:** 14,824 sq mi (38,394 sq km)
**Population:** 766,000
**Capital:** Thimphu, pop. 203,000
**Currencies:** ngultrum, Indian rupee
**Religions:** Lamaistic Buddhist,
Indian- and Nepalese-influenced Hindu
**Languages:** Sharchhopka, Dzongkha, Lhotshamkha

## Bolivia

**Area:** 424,164 sq mi (1,098,581 sq km)
**Population:** 11,306,000
**Capitals:** La Paz, pop. 1,814,000;
Sucre, pop. 278,000
**Currency:** boliviano
**Religions:** Roman Catholic, Protestant
**Languages:** Spanish, Quechua, Aymara

## Bosnia and Herzegovina

**Area:** 19,767 sq mi
(51,197 sq km)
**Population:** 3,850,000
**Capital:** Sarajevo, pop. 343,000
**Currency:** convertible mark
**Religions:** Muslim, Orthodox, Roman Catholic
**Languages:** Bosnian, Serbian, Croatian

## Botswana

**Area:** 224,607 sq mi
(581,730 sq km)
**Population:** 2,249,000
**Capital:** Gaborone, pop. 269,000
**Currency:** pula
**Religions:** Christian, Badimo
**Languages:** Setswana, Sekalanga, Sekgalagadi, English

## Brazil

**Area:** 3,287,956 sq mi
(8,515,770 sq km)
**Population:** 208,847,000
**Capital:** Brasília, pop. 4,470,000
**Currency:** Brazilian real
**Religions:** Roman Catholic, Protestant
**Language:** Portuguese

## Brunei

**Area:** 2,226 sq mi (5,765 sq km)
**Population:** 451,000
**Capital:** Bandar Seri Begawan, pop. 241,000
**Currency:** Brunei dollar
**Religions:** Muslim, Christian, Buddhist, indigenous beliefs
**Languages:** Malay, English, Chinese

## Burkina Faso

**Area:** 105,869 sq mi (274,200 sq km)
**Population:** 19,743,000
**Capital:** Ouagadougou, pop. 2,531,000
**Currency:** Communauté Financière Africaine franc
**Religions:** Muslim, Catholic, animist
**Languages:** French, African languages

## Bulgaria

**Area:** 42,811 sq mi (110,879 sq km)
**Population:** 7,058,000
**Capital:** Sofia, pop. 1,272,000
**Currency:** Bulgarian lev
**Religions:** Eastern Orthodox, Muslim
**Languages:** Bulgarian, Turkish, Romany

## Burundi

**Area:** 10,745 sq mi (27,830 sq km)
**Population:** 11,845,000
**Capital:** Bujumbura, pop. 899,000
**Currency:** Burundi franc
**Religions:** Roman Catholic, Protestant, Muslim
**Languages:** Kirundi, French, Swahili

SNAPSHOT
Bhutan

A sacred site, Paro Taktsang—or Tiger's Nest Monastery—sits at the edge of a cliff some 3,000 feet (915 m) above Paro, Bhutan.

● Asia ● Europe ● North America ● South America

## Cabo Verde

**Area:** 1,557 sq mi (4,033 sq km)
**Population:** 568,000
**Capital:** Praia, pop. 168,000
**Currency:** Cape Verdean escudo
**Religions:** Roman Catholic, Protestant
**Languages:** Portuguese, Crioulo

## Cameroon

**Area:** 183,568 sq mi
(475,440 sq km)
**Population:** 25,641,000
**Capital:** Yaoundé, pop. 3,412,000
**Currency:** Communauté Financière
Africaine franc
**Religions:** Roman Catholic, Protestant, Muslim, animist
**Languages:** African languages, English, French

## Cambodia

**Area:** 69,898 sq mi (181,035 sq km)
**Population:** 16,450,000
**Capital:** Phnom Penh,
pop. 1,952,000
**Currency:** riel
**Religion:** Buddhist
**Language:** Khmer

## Canada

**Area:** 3,855,101 sq mi
(9,984,670 sq km)
**Population:** 35,882,000
**Capital:** Ottawa, pop. 1,363,000
**Currency:** Canadian dollar
**Religions:** Roman Catholic, Protestant
**Languages:** English, French

# SNAPSHOT Colombia

A long-tailed sylph hummingbird feeds on a tropical flower in Colombia.

COLOR KEY    ● Africa    ● Australia, New Zealand, and Oceania

## Central African Republic

**Area:** 240,535 sq mi (622,984 sq km)
**Population:** 5,745,000
**Capital:** Bangui, pop. 851,000
**Currency:** Communauté Financière Africaine franc
**Religions:** indigenous beliefs, Protestant, Roman Catholic, Muslim
**Languages:** French, Sangho, tribal languages

## Chad

**Area:** 495,755 sq mi (1,284,000 sq km)
**Population:** 15,833,000
**Capital:** N'Djamena, pop. 1,323,000
**Currency:** Communauté Financière Africaine franc
**Religions:** Muslim, Protestant, Roman Catholic, animist
**Languages:** French, Arabic, Sara, indigenous languages

## Chile

**Area:** 291,932 sq mi (756,102 sq km)
**Population:** 17,925,000
**Capital:** Santiago, pop. 6,680,000
**Currency:** Chilean peso
**Religions:** Roman Catholic, Protestant
**Languages:** Spanish, English, indigenous languages

## China

**Area:** 3,705,405 sq mi (9,596,960 sq km)
**Population:** 1,384,689,000
**Capital:** Beijing, pop. 19,618,000
**Currency:** yuan
**Religions:** folk religion, Buddhist, Christian
**Languages:** Standard Chinese or Mandarin, Yue or Cantonese, Wu, Minbei, Minnan, Xiang, Gan, Hakka dialects

## Colombia

**Area:** 439,735 sq mi (1,138,910 sq km)
**Population:** 48,169,000
**Capital:** Bogotá, pop. 10,574,000
**Currency:** Colombian peso
**Religions:** Roman Catholic, Protestant
**Language:** Spanish

## Comoros

**Area:** 863 sq mi (2,235 sq km)
**Population:** 821,000
**Capital:** Moroni, pop. 62,000
**Currency:** Comoran franc
**Religion:** Sunni Muslim
**Languages:** Arabic, French, Shikomoro

## Congo

**Area:** 132,047 sq mi (342,000 sq km)
**Population:** 5,062,000
**Capital:** Brazzaville, pop. 2,230,000
**Currency:** Communauté Financière Africaine franc
**Religions:** Christian, animist, Muslim
**Languages:** French, Lingala, local languages

## Costa Rica

**Area:** 19,730 sq mi (51,100 sq km)
**Population:** 4,987,000
**Capital:** San José, pop. 1,358,000
**Currency:** Costa Rican colón
**Religions:** Roman Catholic, Evangelical
**Languages:** Spanish, English

## Côte d'Ivoire (Ivory Coast)

**Area:** 124,504 sq mi (322,463 sq km)
**Population:** 26,261,000
**Capitals:** Abidjan, pop. 4,921,000; Yamoussoukro, pop. 231,000
**Currency:** Communauté Financière Africaine franc
**Religions:** Muslim, Christian, indigenous beliefs
**Languages:** French, Dioula, native dialects

## Croatia

**Area:** 21,581 sq mi (56,594 sq km)
**Population:** 4,270,000
**Capital:** Zagreb, pop. 686,000
**Currency:** kuna
**Religions:** Roman Catholic, Orthodox
**Languages:** Croatian, Serbian

## Cuba

**Area:** 42,803 sq mi (110,860 sq km)
**Population:** 11,116,000
**Capital:** Havana, pop. 2,136,000
**Currencies:** Cuban peso, peso convertible
**Religion:** Roman Catholic
**Language:** Spanish

## Democratic Republic of the Congo

**Area:** 905,354 sq mi (2,344,858 sq km)
**Population:** 85,281,000
**Capital:** Kinshasa, pop. 13,171,000
**Currency:** Congolese franc
**Religions:** Roman Catholic, Protestant, Kimbanguist, Muslim
**Languages:** French, Lingala, Kingwana, Kikongo, Tshiluba

## Cyprus

**Area:** 3,572 sq mi (9,251 sq km)
**Population:** 1,237,000
**Capital:** Nicosia, pop. 269,000
**Currency:** euro
**Religions:** Greek Orthodox, Muslim
**Languages:** Greek, Turkish, English

## Denmark

**Area:** 16,639 sq mi (43,094 sq km)
**Population:** 5,810,000
**Capital:** Copenhagen, pop. 1,321,000
**Currency:** Danish krone
**Religions:** Evangelical Lutheran, Muslim
**Languages:** Danish, Faroese, Greenlandic

## 3 cool things about CYPRUS

1. There were once so many snakes in the country that it was known as Ophiussa, or "abode of snakes." Today, the sight of one of the reptiles slithering around is fairly rare.

2. The earliest evidence of a pet cat was unearthed in an ancient village in Cyprus. Dating back some 9,500 years, the cat's remains were found in a grave next to human bones of the same age, suggesting they were buried together.

3. A massive ferry that sank off the coast of Cyprus in 1980 is now a top spot for scuba divers. The M.S. *Zenobia* wreckage is so popular that divers even decorate it during the holidays.

## Djibouti

**Area:** 8,958 sq mi (23,200 sq km)
**Population:** 884,000
**Capital:** Djibouti, pop. 562,000
**Currency:** Djiboutian franc
**Religions:** Muslim, Christian
**Languages:** French, Arabic, Somali, Afar

## Dominica

**Area:** 290 sq mi (751 sq km)
**Population:** 74,000
**Capital:** Roseau, pop. 15,000
**Currency:** East Caribbean dollar
**Religions:** Roman Catholic, Protestant
**Languages:** English, French patois

## Czechia (Czech Republic)

**Area:** 30,451 sq mi (78,867 sq km)
**Population:** 10,686,000
**Capital:** Prague, pop. 1,292,000
**Currency:** Czech koruny
**Religions:** Roman Catholic, Protestant
**Languages:** Czech, Slovak

## Dominican Republic

**Area:** 18,792 sq mi (48,670 sq km)
**Population:** 10,299,000
**Capital:** Santo Domingo, pop. 3,172,000
**Currency:** Dominican peso
**Religion:** Roman Catholic
**Language:** Spanish

## Ecuador

**Area:** 109,483 sq mi
(283,561 sq km)
**Population:** 16,499,000
**Capital:** Quito, pop. 1,822,000
**Currency:** U.S. dollar
**Religions:** Roman Catholic, Evangelical
**Languages:** Spanish, Quechua, other
Amerindian languages

## Egypt

**Area:** 386,662 sq mi
(1,001,450 sq km)
**Population:** 99,413,000
**Capital:** Cairo, pop. 20,076,000
**Currencies:** Egyptian pound
**Religions:** Muslim (mostly Sunni), Coptic Christian
**Languages:** Arabic, English, French

## El Salvador

**Area:** 8,124 sq mi
(21,041 sq km)
**Population:** 6,187,000
**Capital:** San Salvador,
pop. 1,107,000
**Currencies:** U.S. dollar, El Salvador colón
**Religions:** Roman Catholic, Protestant
**Languages:** Spanish, Nawat

## Equatorial Guinea

**Area:** 10,831 sq mi (28,051 sq km)
**Population:** 797,000
**Capital:** Malabo, pop. 297,000
**Currency:** Communauté
Financière Africaine franc
**Religions:** Roman Catholic, pagan practices
**Languages:** Spanish, French, Fang, Bubi

## Eritrea

**Area:** 45,406 sq mi
(117,600 sq km)
**Population:** 5,971,000
**Capital:** Asmara, pop. 896,000
**Currency:** nakfa
**Religions:** Muslim, Coptic Christian, Roman Catholic
**Languages:** Tigrigna (Tigrinya), Arabic, English, Tigre,
Kunama, Afar, other Cushitic languages

## Estonia

**Area:** 17,463 sq mi (45,228 sq km)
**Population:** 1,244,000
**Capital:** Tallinn, pop. 437,000
**Currency:** euro
**Religions:** Lutheran, Orthodox
**Languages:** Estonian, Russian

## Eswatini (Swaziland)

**Area:** 6,704 sq mi (17,364 sq km)
**Population:** 1,087,000
**Capitals:** Mbabane, pop. 68,000;
Lobamba, pop. 5,800
**Currency:** lilangeni
**Religions:** Christian, Muslim
**Languages:** English, siSwati

## Ethiopia

**Area:** 426,372 sq mi
(1,104,300 sq km)
**Population:** 108,386,000
**Capital:** Addis Ababa,
pop. 4,400,000
**Currency:** Ethiopian birr
**Religions:** Ethiopian Orthodox, Muslim, Protestant
**Languages:** Oromo, Amharic, Somali, Tigrigna (Tigrinya)

## Fiji

**Area:** 7,056 sq mi
(18,274 sq km)
**Population:** 926,000
**Capital:** Suva, pop. 178,000
**Currency:** Fiji dollar
**Religions:** Protestant, Hindu,
Roman Catholic, Muslim
**Languages:** English, Fijian, Hindustani

## Finland

**Area:** 130,558 sq mi
(338,145 sq km)
**Population:** 5,537,000
**Capital:** Helsinki, pop. 1,279,000
**Currency:** euro
**Religion:** Lutheran
**Languages:** Finnish, Swedish

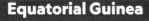

## France

**Area:** 248,573 sq mi
(643,801 sq km)
**Population:** 67,364,000
**Capital:** Paris, pop. 10,901,000
**Currency:** euro
**Religions:** Roman Catholic, Protestant, Muslim, Jewish
**Language:** French

## Gambia

**Area:** 4,363 sq mi (11,300 sq km)
**Population:** 2,093,000
**Capital:** Banjul, pop. 437,000
**Currency:** dalasi
**Religions:** Muslim, Christian
**Languages:** English, Mandinka, Wolof, Fula, other indigenous vernaculars

## Gabon

**Area:** 103,347 sq mi (267,667 sq km)
**Population:** 2,119,000
**Capital:** Libreville, pop. 813,000
**Currency:** Communauté Financière Africaine franc
**Religions:** Christian, Muslim
**Languages:** French, Fang, Myene, Nzebi, Bapounou/Eschira, Bandjabi

## Georgia

**Area:** 26,911 sq mi (69,700 sq km)
**Population:** 4,926,000
**Capital:** Tbilisi, pop. 1,077,000
**Currency:** lari
**Religions:** Orthodox Christian, Muslim, Armenian Apostolic
**Languages:** Georgian, Azeri, Armenian

# SNAPSHOT
# Ghana

A cheerful fisherman repairs a net in Accra, Ghana.

**COLOR KEY**  ● Africa ● Australia, New Zealand, and Oceania

## Germany

**Area:** 137,847 sq mi (357,022 sq km)
**Population:** 80,458,000
**Capital:** Berlin, pop. 3,563,000
**Currency:** euro
**Religions:** Roman Catholic, Protestant, Muslim
**Language:** German

## Guinea

**Area:** 94,926 sq mi (245,857 sq km)
**Population:** 11,855,000
**Capital:** Conakry, pop. 1,843,000
**Currency:** Guinean franc
**Religions:** Muslim, Christian, indigenous beliefs
**Languages:** French, African languages

## Ghana

**Area:** 92,098 sq mi (238,533 sq km)
**Population:** 28,102,000
**Capital:** Accra, pop. 2,439,000
**Currency:** Ghana cedi
**Religions:** Christian, Muslim, traditional beliefs
**Languages:** Asante, Ewe, Fante, Boron (Brong), Dagomba, Dangme, Dagarte (Dagaba), Kokomba, English

## Guinea-Bissau

**Area:** 13,948 sq mi (36,125 sq km)
**Population:** 1,833,000
**Capital:** Bissau, pop. 558,000
**Currency:** Communauté Financière Africaine franc
**Religions:** Muslim, Christian, indigenous beliefs
**Languages:** Crioulu, Portuguese, Pular, Mandingo

## Greece

**Area:** 50,949 sq mi (131,957 sq km)
**Population:** 10,762,000
**Capital:** Athens, pop. 3,156,000
**Currency:** euro
**Religions:** Greek Orthodox, Muslim
**Language:** Greek

## Guyana

**Area:** 83,000 sq mi (214,969 sq km)
**Population:** 741,000
**Capital:** Georgetown, pop. 110,000
**Currency:** Guyanese dollar
**Religions:** Protestant, Hindu, Roman Catholic, Muslim
**Languages:** English, Guyanese Creole, Amerindian languages, Caribbean Hindustani

## Grenada

**Area:** 133 sq mi (344 sq km)
**Population:** 112,000
**Capital:** St. George's, pop. 39,000
**Currency:** East Caribbean dollar
**Religions:** Roman Catholic, Pentacostal, other Protestant
**Languages:** English, French patois

## Haiti

**Area:** 10,714 sq mi (27,750 sq km)
**Population:** 10,788,000
**Capital:** Port-au-Prince, pop. 2,637,000
**Currencies:** gourde, U.S. dollar
**Religions:** Roman Catholic, Protestant, vodou
**Languages:** French, Creole

## Guatemala

**Area:** 42,042 sq mi (108,889 sq km)
**Population:** 16,581,000
**Capital:** Guatemala City, pop. 2,851,000
**Currency:** quetzal
**Religions:** Roman Catholic, Protestant, indigenous Maya beliefs
**Languages:** Spanish, Amerindian languages

## Honduras

**Area:** 43,278 sq mi (112,090 sq km)
**Population:** 9,183,000
**Capital:** Tegucigalpa, pop. 1,363,000
**Currency:** lempira
**Religions:** Roman Catholic, Protestant
**Languages:** Spanish, Amerindian dialects

## Hungary

**Area:** 35,918 sq mi (93,028 sq km)
**Population:** 9,826,000
**Capital:** Budapest, pop. 1,759,000
**Currency:** forint
**Religions:** Roman Catholic, Calvinist, Lutheran
**Language:** Hungarian

## Iraq

**Area:** 169,235 sq mi (438,317 sq km)
**Population:** 40,194,000
**Capital:** Baghdad, pop. 6,634,000
**Currency:** Iraqi dinar
**Religions:** Shiite Muslim, Sunni Muslim
**Languages:** Arabic, Kurdish, Turkmen, Syriac, Armenian

## Iceland

**Area:** 39,769 sq mi (103,000 sq km)
**Population:** 344,000
**Capital:** Reykjavík, pop. 216,000
**Currency:** Icelandic krona
**Religions:** Lutheran, Roman Catholic
**Languages:** Icelandic, English, Nordic languages

## Ireland (Éire)

**Area:** 27,133 sq mi (70,273 sq km)
**Population:** 5,068,000
**Capital:** Dublin (Baile Átha Cliath), pop. 1,201,000
**Currency:** euro
**Religions:** Roman Catholic, Church of Ireland
**Languages:** English, Irish (Gaelic)

## India

**Area:** 1,269,219 sq mi (3,287,263 sq km)
**Population:** 1,296,834,000
**Capital:** New Delhi, pop. 28,514,000
**Currency:** Indian rupee
**Religions:** Hindu, Muslim, Christian, Sikh
**Languages:** Hindi, Bengali, Telugu, Marathi, Tamil, Urdu, Gujarati, Kannada, Malayalam, Oriya, Panjabi, Assamese, Maithili, English

## Israel

**Area:** 8,019 sq mi (20,770 sq km)
**Population:** 8,425,000
**Capital:** Jerusalem, pop. 907,000
**Currency:** new Israeli sheqel
**Religions:** Jewish, Muslim
**Languages:** Hebrew, Arabic, English

## Indonesia

**Area:** 735,358 sq mi (1,904,569 sq km)
**Population:** 262,787,000
**Capital:** Jakarta, pop. 10,517,000
**Currency:** Indonesian rupiah
**Religions:** Muslim, Protestant, Roman Catholic, Hindu
**Languages:** Bahasa Indonesia (modified form of Malay), English, Dutch, Javanese, local dialects

## Italy

**Area:** 116,348 sq mi (301,340 sq km)
**Population:** 62,247,000
**Capital:** Rome, pop. 4,210,000
**Currency:** euro
**Religion:** Roman Catholic
**Languages:** Italian, German, French, Slovene

## Iran

**Area:** 636,371 sq mi (1,648,195 sq km)
**Population:** 83,025,000
**Capital:** Tehran, pop. 8,896,000
**Currency:** Iranian rial
**Religions:** Shiite Muslim, Sunni Muslim
**Languages:** Persian (Farsi), Azeri, Turkic dialects, Kurdish, Gilaki and Mazandarani, Luri, Baluchi, Arabic

## Jamaica

**Area:** 4,244 sq mi (10,991 sq km)
**Population:** 2,812,000
**Capital:** Kingston, pop. 589,000
**Currency:** Jamaican dollar
**Religions:** Protestant, Roman Catholic
**Languages:** English, English patois

## Japan

**Area:** 145,914 sq mi (377,915 sq km)
**Population:** 126,168,000
**Capital:** Tokyo, pop. 37,468,000
**Currency:** yen
**Religions:** Shinto, Buddhist
**Language:** Japanese

## Kazakhstan

**Area:** 1,052,089 sq mi (2,724,900 sq km)
**Population:** 18,745,000
**Capital:** Nur-Sultan, pop. 1,068,000
**Currency:** tenge
**Religions:** Muslim, Russian Orthodox
**Languages:** Kazakh (Qazaq), Russian

## Jordan

**Area:** 34,495 sq mi (89,342 sq km)
**Population:** 10,458,000
**Capital:** Amman, pop. 2,065,000
**Currency:** Jordanian dinar
**Religions:** Sunni Muslim, Christian
**Languages:** Arabic, English

## Kenya

**Area:** 224,081 sq mi (580,367 sq km)
**Population:** 48,398,000
**Capital:** Nairobi, pop. 4,386,000
**Currency:** Kenyan shilling
**Religions:** Protestant, Roman Catholic, Muslim, indigenous beliefs
**Languages:** English, Kiswahili, many indigenous languages

# SNAPSHOT
# Jamaica

Children dance in Kingston, Jamaica, wearing yellow, green, and black—Jamaica's national colors.

● Asia  ● Europe  ● North America  ● **South America**

## Kiribati

**Area:** 313 sq mi (811 sq km)
**Population:** 109,000
**Capital:** Tarawa, pop. 64,000
**Currency:** Australian dollar
**Religions:** Roman Catholic, Protestant
**Languages:** I-Kiribati, English

## Kuwait

**Area:** 6,880 sq mi (17,818 sq km)
**Population:** 2,916,000
**Capital:** Kuwait City, pop. 2,989,000
**Currency:** Kuwaiti dinar
**Religions:** Sunni Muslim, Shiite Muslim, Christian
**Languages:** Arabic, English

## Kosovo

**Area:** 4,203 sq mi (10,887 sq km)
**Population:** 1,908,000
**Capital:** Pristina, pop. 207,062
**Currencies:** euro, Serbian dinar
**Religions:** Muslim, Roman Catholic, Serbian Orthodox
**Languages:** Albanian, Serbian, Bosnian

## Kyrgyzstan

**Area:** 77,201 sq mi (199,951 sq km)
**Population:** 5,849,000
**Capital:** Bishkek, pop. 996,000
**Currency:** som
**Religions:** Muslim, Russian Orthodox
**Languages:** Kyrgyz, Uzbek, Russian

# SNAPSHOT
# Luxembourg

Pretzel from Grevenmacher, Luxembourg

**COLOR KEY** ● Africa ● Australia, New Zealand, and Oceania

## Laos

**Area:** 91,429 sq mi
(236,800 sq km)
**Population:** 7,234,000
**Capital:** Vientiane, pop. 665,000
**Currency:** Lao kip
**Religions:** Buddhist, animist
**Languages:** Lao, French, English,
various ethnic languages

## Libya

**Area:** 679,362 sq mi
(1,759,540 sq km)
**Population:** 6,755,000
**Capital:** Tripoli, pop. 1,158,000
**Currency:** Libyan dinar
**Religions:** Sunni Muslim, Christian
**Languages:** Arabic, Italian, English, Berber

## Latvia

**Area:** 24,938 sq mi
(64,589 sq km)
**Population:** 1,924,000
**Capital:** Riga, pop. 637,000
**Currency:** euro
**Religions:** Lutheran, Orthodox
**Languages:** Latvian, Russian

## Liechtenstein

**Area:** 62 sq mi (160 sq km)
**Population:** 39,000
**Capital:** Vaduz, pop. 5,000
**Currency:** Swiss franc
**Religions:** Roman Catholic, Protestant
**Languages:** German, Italian

## Lebanon

**Area:** 4,015 sq mi (10,400 sq km)
**Population:** 6,100,000
**Capital:** Beirut, pop. 2,385,000
**Currency:** Lebanese pound
**Religions:** Muslim, Christian
**Languages:** Arabic, French, English, Armenian

## Lithuania

**Area:** 25,212 sq mi
(65,300 sq km)
**Population:** 2,793,000
**Capital:** Vilnius, pop. 536,000
**Currency:** euro
**Religions:** Roman Catholic, Russian Orthodox
**Languages:** Lithuanian, Russian, Polish

## Lesotho

**Area:** 11,720 sq mi (30,355 sq km)
**Population:** 1,962,000
**Capital:** Maseru, pop. 202,000
**Currencies:** loti, rand
**Religions:** Protestant, Roman Catholic
**Languages:** Sesotho, English, Zulu, Xhosa

## Luxembourg

**Area:** 998 sq mi (2,586 sq km)
**Population:** 606,000
**Capital:** Luxembourg,
pop. 120,000
**Currency:** euro
**Religion:** Roman Catholic
**Languages:** Luxembourgish,
German, French, Portuguese

## Liberia

**Area:** 43,000 sq mi
(111,369 sq km)
**Population:** 4,810,000
**Capital:** Monrovia,
pop. 1,418,000
**Currency:** Liberian dollar
**Religions:** Christian, Muslim, indigenous beliefs
**Languages:** English, indigenous languages

## Madagascar

**Area:** 226,658 sq mi
(587,041 sq km)
**Population:** 25,684,000
**Capital:** Antananarivo,
pop. 3,058,000
**Currency:** Malagasy ariary
**Religions:** Christian, indigenous beliefs, Muslim
**Languages:** French, Malagasy, English

## Malawi

**Area:** 45,747 sq mi
(118,484 sq km)
**Population:** 19,843,000
**Capital:** Lilongwe, pop. 1,030,000
**Currency:** Malawian kwacha
**Religions:** Christian, Muslim
**Languages:** Chichewa, Chinyanja, Chiyao, Chitumbuka, Chisena, Chilomwe, Chitonga, English

## Malaysia

**Area:** 127,355 sq mi (329,847 sq km)
**Population:** 31,810,000
**Capital:** Kuala Lumpur, pop. 7,564,000
**Currency:** Malaysian ringgit
**Religions:** Muslim, Buddhist, Christian, Hindu
**Languages:** Bahasa Malaysia (Malay), English, Chinese, Tamil, Telugu, Malayalam, Panjabi, Thai

## Maldives

**Area:** 115 sq mi (298 sq km)
**Population:** 392,000
**Capital:** Male, pop. 177,000
**Currency:** rufiyaa
**Religion:** Sunni Muslim
**Languages:** Dhivehi, English

## Mali

**Area:** 478,841 sq mi (1,240,192 sq km)
**Population:** 18,430,000
**Capital:** Bamako, pop. 2,447,000
**Currency:** Communauté Financière Africaine franc
**Religions:** Muslim, Christian, animist
**Languages:** French, Bambara, African languages

## Malta

**Area:** 122 sq mi (316 sq km)
**Population:** 449,000
**Capital:** Valletta, pop. 213,000
**Currency:** euro
**Religion:** Roman Catholic
**Languages:** Maltese, English

## Marshall Islands

**Area:** 70 sq mi (181 sq km)
**Population:** 76,000
**Capital:** Majuro, pop. 31,000
**Currency:** U.S. dollar
**Religions:** Protestant, Roman Catholic, Mormon
**Languages:** Marshallese, English

# 3 cool things about the MARSHALL ISLANDS

1. At just 35 years old, the Marshall Islands is one of the world's youngest nations. The chain of some 1,200 islands and atolls gained its independence from the United States in 1986.

2. There are some 47 sunken ships and 270 airplanes dating back to World War II at the bottom of the Pacific Ocean off the coast of the Marshall Islands. This is a popular spot for scuba divers, who flock to the tropical waters to explore the submerged ships and planes some 100 feet (30 m) below.

3. First debuted in 1946, the bikini is named for the Marshall Islands' Bikini Atoll. The designer of the two-piece bathing suit gave it the unique name as a nod to the ring-shaped reef, which was in the news at the time during World War II.

## Mauritania

**Area:** 397,955 sq mi
(1,030,700 sq km)
**Population:** 3,840,000
**Capital:** Nouakchott, pop. 1,205,000
**Currency:** ouguiya
**Religion:** Muslim
**Languages:** Arabic, Pulaar, Soninke, Wolof, French, Hassaniya

## Mauritius

**Area:** 788 sq mi (2,040 sq km)
**Population:** 1,364,000
**Capital:** Port Louis, pop. 149,000
**Currency:** Mauritius rupee
**Religions:** Hindu, Roman Catholic, Muslim, other Christian
**Languages:** Creole, Bhojpuri, French, English

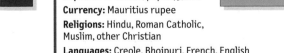

## Mexico

**Area:** 758,449 sq mi
(1,964,375 sq km)
**Population:** 125,959,000
**Capital:** Mexico City,
pop. 21,581,000
**Currency:** Mexican peso
**Religions:** Roman Catholic, Protestant
**Languages:** Spanish, indigenous languages

## The CHIHUAHUA, the WORLD'S SMALLEST DOG, is named for a STATE in MEXICO.

## Micronesia

**Area:** 271 sq mi (702 sq km)
**Population:** 104,000
**Capital:** Palikir, pop. 7,000
**Currency:** U.S. dollar
**Religions:** Roman Catholic, Protestant
**Languages:** English, Chuukese, Kosrean, Pohnpeian, Yapese, other indigenous languages

## Moldova

**Area:** 13,070 sq mi
(33,851 sq km)
**Population:** 3,438,000
**Capital:** Chișinău,
pop. 510,000
**Currency:** Moldovan leu
**Religion:** Eastern Orthodox
**Languages:** Moldovan, Russian, Gagauz

## Monaco

**Area:** 1 sq mi (2 sq km)
**Population:** 38,000
**Capital:** Monaco, pop. 38,000
**Currency:** euro
**Religion:** Roman Catholic
**Languages:** French, English, Italian, Monegasque

## Mongolia

**Area:** 603,908 sq mi
(1,564,116 sq km)
**Population:** 3,103,000
**Capital:** Ulaanbaatar,
pop. 1,520,000
**Currency:** tugrik
**Religions:** Buddhist, Muslim, Shamanist, Christian
**Languages:** Mongolian, Turkic, Russian

## Montenegro

**Area:** 5,333 sq mi
(13,812 sq km)
**Population:** 614,000
**Capital:** Podgorica, pop. 177,000
**Currency:** euro
**Religions:** Orthodox, Muslim, Roman Catholic
**Languages:** Serbian, Montenegrin, Bosnian, Albanian

## Morocco

**Area:** 172,414 sq mi
(446,550 sq km)
**Population:** 34,314,000
**Capital:** Rabat, pop. 1,847,000
**Currency:** Moroccan dirham
**Religion:** Muslim
**Languages:** Arabic, Tamazight, other Berber languages, French

## Mozambique

**Area:** 308,642 sq mi
(799,380 sq km)
**Population:** 27,234,000
**Capital:** Maputo, pop. 1,102,000
**Currency:** Mozambique metical
**Religions:** Christian, Muslim
**Languages:** Emakhuwa, Portuguese, Xichangana, Cisena, Elomwe, Echuwabo, other local languages

## Myanmar (Burma)

**Area:** 261,228 sq mi
(676,578 sq km)
**Population:** 55,623,000
**Capital:** Nay Pyi Taw,
pop. 1,176,000
**Currency:** kyat
**Religions:** Buddhist, Christian, Muslim
**Languages:** Burmese, ethnic languages

## Namibia

**Area:** 318,261 sq mi
(824,292 sq km)
**Population:** 2,533,000
**Capital:** Windhoek, pop. 404,000
**Currencies:** Namibian dollar,
South African rand
**Religion:** Christian
**Languages:** Indigenous languages, Afrikaans, English

## Nepal

**Area:** 56,827 sq mi
(147,181 sq km)
**Population:** 29,718,000
**Capital:** Kathmandu, pop. 1,330,000
**Currency:** Nepalese rupee
**Religions:** Hindu, Buddhist, Muslim, Kirant
**Languages:** Nepali, Maithali, Bhojpuri, Tharu, Tamang, Newar, Magar, Bajjika, Awadhi

## Nauru

**Area:** 8 sq mi (21 sq km)
**Population:** 10,000
**Capital:** Yaren, pop. 1,000
**Currency:** Australian dollar
**Religions:** Protestant, Roman Catholic
**Languages:** Nauruan, English

## Netherlands

**Area:** 16,040 sq mi
(41,543 sq km)
**Population:** 17,151,000
**Capitals:** Amsterdam, pop. 1,132,000;
The Hague, pop. 685,000
**Currency:** euro
**Religions:** Roman Catholic, Protestant, Muslim
**Languages:** Dutch, Frisian

# SNAPSHOT
# Norway

The brightly painted buildings along the Nidelva River in Trondheim, Norway, date back to the 18th century.

**COLOR KEY** ● Africa ● Australia, New Zealand, and Oceania

## New Zealand

**Area:** 103,799 sq mi
(268,838 sq km)
**Population:** 4,546,000
**Capital:** Wellington, pop. 411,000
**Currency:** New Zealand dollar
**Religions:** Protestant, Roman Catholic,
Hindu, Buddhist, Maori Christian
**Languages:** English, Maori

## Nicaragua

**Area:** 50,336 sq mi
(130,370 sq km)
**Population:** 6,085,000
**Capital:** Managua, pop. 1,048,000
**Currency:** córdoba oro
**Religions:** Roman Catholic, Protestant
**Languages:** Spanish, Miskito

## Niger

**Area:** 489,191 sq mi (1,267,000 sq km)
**Population:** 19,866,000
**Capital:** Niamey, pop. 1,214,000
**Currency:** Communauté
Financière Africaine franc
**Religion:** Muslim
**Languages:** French, Hausa, Djerma

## Nigeria

**Area:** 356,669 sq mi
(923,768 sq km)
**Population:** 203,453,000
**Capital:** Abuja, pop. 2,919,000
**Currency:** naira
**Religions:** Muslim, Christian, indigenous beliefs
**Languages:** English, Hausa, Yoruba, Igbo (Ibo), Fulani

## North Korea

**Area:** 46,540 sq mi
(120,538 sq km)
**Population:** 25,381,000
**Capital:** Pyongyang,
pop. 3,038,000
**Currency:** North Korean won
**Religions:** Buddhist, Confucianist, some Christian
and syncretic Chondogyo
**Language:** Korean

## North Macedonia

**Area:** 9,928 sq mi
(25,713 sq km)
**Population:** 2,119,000
**Capital:** Skopje, pop. 584,000
**Currency:** denar
**Religions:** Macedonian Orthodox, Muslim
**Languages:** Macedonian, Albanian, Turkish, Romany,
Aromanian, Serbian

## Norway

**Area:** 125,021 sq mi
(323,802 sq km)
**Population:** 5,372,000
**Capital:** Oslo, pop. 1,012,000
**Currency:** Norwegian krone
**Religion:** Lutheran
**Languages:** Bokmal Norwegian, Nynorsk
Norwegian, Sami, Finnish

## Oman

**Area:** 119,499 sq mi
(309,500 sq km)
**Population:** 3,494,000
**Capital:** Muscat, pop. 1,447,000
**Currency:** Omani rial
**Religions:** Muslim, Christian, Hindu
**Languages:** Arabic, English, Baluchi,
Urdu, Indian dialects

## Pakistan

**Area:** 307,374 sq mi
(796,095 sq km)
**Population:** 207,863,000
**Capital:** Islamabad, pop. 1,061,000
**Currency:** Pakistani rupee
**Religions:** Sunni Muslim, Shiite Muslim
**Languages:** Punjabi, Sindhi, Saraiki, Pashto, Urdu,
Baluchi, Hindko, Brahui, English, Burushaski

## Palau

**Area:** 177 sq mi (459 sq km)
**Population:** 22,000
**Capital:** Melekeok
(on Babelthuap), pop. 299
**Currency:** U.S. dollar
**Religions:** Roman Catholic, Protestant, Modekngei
**Languages:** Palauan, Filipino, English, Chinese

## Panama

**Area:** 29,120 sq mi (75,420 sq km)
**Population:** 3,801,000
**Capital:** Panama City, pop. 1,783,000
**Currency:** U.S. dollar
**Religions:** Roman Catholic, Protestant
**Languages:** Spanish, English

## Poland

**Area:** 120,728 sq mi (312,685 sq km)
**Population:** 38,421,000
**Capital:** Warsaw, pop. 1,768,000
**Currency:** zloty
**Religion:** Roman Catholic
**Language:** Polish

## Papua New Guinea

**Area:** 178,703 sq mi (462,840 sq km)
**Population:** 7,027,000
**Capital:** Port Moresby, pop. 367,000
**Currency:** kina
**Religions:** Protestant, Roman Catholic
**Languages:** Tok Pisin, English, Hiri Motu, other indigenous languages

## Portugal

**Area:** 35,556 sq mi (92,090 sq km)
**Population:** 10,355,000
**Capital:** Lisbon, pop. 2,927,000
**Currency:** euro
**Religion:** Roman Catholic
**Languages:** Portuguese, Mirandese

## Paraguay

**Area:** 157,048 sq mi (406,752 sq km)
**Population:** 7,026,000
**Capital:** Asunción, pop. 3,222,000
**Currency:** guaraní
**Religions:** Roman Catholic, Protestant
**Languages:** Spanish, Guarani

## Qatar

**Area:** 4,473 sq mi (11,586 sq km)
**Population:** 2,364,000
**Capital:** Doha, pop. 633,000
**Currency:** Qatari rial
**Religions:** Muslim, Christian
**Languages:** Arabic, English

## Peru

**Area:** 496,224 sq mi (1,285,216 sq km)
**Population:** 31,331,000
**Capital:** Lima, pop. 10,391,000
**Currency:** sol
**Religions:** Roman Catholic, Evangelical
**Languages:** Spanish, Quechua, Aymara, Ashaninka, other indigenous languages

## Romania

**Area:** 92,043 sq mi (238,391 sq km)
**Population:** 21,457,000
**Capital:** Bucharest, pop. 1,821,000
**Currency:** Romanian leu
**Religions:** Eastern Orthodox, Protestant, Roman Catholic
**Languages:** Romanian, Hungarian, Romany

## Philippines

**Area:** 115,831 sq mi (300,000 sq km)
**Population:** 105,893,000
**Capital:** Manila, pop. 13,482,000
**Currency:** Philippine peso
**Religions:** Roman Catholic, Protestant, Muslim
**Languages:** Filipino (Tagalog), English

## Russia

**Area:** 6,601,665 sq mi (17,098,242 sq km)
**Population:** 142,123,000
**Capital:** Moscow, pop. 12,410,000
**Currency:** Russian ruble
**Religions:** Russian Orthodox, Muslim
**Languages:** Russian, Tatar, other local languages
*Note: Russia is in both Europe and Asia, but its capital is in Europe, so it is classified here as a European country.*

## Rwanda

**Area:** 10,169 sq mi
(26,338 sq km)
**Population:** 12,187,000
**Capital:** Kigali, pop. 1,058,000
**Currency:** Rwandan franc
**Religions:** Protestant, Roman Catholic, Muslim
**Languages:** Kinyarwanda, French, English,
Kiswahili (Swahili)

## San Marino

**Area:** 24 sq mi (61 sq km)
**Population:** 34,000
**Capital:** San Marino, pop. 4,000
**Currency:** euro
**Religion:** Roman Catholic
**Language:** Italian

## Samoa

**Area:** 1,093 sq mi
(2,831 sq km)
**Population:** 201,000
**Capital:** Apia, pop. 36,000
**Currency:** tala
**Religions:** Protestant, Roman Catholic, Mormon
**Languages:** Samoan (Polynesian), English

## Sao Tome and Principe

**Area:** 372 sq mi (964 sq km)
**Population:** 204,000
**Capital:** São Tomé,
pop. 80,000
**Currency:** dobra
**Religions:** Roman Catholic, Protestant
**Languages:** Portuguese, Forro

# SNAPSHOT
# Papua New Guinea

Children ride in a homemade canoe in
Kavieng, New Ireland, Papua New Guinea.

● Asia   ● Europe   ● North America   ● South America

## Saudi Arabia

**Area:** 830,000 sq mi
(2,149,690 sq km)
**Population:** 33,091,000
**Capital:** Riyadh, pop. 6,907,000
**Currency:** Saudi riyal
**Religion:** Muslim
**Language:** Arabic

## Singapore

**Area:** 269 sq mi (697 sq km)
**Population:** 5,996,000
**Capital:** Singapore,
pop. 5,792,000
**Currency:** Singapore dollar
**Religions:** Buddhist, Christian, Muslim, Taoist, Hindu
**Languages:** English, Mandarin, Malay, Tamil

## Senegal

**Area:** 75,955 sq mi
(196,722 sq km)
**Population:** 15,021,000
**Capital:** Dakar, pop. 2,978,000
**Currency:** Communauté
Financière Africaine franc
**Religions:** Muslim, Roman Catholic
**Languages:** French, Wolof, Pulaar, Jola, Mandinka

## Slovakia

**Area:** 18,933 sq mi
(49,035 sq km)
**Population:** 5,445,000
**Capital:** Bratislava, pop. 430,000
**Currency:** euro
**Religions:** Roman Catholic, Protestant, Greek Catholic
**Languages:** Slovak, Hungarian, Romany

## Serbia

**Area:** 29,913 sq mi (77,474 sq km)
**Population:** 7,078,000
**Capital:** Belgrade, pop. 1,389,000
**Currency:** Serbian dinar
**Religions:** Serbian Orthodox,
Roman Catholic, Protestant
**Languages:** Serbian, Hungarian, Bosniak, Romany

## Slovenia

**Area:** 7,827 sq mi
(20,273 sq km)
**Population:** 2,102,000
**Capital:** Ljubljana,
pop. 286,000
**Currency:** euro
**Religions:** Roman Catholic, Muslim, Orthodox
**Languages:** Slovene, Serbo-Croatian, Italian, Hungarian

## Seychelles

**Area:** 176 sq mi (455 sq km)
**Population:** 95,000
**Capital:** Victoria, pop. 28,000
**Currency:** Seychelles rupee
**Religions:** Roman Catholic, Protestant,
Hindu, Muslim
**Languages:** Seychellois Creole, English, French

# 3 cool things about SLOVENIA

1. Some 54 percent of Slovenia's land is forest. Kočevje, a town that is made up of about 90 percent forest, is also known as Slovenia's Bear Forest, as it's home to much of the country's 500-strong brown bear population.

2. There are about 10,000 caves in Slovenia, including Postojna Cave, which has 15 miles (24 km) of passages, galleries, and chambers that started forming some three million years ago.

3. A 1,181-foot (360-m)-tall chimney soars above the city of Trbovlje, Slovenia. The tallest chimney in Europe, it's part of the old Trbovlje Power Station and is a destination for climbers, who scale the more than 50-year-old tower.

## Sierra Leone

**Area:** 27,699 sq mi (71,740 sq km)
**Population:** 6,312,000
**Capital:** Freetown, pop. 1,136,000
**Currency:** leone
**Religions:** Muslim, Christian
**Languages:** English, Mende, Temne, Krio

**COLOR KEY** ● Africa ● Australia, New Zealand, and Oceania

## Solomon Islands

**Area:** 11,157 sq mi
(28,896 sq km)
**Population:** 660,000
**Capital:** Honiara, pop. 82,000
**Currency:** Solomon Islands dollar
**Religions:** Protestant, Roman Catholic
**Languages:** Melanesian pidgin, English, indigenous languages

## Somalia

**Area:** 246,201 sq mi
(637,657 sq km)
**Population:** 11,259,000
**Capital:** Mogadishu, pop. 2,082,000
**Currency:** Somali shilling
**Religion:** Sunni Muslim
**Languages:** Somali, Arabic, Italian, English

## South Africa

**Area:** 470,693 sq mi (1,219,090 sq km)
**Population:** 55,380,000
**Capitals:** Pretoria (Tshwane),
pop. 2,378,000; Cape Town, pop.
4,430,000; Bloemfontein, pop. 465,000
**Currency:** rand
**Religions:** Christian, indigenous religions
**Languages:** isiZulu, isiXhosa, Afrikaans, Sepedi, Setswana, English, Sesotho, Xitsonga, siSwati, Tshivenda isiNdebele

## South Korea

**Area:** 38,502 sq mi
(99,720 sq km)
**Population:** 51,418,000
**Capital:** Seoul, pop. 9,963,000
**Currency:** won
**Religions:** Christian, Buddhist
**Languages:** Korean, English

## South Sudan

**Area:** 248,777 sq mi
(644,329 sq km)
**Population:** 10,205,000
**Capital:** Juba, pop. 369,000
**Currency:** South Sudanese pound
**Religions:** animist, Christian
**Languages:** English, Arabic, Dinke, Nuer, Bari, Zande, Shilluk

## Spain

**Area:** 195,124 sq mi (505,370 sq km)
**Population:** 49,331,000
**Capital:** Madrid, pop. 6,497,000
**Currency:** euro
**Religion:** Roman Catholic
**Languages:** Castilian Spanish, Catalan, Galician, Basque

## Sri Lanka

**Area:** 25,332 sq mi
(65,610 sq km)
**Population:** 22,577,000
**Capitals:** Colombo, pop. 600,000;
Sri Jayewardenepura Kotte, pop. 103,000
**Currency:** Sri Lankan rupee
**Religions:** Buddhist, Muslim, Hindu, Christian
**Languages:** Sinhala, Tamil

## St. Kitts and Nevis

**Area:** 101 sq mi (261 sq km)
**Population:** 53,000
**Capital:** Basseterre, pop. 14,000
**Currency:** East Caribbean dollar
**Religions:** Protestant, Roman Catholic
**Language:** English

## St. Lucia

**Area:** 238 sq mi (616 sq km)
**Population:** 166,000
**Capital:** Castries,
pop. 22,000
**Currency:** East Caribbean dollar
**Religions:** Roman Catholic, Protestant, Rastafarian
**Languages:** English, French patois

## St. Vincent and the Grenadines

**Area:** 150 sq mi (389 sq km)
**Population:** 102,000
**Capital:** Kingstown, pop. 27,000
**Currency:** East Caribbean dollar
**Religions:** Protestant, Roman Catholic
**Languages:** English, Vincentian Creole English, French patois

## Sudan

**Area:** 718,723 sq mi (1,861,484 sq km)
**Population:** 43,121,000
**Capital:** Khartoum, pop. 5,534,000
**Currency:** Sudanese pound
**Religions:** Sunni Muslim, Christian
**Languages:** Arabic, English, Nubian, Ta BedawieFur

## Syria

**Area:** 71,498 sq mi (185,180 sq km)
**Population:** 19,454,000
**Capital:** Damascus, pop. 2,320,000
**Currency:** Syrian pound
**Religions:** Sunni Muslim, other Muslim (includes Alawite), Christian, Druze
**Languages:** Arabic, Kurdish, Armenian, Aramaic, Circassian, French

## Suriname

**Area:** 63,251 sq mi (163,820 sq km)
**Population:** 598,000
**Capital:** Paramaribo, pop. 239,000
**Currency:** Suriname dollar
**Religions:** Protestant, Hindu, Roman Catholic, Muslim
**Languages:** Dutch, English, Sranang Tongo, Caribbean Hindustani, Javanese

## Tajikistan

**Area:** 55,637 sq mi (144,100 sq km)
**Population:** 8,605,000
**Capital:** Dushanbe, pop. 873,000
**Currency:** somoni
**Religions:** Sunni Muslim, Shia Muslim
**Languages:** Tajik, Uzbek

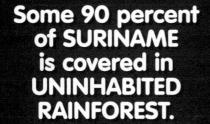

**Some 90 percent of SURINAME is covered in UNINHABITED RAINFOREST.**

## Tanzania

**Area:** 365,754 sq mi (947,300 sq km)
**Population:** 55,451,000
**Capitals:** Dar es Salaam, pop. 6,048,000; Dodoma, pop. 262,000
**Currency:** Tanzanian shilling
**Religions:** Christian, Muslim, indigenous beliefs
**Languages:** Kiswahili (Swahili), Kiunguja (Swahili in Zanzibar), English, Arabic, local languages

## Sweden

**Area:** 173,860 sq mi (450,295 sq km)
**Population:** 10,041,000
**Capital:** Stockholm, pop. 1,583,000
**Currency:** Swedish krona
**Religion:** Lutheran
**Languages:** Swedish, Sami, Finnish

**More than 1.5 MILLION WILDEBEESTS migrate through TANZANIA each year.**

## Switzerland

**Area:** 15,937 sq mi (41,277 sq km)
**Population:** 8,293,000
**Capital:** Bern, pop. 422,000
**Currency:** Swiss franc
**Religions:** Roman Catholic, Protestant, Muslim
**Languages:** German, French, Italian, English, Romansh

## Thailand

**Area:** 198,117 sq mi (513,120 sq km)
**Population:** 68,616,000
**Capital:** Bangkok, pop. 10,156,000
**Currency:** baht
**Religions:** Buddhist, Muslim, Christian
**Languages:** Thai, English, ethnic dialects

**COLOR KEY** ● Africa ● Australia, New Zealand, and Oceania

## Timor-Leste (East Timor)

**Area:** 5,743 sq mi
(14,874 sq km)
**Population:** 1,322,000
**Capital:** Dîli, pop. 281,000
**Currency:** U.S. dollar
**Religions:** Roman Catholic, Protestant
**Languages:** Tetum, Portuguese, Indonesian, English

## Turkey

**Area:** 302,535 sq mi
(783,562 sq km)
**Population:** 81,257,000
**Capital:** Ankara, pop. 4,919,000
**Currency:** Turkish lira
**Religion:** Muslim
**Languages:** Turkish, Kurdish,
other minority languages

## Togo

**Area:** 21,925 sq mi (56,785 sq km)
**Population:** 8,176,000
**Capital:** Lomé, pop. 1,746,000
**Currency:** Communauté
Financière Africaine franc
**Religions:** indigenous beliefs, Christian, Muslim
**Languages:** French, Ewe, Mina, Kabye, Dagomba

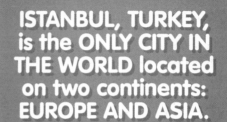

**ISTANBUL, TURKEY, is the ONLY CITY IN THE WORLD located on two continents: EUROPE AND ASIA.**

## Tonga

**Area:** 288 sq mi (747 sq km)
**Population:** 106,000
**Capital:** Nukuʻalofa
(on Tongatapu), pop. 23,000
**Currency:** paʻanga
**Religions:** Protestant, Church of Latter Day Saints,
Roman Catholic
**Languages:** Tongan, English

## Turkmenistan

**Area:** 188,456 sq mi
(488,100 sq km)
**Population:** 5,411,000
**Capital:** Ashgabat, pop. 810,000
**Currency:** Turkmenistan new manat
**Religions:** Muslim, Eastern Orthodox
**Languages:** Turkmen, Russian, Uzbek

## Trinidad and Tobago

**Area:** 1,980 sq mi (5,128 sq km)
**Population:** 1,216,000
**Capital:** Port of Spain
(on Trinidad), pop. 544,000
**Currency:** Trinidad and Tobago dollar
**Religions:** Protestant, Roman Catholic, Hindu, Muslim
**Languages:** English, Creole, Caribbean Hindustani

## Tuvalu

**Area:** 10 sq mi (26 sq km)
**Population:** 11,000
**Capital:** Funafuti
(on Funafuti Atoll), pop. 7,000
**Currency:** Australian dollar
**Religions:** Protestant, Baha'i
**Languages:** Tuvaluan, English, Samoan, Kiribati

## Tunisia

**Area:** 63,170 sq mi
(163,610 sq km)
**Population:** 11,516,000
**Capital:** Tunis, pop. 2,291,000
**Currency:** Tunisian dinar
**Religion:** Muslim
**Languages:** Arabic, French, Berber (Tamazight)

## Uganda

**Area:** 93,065 sq mi
(241,038 sq km)
**Population:** 40,854,000
**Capital:** Kampala, pop. 2,986,000
**Currency:** Ugandan shilling
**Religions:** Protestant, Roman Catholic, Muslim
**Languages:** English, Ganda (Luganda), other local
languages, Swahili, Arabic

## Ukraine

**Area:** 233,032 sq mi
(603,550 sq km)
**Population:** 43,952,000
**Capital:** Kiev, pop. 2,957,000
**Currency:** hryvnia
**Religions:** Ukrainian Orthodox, Ukrainian Greek Catholic, Roman Catholic, Protestant, Jewish
**Languages:** Ukrainian, Russian

## United Arab Emirates

**Area:** 32,278 sq mi
(83,600 sq km)
**Population:** 9,701,000
**Capital:** Abu Dhabi,
pop. 1,420,000
**Currency:** United Arab Emirates dirham
**Religions:** Muslim, Christian, Hindu
**Languages:** Arabic, Persian, English, Hindi, Urdu

Some 350 feet (105 m) underground, the Arsenalna Metro Station in KIEV, UKRAINE, is the WORLD'S DEEPEST SUBWAY STOP.

## United Kingdom

**Area:** 94,058 sq mi
(243,610 sq km)
**Population:** 65,105,000
**Capital:** London, pop. 9,046,000
**Currency:** pound sterling
**Religions:** Anglican, Roman Catholic, Presbyterian, Methodist, Muslim, Hindu
**Languages:** English, Scottish Gaelic, Welsh, Irish

SNAPSHOT Vietnam

Outdoor market in the streets of Hoi An, Vietnam

**COLOR KEY** ● Africa ● Australia, New Zealand, and Oceania

## United States

**Area:** 3,796,741 sq mi (9,833,517 sq km)
**Population:** 329,256,000
**Capital:** Washington, D.C., pop. 5,207,000
**Currency:** U.S. dollar
**Religions:** Protestant, Roman Catholic, Jewish
**Languages:** English, Spanish, Native American languages

## Uruguay

**Area:** 68,037 sq mi (176,215 sq km)
**Population:** 3,369,000
**Capital:** Montevideo, pop. 1,737,000
**Currency:** Uruguayan peso
**Religions:** Roman Catholic, Protestant
**Language:** Spanish

## Uzbekistan

**Area:** 172,742 sq mi (447,400 sq km)
**Population:** 30,024,000
**Capital:** Tashkent, pop. 2,464,000
**Currency:** Uzbekistan sum
**Religions:** Muslim (mostly Sunni), Eastern Orthodox
**Languages:** Uzbek, Russian, Tajik

## Vanuatu

**Area:** 4,706 sq mi (12,189 sq km)
**Population:** 288,000
**Capital:** Port Vila, pop. 53,000
**Currency:** Vatu
**Religions:** Protestant, Roman Catholic, other indigenous beliefs
**Languages:** Bislama, English, French, local languages

## Vatican City

**Area:** .17 sq mi (.44 sq km)
**Population:** 1,000
**Capital:** Vatican City, pop. 1,000
**Currency:** euro
**Religion:** Roman Catholic
**Languages:** Italian, Latin, French

## Venezuela

**Area:** 352,144 sq mi (912,050 sq km)
**Population:** 31,689,000
**Capital:** Caracas, pop. 2,935,000
**Currency:** bolívar soberano
**Religion:** Roman Catholic
**Languages:** Spanish, numerous indigenous dialects

## Vietnam

**Area:** 127,881 sq mi (331,210 sq km)
**Population:** 97,040,000
**Capital:** Hanoi, pop. 1,064,000
**Currency:** dong
**Religions:** Buddhist, Roman Catholic, Hoa Hao, Cao Dai, Protestant, Muslim
**Languages:** Vietnamese, English, French, Chinese, Khmer

## Yemen

**Area:** 203,850 sq mi (527,968 sq km)
**Population:** 28,667,000
**Capital:** Sanaa, pop. 2,779,000
**Currency:** Yemeni rial
**Religion:** Muslim
**Language:** Arabic

## Zambia

**Area:** 290,587 sq mi (752,618 sq km)
**Population:** 16,445,000
**Capital:** Lusaka, pop. 2,524,000
**Currency:** Zambian kwacha
**Religions:** Protestant, Roman Catholic
**Languages:** Bemba, Nyanja,Tonga, Lozi, Chewa, Nsenga, Tumbuka, English

## Zimbabwe

**Area:** 150,872 sq mi (390,757 sq km)
**Population:** 14,030,000
**Capital:** Harare, pop. 1,515,000
**Currency:** Zimbabwe dollar
**Religions:** Protestant, Roman Catholic, indigenous beliefs
**Languages:** Shona, Ndebele, English

# THE POLITICAL UNITED STATES

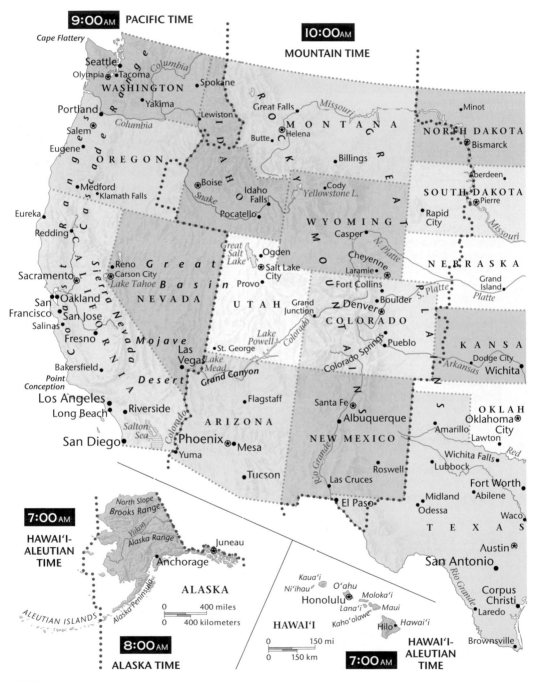

**9:00** AM  PACIFIC TIME

**10:00** AM  MOUNTAIN TIME

Cape Flattery

Seattle
Olympia · Tacoma
WASHINGTON · Spokane
· Yakima
Portland
Columbia
Salem
Eugene
OREGON
Medford · Klamath Falls
Lewiston
IDAHO
Snake
· Boise
Idaho Falls
Pocatello

Great Falls
Missouri
MONTANA
Butte · Helena
Billings
Cody
Yellowstone L.

Minot
NORTH DAKOTA
· Bismarck

Aberdeen
SOUTH DAKOTA
· Pierre
Rapid City
Missouri

Eureka
Redding

WYOMING
Casper
N. Platte
Cheyenne
Laramie
Fort Collins
S. Platte
NEBRASKA
Grand Island
Platte

Reno · Carson City
Great
Lake Tahoe
Basin
NEVADA
Sacramento
San Oakland
Francisco San Jose
Salinas
Fresno
Bakersfield
Point Conception
Los Angeles
Long Beach
San Diego

Sierra Nevada
Great Salt Lake
Ogden
· Salt Lake City
Provo
UTAH
Lake Powell
Colorado
Grand Junction
COLORADO
Denver · Boulder
Colorado Springs · Pueblo
KANSA
Dodge City
Arkansas
Wichita

Mojave
Las Vegas
Lake Mead
Desert
Grand Canyon
St. George
Flagstaff
ARIZONA
Phoenix · Mesa
Yuma
Tucson

Salton Sea
Colorado
Riverside

Santa Fe
Albuquerque
NEW MEXICO
Las Cruces
Rio Grande
El Paso
Roswell

OKLAH
Oklahoma City
Amarillo · Lawton
Wichita Falls
Red
Lubbock
Fort Worth
Midland · Abilene
Odessa
Waco
TEXAS
Austin
San Antonio
Rio Grande
Corpus Christi
Laredo
Brownsville

**7:00** AM
HAWAI'I-ALEUTIAN TIME

North Slope
Brooks Range
Yukon
Alaska Range
Juneau
Anchorage
ALASKA
ALEUTIAN ISLANDS
Alaska Peninsula

0     400 miles
0     400 kilometers

**8:00** AM
ALASKA TIME

Kaua'i
Ni'ihau
O'ahu
Moloka'i
Honolulu
Lana'i Maui
HAWAI'I
Kaho'olawe
Hilo Hawai'i

0     150 mi
0     150 km

**7:00** AM
HAWAI'I-ALEUTIAN TIME

The United States is made up of 50 states joined like a giant quilt. Each is unique, but together they make a national fabric held together by a constitution and a federal government. State boundaries, outlined in dotted lines on the map, set apart internal political units within the country. The national capital—Washington, D.C.—is marked by a star in a double circle. The capital of each state is marked by a star in a single circle.

**11:00 AM**
**CENTRAL TIME**

**12:00 NOON**
**EASTERN TIME**

TIME ZONES: Earth is divided into 24 time zones, each about 15 degrees of longitude wide, reflecting the distance Earth turns from west to east each hour. The U.S. is divided into six time zones, indicated by red dotted lines on the map.

# THE PHYSICAL UNITED STATES

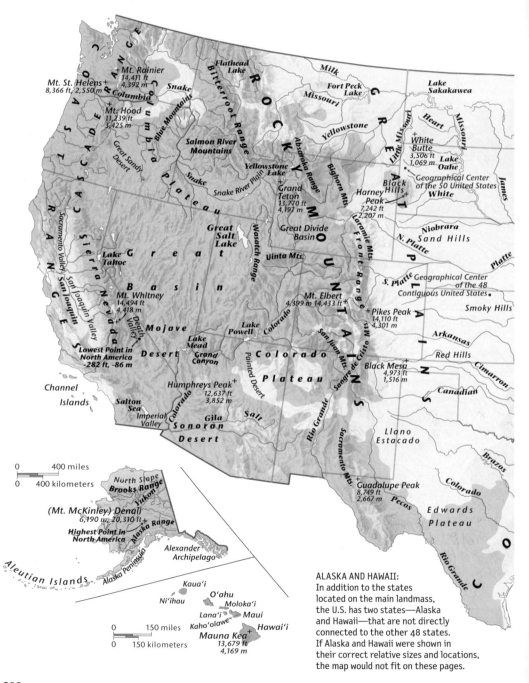

Mt. Rainier
14,411 ft
4,392 m

Mt. St. Helens
8,366 ft, 2,550 m

Columbia

Mt. Hood
11,239 ft
3,425 m

CASCADE RANGE

Columbia Plateau

Great Sandy Desert

Snake

Bitterroot Range

Blue Mountains

Flathead Lake

ROCKY

Salmon River Mountains

Snake River Plain

Snake

Yellowstone Lake

Absaroka Range

Grand Teton
13,770 ft
4,197 m

MOUNTAINS

Bighorn Mts.

Milk

Missouri

Fort Peck Lake

Yellowstone

Little Missouri

Lake Sakakawea

Heart

Missouri

White Butte
3,506 ft
1,069 m

Lake Oahe

Geographical Center of the 50 United States

James

White

Great Salt Lake

Wasatch Range

Uinta Mts.

Great Divide Basin

Front Range

Harney Peak
7,242 ft
2,207 m

Black Hills

Laramie Mts.

Niobrara

N. Platte

Sand Hills

GREAT

Sierra Nevada

Sacramento Valley

San Joaquin

San Joaquin Valley

Lake Tahoe

Great

Basin

Mojave

Death Valley

Mt. Whitney
14,494 ft
4,418 m

Lowest Point in North America
-282 ft, -86 m

Desert

Lake Mead

Grand Canyon

Lake Powell

Colorado

Painted Desert

Colorado Plateau

Mt. Elbert
4,399 m 14,433 ft

Pikes Peak
14,110 ft
4,301 m

San Juan Mts.

Sangre de Cristo Mts.

S. Platte

Geographical Center of the 48 Contiguous United States.

Smoky Hills

Arkansas

Red Hills

Platte

PLAINS

Channel Islands

Salton Sea

Imperial Valley

Humphreys Peak
12,637 ft
3,852 m

Colorado

Gila

Sonoran Desert

Salt

Rio Grande

Black Mesa
4,973 ft
1,516 m

Canadian

Cimarron

Llano Estacado

0    400 miles
0    400 kilometers

North Slope
Brooks Range

Yukon

(Mt. McKinley) Denali
6,190 m, 20,310 ft

Highest Point in North America

Alaska Range

Alexander Archipelago

Aleutian Islands

Alaska Peninsula

Guadalupe Peak
8,749 ft
2,667 m

Pecos

Edwards Plateau

Brazos

Colorado

Sacramento Mts.

Rio Grande

Kaua'i

Ni'ihau

O'ahu

Moloka'i

Lana'i    Maui

Kaho'olawe

Mauna Kea
13,679 ft
4,169 m

Hawai'i

0    150 miles
0    150 kilometers

**ALASKA AND HAWAII:**
In addition to the states located on the main landmass, the U.S. has two states—Alaska and Hawaii—that are not directly connected to the other 48 states. If Alaska and Hawaii were shown in their correct relative sizes and locations, the map would not fit on these pages.

Stretching from the Atlantic Ocean in the east to the Pacific Ocean in the west, the United States is the third largest country (by area) in the world. Its physical diversity ranges from mountains to fertile plains and dry deserts. Shading on the map indicates changes in elevation, while colors show different vegetation patterns.

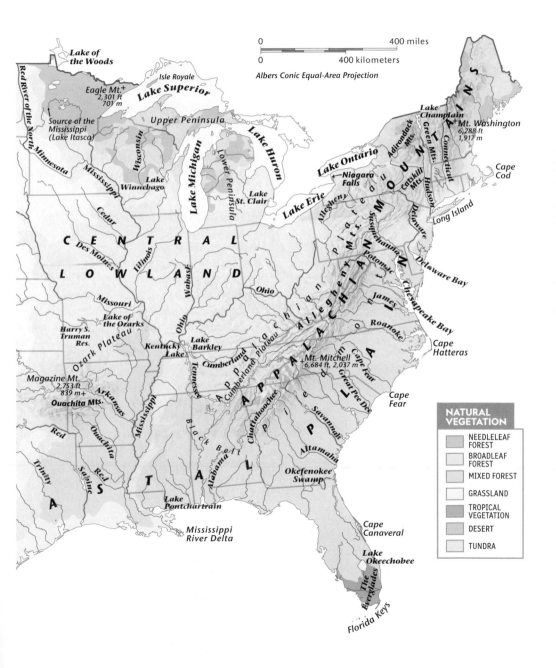

0                400 miles

0                400 kilometers

*Albers Conic Equal-Area Projection*

Lake of the Woods

Isle Royale

Eagle Mt.
2,301 ft
701 m

Lake Superior

Red River of the North

Source of the Mississippi (Lake Itasca)

Upper Peninsula

Lake Champlain

Mt. Washington
6,288 ft
1,917 m

Minnesota

Wisconsin

Lake Michigan

Lower Peninsula

Lake Huron

Lake Ontario

Adirondack Mts.

Green Mts.

MOUNTAINS

Connecticut

Cape Cod

Mississippi

Cedar

Lake Winnebago

Lake St. Clair

Lake Erie

Niagara Falls

Allegheny

Catskill Mts.

Hudson

Delaware

Long Island

CENTRAL

Des Moines

Illinois

Wabash

Ohio

Appalachian Plateau

Susquehanna

Potomac

Delaware Bay

LOWLAND

Missouri

Lake of the Ozarks

Kentucky Lake

Lake Barkley

Cumberland

Ohio

Tennessee

Appalachian

APPALACHIAN

Cumberland Plateau

James

Chesapeake Bay

Roanoke

Cape Hatteras

Harry S. Truman Res.

Ozark Plateau

Mt. Mitchell
6,684 ft, 2,037 m

Cape Fear

Great Pee Dee

Magazine Mt.
2,753 ft
839 m

Arkansas

Ouachita Mts.

Chattahoochee

Black Belt

MOUNTAINS

Cape Fear

Red

Ouachita

Mississippi

Alabama

Savannah

Altamaha

Trinity

Sabine

Red

COASTAL

Okefenokee Swamp

Cape Canaveral

Lake Pontchartrain

Mississippi River Delta

Lake Okeechobee

The Everglades

Florida Keys

## NATURAL VEGETATION

- NEEDLELEAF FOREST
- BROADLEAF FOREST
- MIXED FOREST
- GRASSLAND
- TROPICAL VEGETATION
- DESERT
- TUNDRA

# THE STATES

**From sea to shining sea,** the United States of America is a nation of diversity. In the 244 years since its creation, the nation has grown to become home to a wide range of peoples, industries, and cultures. The following pages present a general overview of all 50 states in the U.S.

The country is generally divided into five large regions: the Northeast, the Southeast, the Midwest, the Southwest, and the West. Though loosely defined, these zones tend to share important similarities, including climate, history, and geography. The color key below provides a guide to which states are in each region.

The flag of each state and highlights of demography and industry are also included. These details offer a brief overview of each state.

In addition, each state's official flower and bird are identified.

**Color Key by Region**

## Alabama

**Nickname:** Heart of Dixie
**Area:** 52,419 sq mi (135,765 sq km)
**Population:** 4,887,871
**Capital:** Montgomery; population 198,218
**Statehood:** December 14, 1819; 22nd state
**State flower/bird:** Camellia/northern flicker

## Alaska

**Nickname:** Last Frontier
**Area:** 663,267 sq mi (1,717,854 sq km)
**Population:** 737,438
**Capital:** Juneau; population 32,113
**Statehood:** January 3, 1959; 49th state
**State flower/bird:** Forget-me-not/willow ptarmigan

## Arizona

**Nickname:** Grand Canyon State
**Area:** 113,998 sq mi (295,254 sq km)
**Population:** 7,171,646
**Capital:** Phoenix; population 1,660,272
**Statehood:** February 14, 1912; 48th state
**State flower/bird:** Saguaro cactus blossom/cactus wren

## Arkansas

**Nickname:** Natural State
**Area:** 53,179 sq mi (137,732 sq km)
**Population:** 3,013,825
**Capital:** Little Rock; population 197,881
**Statehood:** June 15, 1836; 25th state
**State flower/bird:** Apple blossom/northern mockingbird

## California

**Nickname:** Golden State
**Area:** 163,696 sq mi (423,970 sq km)
**Population:** 39,557,045
**Capital:** Sacramento; population 508,529
**Statehood:** September 9, 1850; 31st state
**State flower/bird:** California poppy/California quail

## Colorado

**Nickname:** Centennial State
**Area:** 104,094 sq mi (269,601 sq km)
**Population:** 5,695,564
**Capital:** Denver; population 716,492
**Statehood:** August 1, 1876; 38th state
**State flower/bird:** Rocky Mountain columbine/lark bunting

**A town in Colorado hosts a FRUITCAKE TOSS COMPETITION each January.**

**COLOR KEY** ● Northeast ● Southeast

## Connecticut

**Nickname:** Constitution State
**Area:** 5,543 sq mi (14,357 sq km)
**Population:** 3,572,665
**Capital:** Hartford; population 122,587
**Statehood:** January 9, 1788; 5th state
**State flower/bird:** Mountain laurel/
American robin

## Hawaii

**Nickname:** Aloha State
**Area:** 10,931 sq mi (28,311 sq km)
**Population:** 1,420,491
**Capital:** Honolulu; population 980,080
**Statehood:** August 21, 1959; 50th state
**State flower/bird:** Pua aloalo/
Nene (Hawaiian goose)

## Delaware

**Nickname:** First State
**Area:** 2,489 sq mi (6,447 sq km)
**Population:** 967,171
**Capital:** Dover; population 38,079
**Statehood:** December 7, 1787; 1st state
**State flower/bird:** Peach blossom/
blue hen chicken

## Idaho

**Nickname:** Gem State
**Area:** 83,570 sq mi (216,446 sq km)
**Population:** 1,754,208
**Capital:** Boise; population 228,790
**Statehood:** July 3, 1890; 43rd state
**State flower/bird:** Syringa (mock orange)/
mountain bluebird

## Florida

**Nickname:** Sunshine State
**Area:** 65,755 sq mi (170,304 sq km)
**Population:** 21,299,325
**Capital:** Tallahassee; population 193,551
**Statehood:** March 3, 1845; 27th state
**State flower/bird:** Orange blossom/
northern mockingbird

## Illinois

**Nickname:** Prairie State
**Area:** 57,914 sq mi (149,998 sq km)
**Population:** 12,741,080
**Capital:** Springfield; population 114,694
**Statehood:** December 3, 1818; 21st state
**State flower/bird:** Purple violet/
northern cardinal

**South Florida is the ONLY PLACE where CROCODILES and ALLIGATORS COEXIST IN THE WILD.**

## Indiana

**Nickname:** Hoosier State
**Area:** 36,418 sq mi (94,321 sq km)
**Population:** 6,691,878
**Capital:** Indianapolis; population 867,125
**Statehood:** December 11, 1816; 19th state
**State flower/bird:** Peony/northern cardinal

## Georgia

**Nickname:** Peach State
**Area:** 59,425 sq mi (153,909 sq km)
**Population:** 10,519,475
**Capital:** Atlanta; population 498,044
**Statehood:** January 2, 1788; 4th state
**State flower/bird:** Cherokee rose/brown thrasher

## Iowa

**Nickname:** Hawkeye State
**Area:** 56,272 sq mi (145,743 sq km)
**Population:** 3,156,145
**Capital:** Des Moines; population 216,853
**Statehood:** December 28, 1846; 29th state
**State flower/bird:** Wild prairie rose/
American goldfinch

 ● Midwest ● Southwest ● West

## Kansas

**Nickname:** Sunflower State
**Area:** 82,277 sq mi (213,096 sq km)
**Population:** 2,911,505
**Capital:** Topeka; population 125,904
**Statehood:** January 29, 1861; 34th state
**State flower/bird:** Sunflower/
western meadowlark

## Kentucky

**Nickname:** Bluegrass State
**Area:** 40,409 sq mi
(104,659 sq km)
**Population:** 4,468,402
**Capital:** Frankfort; population 27,679
**Statehood:** June 1, 1792; 15th state
**State flower/bird:** Goldenrod/northern cardinal

## Louisiana

**Nickname:** Pelican State
**Area:** 51,840 sq mi
(134,264 sq km)
**Population:** 4,659,978
**Capital:** Baton Rouge; population 221,599
**Statehood:** April 30, 1812; 18th state
**State flower/bird:** Magnolia/brown pelican

## Maine

**Nickname:** Pine Tree State
**Area:** 35,385 sq mi (91,646 sq km)
**Population:** 1,338,404
**Capital:** Augusta; population 18,681
**Statehood:** March 15, 1820; 23rd state
**State flower/bird:** Eastern white pine tassel
and cone/chickadee

## EARMUFFS were invented in MAINE.

## Maryland

**Nickname:** Old Line State
**Area:** 12,407 sq mi (32,133 sq km)
**Population:** 6,042,718
**Capital:** Annapolis; population 39,174
**Statehood:** April 28, 1788; 7th state
**State flower/bird:** Black-eyed Susan/
Baltimore oriole

## Massachusetts

**Nickname:** Bay State
**Area:** 10,555 sq mi (27,336 sq km)
**Population:** 6,902,149
**Capital:** Boston; population 694,583
**Statehood:** February 6, 1788; 6th state
**State flower/bird:** Mayflower/
black-capped chickadee

## Michigan

**Nickname:** Great Lakes State
**Area:** 96,716 sq mi
(250,494 sq km)
**Population:** 9,995,915
**Capital:** Lansing; population 118,427
**Statehood:** January 26, 1837; 26th state
**State flower/bird:** Apple blossom/
American robin

## Minnesota

**Nickname:** Land of 10,000 Lakes
**Area:** 86,939 sq mi (225,171 sq km)
**Population:** 5,611,179
**Capital:** St. Paul; population 307,695
**Statehood:** May 11, 1858; 32nd state
**State flower/bird:** Pink and white ladyslipper/
common loon

## Mississippi

**Nickname:** Magnolia State
**Area:** 48,430 sq mi (125,434 sq km)
**Population:** 2,986,530
**Capital:** Jackson; population 164,422
**Statehood:** December 10, 1817; 20th state
**State flower/bird:** Magnolia/
northern mockingbird

**COLOR KEY** ● Northeast ● Southeast

## Missouri

**Nickname:** Show-Me State
**Area:** 69,704 sq mi (180,533 sq km)
**Population:** 6,126,452
**Capital:** Jefferson City; population 42,838
**Statehood:** August 10, 1821; 24th state
**State flower/bird:** Hawthorn/eastern bluebird

## More than 6,300 CAVES have been DISCOVERED in MISSOURI.

## Montana

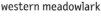

**Nickname:** Treasure State
**Area:** 147,042 sq mi (380,838 sq km)
**Population:** 1,062,305
**Capital:** Helena; population 32,315
**Statehood:** November 8, 1889; 41st state
**State flower/bird:** Bitterroot/ western meadowlark

## Nebraska

**Nickname:** Cornhusker State
**Area:** 77,354 sq mi (200,345 sq km)
**Population:** 1,929,268
**Capital:** Lincoln; population 287,401
**Statehood:** March 1, 1867; 37th state
**State flower/bird:** Goldenrod/ western meadowlark

## Nevada

**Nickname:** Silver State
**Area:** 110,561 sq mi (286,351 sq km)
**Population:** 3,034,392
**Capital:** Carson City; population 55,414
**Statehood:** October 31, 1864; 36th state
**State flower/bird:** Sagebrush/ mountain bluebird

## New Hampshire

**Nickname:** Granite State
**Area:** 9,350 sq mi (24,216 sq km)
**Population:** 1,356,458
**Capital:** Concord; population 43,412
**Statehood:** June 21, 1788; 9th state
**State flower/bird:** Purple lilac/purple finch

## New Jersey

**Nickname:** Garden State
**Area:** 8,721 sq mi (22,588 sq km)
**Population:** 8,908,520
**Capital:** Trenton; population 83,974
**Statehood:** December 18, 1787; 3rd state
**State flower/bird:** Violet/American goldfinch

## New Mexico

**Nickname:** Land of Enchantment
**Area:** 121,590 sq mi (314,915 sq km)
**Population:** 2,095,428
**Capital:** Santa Fe; population 84,612
**Statehood:** January 6, 1912; 47th state
**State flower/bird:** Yucca/greater roadrunner

## New York

**Nickname:** Empire State
**Area:** 54,556 sq mi (141,299 sq km)
**Population:** 19,542,209
**Capital:** Albany; population 97,279
**Statehood:** July 26, 1788; 11th state
**State flower/bird:** Rose/eastern bluebird

## North Carolina

**Nickname:** Tar Heel State
**Area:** 53,819 sq mi (139,389 sq km)
**Population:** 10,383,620
**Capital:** Raleigh; population 469,298
**Statehood:** November 21, 1789; 12th state
**State flower/bird:** Flowering dogwood/ northern cardinal

● Midwest  ● Southwest  ● West

**323**

## North Dakota

**Nickname:** Peace Garden State
**Area:** 70,700 sq mi (183,112 sq km)
**Population:** 760,077
**Capital:** Bismarck; population 73,112
**Statehood:** November 2, 1889; 39th state
**State flower/bird:** Wild prairie rose/
western meadowlark

## Ohio

**Nickname:** Buckeye State
**Area:** 44,825 sq mi (116,096 sq km)
**Population:** 11,689,442
**Capital:** Columbus; population 892,533
**Statehood:** March 1, 1803; 17th state
**State flower/bird:** Scarlet carnation/
northern cardinal

## Oklahoma

**Nickname:** Sooner State
**Area:** 69,898 sq mi (181,036 sq km)
**Population:** 3,943,079
**Capital:** Oklahoma City; population 649,021
**Statehood:** November 16, 1907; 46th state
**State flower/bird:** Oklahoma rose/
scissor-tailed flycatcher

### There is an annual BIGFOOT FESTIVAL in eastern Oklahoma each OCTOBER.

## Oregon

**Nickname:** Beaver State
**Area:** 98,381 sq mi (254,805 sq km)
**Population:** 4,190,713
**Capital:** Salem; population 173,442
**Statehood:** February 14, 1859; 33rd state
**State flower/bird:** Oregon grape/
western meadowlark

## Pennsylvania

**Nickname:** Keystone State
**Area:** 46,055 sq mi (119,283 sq km)
**Population:** 12,807,060
**Capital:** Harrisburg; population 49,229
**Statehood:** December 12, 1787; 2nd state
**State flower/bird:** Mountain laurel/
ruffed grouse

## Rhode Island

**Nickname:** Ocean State
**Area:** 1,545 sq mi (4,002 sq km)
**Population:** 1,057,315
**Capital:** Providence; population 179,335
**Statehood:** May 29, 1790; 13th state
**State flower/bird:** Violet/
Rhode Island red chicken

## South Carolina

**Nickname:** Palmetto State
**Area:** 32,020 sq mi (82,932 sq km)
**Population:** 5,084,127
**Capital:** Columbia; population 133,451
**Statehood:** May 23, 1788; 8th state
**State flower/bird:** Yellow jessamine/
Carolina wren

## South Dakota

**Nickname:** Mount Rushmore State
**Area:** 77,117 sq mi (199,731 sq km)
**Population:** 882,235
**Capital:** Pierre; population 13,980
**Statehood:** November 2, 1889; 40th state
**State flower/bird:** Pasque flower/
ring-necked pheasant

## Tennessee

**Nickname:** Volunteer State
**Area:** 42,143 sq mi (109,151 sq km)
**Population:** 6,770,010
**Capital:** Nashville; population 669,053
**Statehood:** June 1, 1796; 16th state
**State flower/bird:** Iris/
northern mockingbird

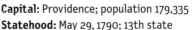

## Texas

**Nickname:** Lone Star State
**Area:** 268,581 sq mi (695,621 sq km)
**Population:** 28,701,845
**Capital:** Austin; population 964,254
**Statehood:** December 29, 1845; 28th state
**State flower/bird:** Texas bluebonnet/
northern mockingbird

## Utah

**Nickname:** Beehive State
**Area:** 84,899 sq mi
(219,887 sq km)
**Population:** 3,161,105
**Capital:** Salt Lake City; population 200,591
**Statehood:** January 4, 1896; 45th state
**State flower/bird:** Sego lily/California gull

## Vermont

**Nickname:** Green Mountain State
**Area:** 9,614 sq mi (24,901 sq km)
**Population:** 626,299
**Capital:** Montpelier; population 7,436
**Statehood:** March 4, 1791; 14th state
**State flower/bird:** Red clover/hermit thrush

## Virginia

**Nickname:** Old Dominion State
**Area:** 42,774 sq mi (110,785 sq km)
**Population:** 8,517,685
**Capital:** Richmond; population 228,783
**Statehood:** June 25, 1788; 10th state
**State flower/bird:** Flowering dogwood/
northern cardinal

## Washington

**Nickname:** Evergreen State
**Area:** 71,300 sq mi (184,665 sq km)
**Population:** 7,535,591
**Capital:** Olympia; population 52,555
**Statehood:** November 11, 1889; 42nd state
**State flower/bird:** Coast rhododendron/
American goldfinch

## West Virginia

**Nickname:** Mountain State
**Area:** 24,230 sq mi (62,755 sq km)
**Population:** 1,805,832
**Capital:** Charleston; population 47,215
**Statehood:** June 20, 1863; 35th state
**State flower/bird:** Rhododendron/
northern cardinal

## Wisconsin

**Nickname:** Badger State
**Area:** 65,498 sq mi (169,639 sq km)
**Population:** 5,813,568
**Capital:** Madison; population 258,054
**Statehood:** May 29, 1848; 30th state
**State flower/bird:** Wood violet/
American robin

# 3 cool things about WISCONSIN

1. Green Bay, Wisconsin, is known as the "Toilet Paper Capital of the World." A factory there began producing rolls in 1901.

2. Wisconsin is home to a museum all about mustard. Open since 1992, the popular attraction features more than 6,000 mustards from all 50 states and more than 70 countries.

3. Surfers seek swells on Wisconsin's Lake Sheboygan, where high, steady winds of up to 25 miles an hour (40 km/h) whip up waves as high as eight feet (2.4 m) tall.

## Wyoming

**Nickname:** Equality State
**Area:** 97,814 sq mi (253,336 sq km)
**Population:** 577,737
**Capital:** Cheyenne; population 63,957
**Statehood:** July 10, 1890; 44th state
**State flower/bird:** Indian paintbrush/
western meadowlark

● Midwest ● Southwest ● West

# THE TERRITORIES

**The United States has 14 territories—** political divisions that are not states. Three of these are in the Caribbean Sea, and the other 11 are in the Pacific Ocean.

St. John, U.S. Virgin Islands

Convention Center, San Juan, Puerto Rico

Talofofo Falls, Guam

## U.S. CARIBBEAN TERRITORIES

### Puerto Rico

**Area:** 3,515 sq mi (9,104 sq km)
**Population:** 3,294,626
**Capital:** San Juan; population 2,454,000
**Languages:** Spanish, English

### U.S. Virgin Islands

**Area:** 737 sq mi (1,910 sq km)
**Population:** 106,977
**Capital:** Charlotte Amalie; population 52,000
**Languages:** English, Spanish, Spanish French

## U.S. PACIFIC TERRITORIES

### American Samoa

**Area:** 77 sq mi (199 sq km)
**Population:** 50,826
**Capital:** Pago Pago; population 49,000
**Language:** Samoan, English, Tongan

### Guam

**Area:** 210 sq mi (544 sq km)
**Population:** 167,772
**Capital:** Hagåtña (Agana); population 147,000
**Languages:** English, Filipino, Chamorro, other Pacific island and Asian languages

### Northern Mariana Islands

**Area:** 184 sq mi (477 sq km)
**Population:** 51,994
**Capital:** Capital Hill; population 51,000
**Languages:** Philippine languages, Chinese, Chamorro, English

### Other U.S. Territories

Baker Island, Howland Island, Jarvis Island, Johnston Atoll, Kingman Reef, Midway Islands, Palmyra Atoll, Wake Island, Navassa Island (in the Caribbean)

*Figures for capital cities vary widely between sources because of differences in the way the area is defined and other projection methods.*

## THE U.S. CAPITAL

### District of Columbia

**Area:** 68 sq mi (177 sq km)
**Population:** 5,207,000

Abraham Lincoln, who was president during the Civil War and a strong opponent of slavery, is remembered in the Lincoln Memorial, located at the opposite end of the National Mall from the U.S. Capitol Building.

**COLOR KEY** ● Territories ● Northeast

# Check out these outrageous U.S.A. facts.

The state "FLOWER" of Maine is the WHITE PINE CONE.

A ball of **twine** in Kansas **weighs more** than **19,000 pounds** (8,618 kg) and could stretch **halfway across** the **United States.**

Halló! Hallo! Здравствуйте!
Hej! Laba diena!
Guten Tag! Sveicināti!
He **More than** Вітаю!
Goddag! Gr **200** Добридень!
Dia duit! aj!
Helô! **languages** Halló!
Olá! B **are spoken in** Pershenderje!
**New York City.**
Kaixo! Здравейте! Здраво!
Hola! ¡Hola! Salve! Γεια σας! Zdravo!

IN ONE SECOND, A WATER PIPE FROM THE HOOVER DAM COULD FILL 960,000 SODA CANS.

**321** is the **area code** for where the **space shuttle** used to **blast off** in Florida.

A building in Nashville, Tennessee, has towers that look like the ears of BATMAN'S MASK.

THE CITY OF PORTLAND, OREGON, WAS NAMED IN A COIN TOSS —IT HAD A FIFTY-FIFTY CHANCE OF BECOMING BOSTON, OREGON.

More than **700 flavors** of soda are sold at a Los Angeles soda pop store.

Most of Mount Rushmore was carved with dynamite.

# Bet You Didn't Know!

# 10 fast facts about

**1** Japan is the only country with an **emperor** and an **empress.**

**2** Karaoke, which means "empty orchestra" in Japanese, originated in Japan in the early 1970s.

**3** Japan has the highest number of **vending machines** per capita in the world, with some **5.5 million machines.**

**4** Japan's Akashi Kaikyō Bridge can handle up to **180-mile-an-hour** (290-km/h) winds **and withstand earthquakes.**

A bullet train speeds past Mount Fuji in Japan.

# Japan

**5** There are more than **100 active volcanoes** in Japan.

**7** In Japan, it's possible to buy **watermelons** shaped like **pyramids.**

**6** About **73 percent** of Japan is covered with **mountains.**

**8** Japanese kids start the school year in **April,** at about the time when the cherry blossoms bloom.

**9** Japan's bullet trains, called **Shinkansen,** carry passengers at speeds of **200 miles an hour** (320 km/h).

**10** A 2011 earthquake in Japan was so powerful, it moved the entire **island of Honshu as much as 15 feet** (4.7 m).

# EXTREME
# WEIRDNESS

## VADER RULES THE SKY

**WHAT** León International Balloon Festival

**WHERE** León, Mexico

**DETAILS** This might be the Rebels' worst nightmare. Participants at this festival soared across the sky in giant hot-air balloons, such as this one shaped like Darth Vader's mask. More than a hundred balloons fly each year—anything from pandas to bees to scarecrows. But don't worry. This Vader's only full of hot air.

THE FORCE IS STRONG WITH THIS ONE.

DON'T MOW THIS GRASS.

## WEAR YOUR LAWN

**WHAT** Grass-covered flip-flops

**WHERE** New South Wales Coast, Australia

**DETAILS** Want to feel the grass between your toes? Just plant your feet in these grass-topped flip-flops, designed to give you the sensation of being outdoors anytime. Don't worry about watering the sandals—the grass is actually a layer of artificial turf. You'll have some happy feet!

YOU'RE IN THE COLD SEAT.

## ICE CUBE ON WHEELS

**WHAT** Truck made of ice

**WHERE** Hensall, Canada

**DETAILS** It's going to be an icy ride. This functional truck has a body made of 11,000 pounds (4,990 kg) of ice. Built over a base frame with wheels, the icy exterior covers a real engine, brakes, and steering wheel. It runs on a battery that's specially designed to start in frigid conditions that would keep most cars from revving up. The car can only go short distances—but what a great place to chill!

# COOL INVENTIONS

## A SUPERSMART BUILDING THAT COULD CHANGE YOUR LIFE

## THE STRAWSCRAPER »

For some people, a windy day means a bad hair day. But for the folks designing this odd-looking building, a windy day is a *good* hair day. For them, windy days will mean the hairy fibers on their building are capturing loads of free energy. A Swedish architectural firm is working on plans to transform an existing Stockholm building into a futuristic, 40-floor skyscraper that will create energy. The design for this project, known as the Strawscraper, encloses the building in a casing covered with long, flexible straws that turn wind motion into electrical energy. From gentle breezes to strong winds, the friction on the straws will produce and store electricity much like a wind power plant does. The Strawscraper will be much quieter than a wind turbine, though, and will be bird-friendly, too.

Plans include a restaurant and a viewing platform in the Strawscraper.

**WANT MORE EARTH-SAVING ACTION?**
Go online to find out how you can protect our planet.
natgeokids.com/SaveTheEarth

331

# THIS or THAT?

## CHOOSE THIS:

Stack monuments all the way to the moon's surface.

**or**

## CHOOSE THAT:

Stack hamsters to the height of a famous monument.

## If you CHOSE THIS

You're reaching for the stars if you try to get to the moon by stacking **Eiffel Towers** on top of each other. Not counting its antennas, the height of the Eiffel Tower in Paris, France, is **986 feet (300 m)**. The distance from the Earth's surface to the **moon** at its closest is about **223,700 miles (360,010 km)**. If you were to stack Eiffel Tower upon Eiffel Tower all the way to the moon, it would require more than **1.1 million monuments!** Be sure to build an elevator while you're at it.

# If you CHOSE THAT

You've got quite a **balancing act** if you try to stack **hamsters** to the top of the **Statue of Liberty** in New York City, U.S.A. The height of the monument—from base to torch—is about **151 feet (46 m)**. The average height of a hamster standing on its hind legs is **six inches (15 cm)**. That means if you created a tower of hamsters that reached the top of Lady Liberty, you'd need **302 hamsters** in all! It would stink to be the hamster on the bottom, wouldn't it?

## BONUS FACT

If you lined up 45 crocodiles tail to snout, they'd stretch as long as one side of the Great Pyramid at Giza.

THIS OR THAT? 3

EVEN MORE
YOU

CHECK OUT THIS BOOK!

# WILD VACATION

ENTER HERE!

SLEEP HERE!

## Tree Hotel
### NESTLING INTO NATURE

**WHERE** Dalat, Vietnam

**HOW MUCH** About $45 to $116 a night

**WHY IT'S COOL** One look at this hotel and you'll understand its nickname: "Crazy House." The bizarre lodging is designed to resemble a giant tree stump from the outside. The structure's cozy interior is filled with twisting passageways and 10 cavelike rooms, each with a different animal, insect, or plant theme. Visitors can unwind next to a fireplace shaped like a kangaroo or drift to sleep while staring at the stars through skylights in the Gourd Room. Guests can also wander through the garden, where eerie metal spiderwebs hang. More daring individuals can climb the winding walkways to the roof of the building and take in views of the surrounding city. From top to bottom, this hotel is insanely awesome.

## COOL THINGS ABOUT VIETNAM

About 40 percent of the people in Vietnam have the last name Nguyen.

Grilled squid teeth are a popular snack in the country's coastal towns.

Vietnam is only 30 miles (48 km) wide at its narrowest point.

## THINGS TO DO IN VIETNAM

Explore the bustling Cai Rang floating market, where boats are colorfully packed with fruits and vegetables for sale.

Sample traditional noodle soup called pho (pronounced FUH) from shops in Hanoi, the country's capital city.

Discover the palaces of former emperors inside the walls of the Hue Citadel, along the Perfume River.

# HOW TALL IS IT?

**Burj Khalifa, located in Dubai** in the United Arab Emirates, soars over half a mile (0.8 km) high. But how does that compare to other cool sights around the globe? Check out this lineup to find out!

The Willis Tower has **16,100** windows.

More than **36,000** stones make up the Washington Monument.

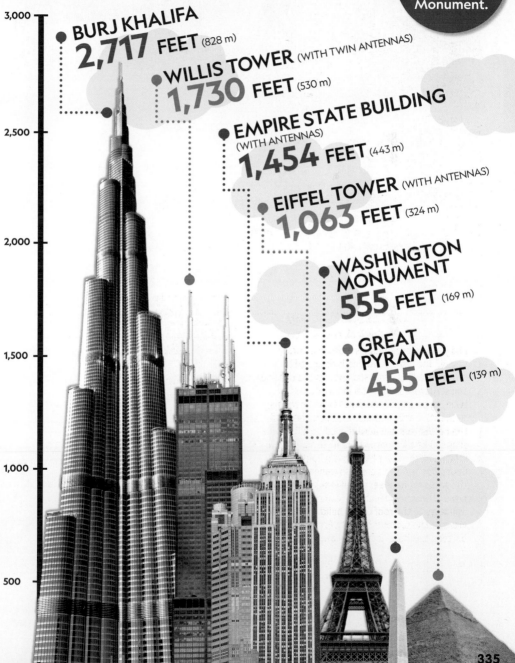

BURJ KHALIFA
**2,717** FEET (828 m)

WILLIS TOWER (WITH TWIN ANTENNAS)
**1,730** FEET (530 m)

EMPIRE STATE BUILDING
(WITH ANTENNAS)
**1,454** FEET (443 m)

EIFFEL TOWER (WITH ANTENNAS)
**1,063** FEET (324 m)

WASHINGTON MONUMENT
**555** FEET (169 m)

GREAT PYRAMID
**455** FEET (139 m)

3,000
2,500
2,000
1,500
1,000
500

# QUIZ WHIZ

## Is your geography knowledge off the map? Quiz yourself to find out!

Write your answers on a piece of paper. Then check them below.

**1** You'd have to stack _____ Eiffel Towers on top of each other to reach the moon.
a. 111
b. 1,100
c. 11,100
d. 1.1 million

**2** Besides being the tallest mountain on Earth, what else is unique about Mauna Loa?
a. It's an active volcano.
b. It's a glacier.
c. It's entirely underwater.
d. It's an ancient burial ground.

**3** What's the bikini bathing suit named after?
a. Bikini, Germany
b. Bikini Atoll in the Marshall Islands
c. Bikini, California, U.S.A.
d. Bikini Island in Hawaii, U.S.A.

**4** **True or false?** Bullet trains in Japan travel at speeds of 200 miles an hour (320 km/h).

**5** There's a _____ at the top of Mount Mabu in Mozambique.
a. crater
b. rainforest
c. village
d. desert

Not **STUMPED** yet? Check out the *NATIONAL GEOGRAPHIC KIDS QUIZ WHIZ* collection for more crazy **GEOGRAPHY** questions!

**ANSWERS:**
1. d; 2. a; 3. b; 4. True; 5. b

## HOMEWORK HELP

# Finding Your Way Around

**Every map has a story to tell,**
but first you have to know how to read one. Maps represent information by using a language of symbols. Knowing how to read these symbols provides access to a wide range of information. Look at the scale and compass rose or arrow to understand distance and direction (see box below).

To find out what each symbol on a map means, you must use the key. It's your secret decoder—identifying information by each symbol on the map.

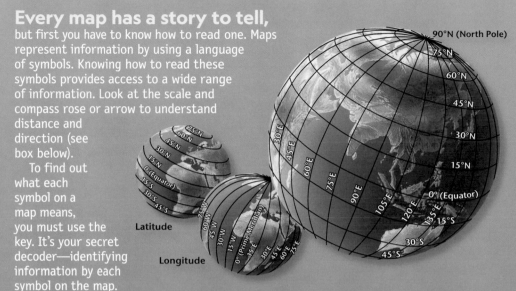

---

## LATITUDE AND LONGITUDE

Latitude and longitude lines (above) help us determine locations on Earth. Every place on Earth has a special address called absolute location. Imaginary lines called lines of latitude run west to east, parallel to the Equator. These lines measure distance in degrees north or south from the Equator (0° latitude) to the North Pole (90° N) or to the South Pole (90° S). One degree of latitude is approximately 70 miles (113 km).

Lines of longitude run north to south, meeting at the poles. These lines measure distance in degrees east or west from 0° longitude (prime meridian) to 180° longitude. The prime meridian runs through Greenwich, England.

---

## SCALE AND DIRECTION

The scale on a map can be shown as a fraction, as words, or as a line or bar. It relates distance on the map to distance in the real world. Sometimes the scale identifies the type of map projection. Maps may include an arrow to indicate north on the map or a compass rose to show all principal directions.

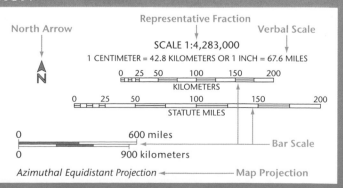

# GAME ANSWERS

## We Gave It a Swirl
page 136

1. flamingo, 2. chameleon, 3. koala,
4. cow, 5. fish

## What in the World?
page 137

Top row: **pineapples, leis, coconut**
Middle row: **Hawaiian shirt, sea turtle**
Bottom row: **volcano, surfboard, ukulele**

## Galaxy Quest
pages 138–139

## Bark Park
page 141

## What in the World?
page 142

Top row: **sweaters, rainbow, sprinkles**
Middle row: **colored pencils, umbrella, toothbrushes**
Bottom row: **licorice, towels, feathers**

## Undersea Stars
page 144

## Find the Hidden Animals
page 146

1. D, 2. C, 3. B, 4. F, 5. A, 6. E

## Signs of the Times
page 149

Sign #2 is fake.

## Windy Jumble
page 150

Eleanor, **A**; Sam, **J**; Nicole, **E**; Steve, **H**;
Carlos, **F**; Zak, **B**; Ava, **C**; Jill, **I**; Isabel, **G**;
Daniel, **D**

# Want to Learn More?

Find more information about topics in this book in these National Geographic Kids resources.

**Absolute Expert series**

**Weird But True! series**

**Just Joking series**

**5,000 Awesome Facts (About Everything!) series**

**Bet You Didn't Know! series**

**Make This!**
*Ella Schwartz*
February 2019

**Don't Read This Book Before Dinner**
*Anna Claybourne*
July 2019

**Nerd A to Z**
*T. J. Resler*
August 2019

**Sharks vs. Sloths**
*Julie Beer*
September 2019

**The Big Book of Bling**
*Rose Davidson*
September 2019

**Surprising Stories Behind Everyday Stuff**
*Stephanie Warren Drimmer*
September 2019

**Encyclopedia of American Indian History and Culture**
*Cynthia O'Brien*
October 2019

**It's a Numbers Game! Basketball**
*James Buckley, Jr.*
February 2020

**1,000 Facts About Dinosaurs, Fossils, and Prehistoric Life**
*Patricia Daniels*
February 2020

## Abbreviations:
AL: Alamy Stock Photo
DRMS: Dreamstime
GI: Getty Images
IS: iStockphoto
MP: Minden Pictures
NGIC: National Geographic Image Collection
SS: Shutterstock

## All Maps
By National Geographic unless otherwise noted

## All Illustrations & Charts
By Stuart Armstrong unless otherwise noted

## Front Cover
(leopard), Gèrard Lacz/Biosphoto; (diver), Mark D. Conlin; (robot), Julian Stratenschulte/dpa/GI

## Spine
(leopard), Gèrard Lacz/Biosphoto

## Back Cover
(Earth), ixpert/SS; (puffin), Mlenny/E+/GI; (satellite), NASA/JPL; (frog), kuritafsheen/RooM/GI; (pyramids), Yann Arthus-Bertrand/GI Plus/GI; (explorer), Edward Selfe; (butterfly), Steven Russell Smith/AL

## Front Matter (2-7)
2-3, Dave Fleetham/Perspectives/GI; 5 (Your World), Benoit Tessier/Reuters; 5 (Awesome Exploration), Jennifer Adler/NGIC; 5 (Amazing Animals), Ron Kimball/Kimball Stock; 5 (Wonders of Nature, LE), Preto_perola/GI; 5 (Wonders of Nature, RT), SpectrumPhotofile.com; 6 (Space and Earth, LE), NASA/JPL; 6 (Space and Earth, RT), Sven Sjöström/EyeEm/GI; 6 (Fun and Games, LE), David Madison/GI; 6 (Fun and Games, RT), Dan Sipple; 6 (Science and Technology), Alexander Miridonov/Kommersant Photo/Polaris/Newscom; 6 (Culture Connection, LE), Stefano Gentile/EyeEm/GI; 6 (Culture Connection, RT), Dinodia/GI; 7 (Going Green), Rana Sajid Hussain/Pacific Press/LightRocket/GI; 7 (History Happens), David Lazar/GI; 7 (Geography Rocks), Layne Kennedy/GI

## Your World 2021 (8-17)
8-9, Benoit Tessier/Reuters; 10 (UP LE), Nicola Maplres and Sean Kelly; 10 (CTR RT), Dr. Luiz Rocha; 10 (CTR LE), Tim Laman/MP; 10 (LO RT), Ron Santiago, BioWeb PUCE; 11 (UP), HUBBLESITE; 11 (CTR), Kazuhiro Nogi/AFP/GI; 11 (LO), Kazuhiro Nogi/AFP/GI; 12 (UP), Joel Sartore/NGIC; 12 (LO), Fabio Pupin/MP; 13 (UP), AP Images/Carolyn Thompson; 13 (LO), Aflac Worldwide; 14 (UP), Photo courtesy of K-9 Country Inn; 14 (CTR), Photo courtesy of K-9 Country Inn; 14 (LO), Susan Schmitz/SS; 14 (LO), John Lund/GI; 15 (UP LE), Wildlife Reserves Singapore; 15 (UP RT), Wildlife Reserves Singapore; 15 (LO), Rothy's/photo by Mark Thiessen and Becky Hale/NGP Staff; 16 (UP RT), markgoddard/GI; 16 (UP CTR RT), a_v_d/SS; 16 (CTR LE), © Warner Bros./courtesy Everett Collection; 16 (CTR RT), Melinda Nagy/SS; 16 (LO CTR LE), stanley45/IS; 16 (LO CTR RT), MariaKovaleva/SS; 16 (LO LE), Kabayan Mark/500px/GI; 16 (LO RT), Jill Brady/GI; 17 (UP), Compass Pools UK; 17 (CTR), National Weather Service/AP Images/SS; 17 (LO), Michael Sewell Visual Pursuit/GI

## Awesome Exploration (18-35)
18-19, Jennifer Adler/NGIC; 20 (LE), Tyler Roemer; 20 (inset), Tyler Roemer; 20 (LO RT), courtesy Rainforest Connection; 21 (UP LE), Jacqueline Faherty/NGIC; 21 (LO LE), Randall Scott/NGIC; 21 (UP RT), Randall Scott/NGIC; 21 (LO RT), jeep2499/SS; 22 (LE), Ali Cansino, courtesy Jamal Galves; 22 (UP RT), Mark Thiessen, NGP Staff; 22 (LO), Celeshia Guy, courtesy Jamal Galves; 23, Vladimir Wrangel/SS; 24, University of Georgia Marketing & Communications. All rights reserved.; 25 (UP LE), Pixel-Shot/Adobe Stock; 25 (UP RT), Chones/SS; 25 (CTR), Arthur Tilley/GI; 25 (LO CTR LE), Strekoza64/SS; 25 (LO CTR RT), EasternLightcraft/iStock/GI; 25 (LO), PBorowka/iStockphoto/Getty Images; 26-27 (UP), Brian J. Skerry/NGIC; 26 (LO), Brian J. Skerry/NGIC; 27 (CTR), Mark D. Conlin/NGIC; 27 (LO), Brian J. Skerry/NGIC; 28 (UP LE), Pictures Colour Library/Newscom; 28 (UP RT), jarino47/istock/GI; 28 (LO LE), Channi Anand/AP Photo; 28 (LO RT), Bigfoot Hostel/Barcroft Media/GI; 29 (UP LE), Michael Clark/AL; 29 (UP RT), EPA/Newscom; 29 (CTR), Anthony Devlin/PA Images/AL; 29 (LO), Adam Pretty/GI; 30 (UP), courtesy Colin O'Brady; 30 (CTR LE), photo by Samuel A. Harrison, courtesy Colin O'Brady; 30 (CTR RT), courtesy Colin O'Brady; 30 (LO LE), courtesy Louis Rudd; 30 (LO RT), courtesy Louis Rudd; 31 (UP), Tony Campbell/SS; 31 (LO), SS; 32 (UP), Annie Griffiths; 32 (LO), Annie Griffiths; 33 (UP), Annie Griffiths; 33 (CTR LE), Annie Griffiths; 33 (CTR RT), Annie Griffiths; 33 (LO), Annie Griffiths; 34 (UP RT), Vladimir Wrangel/SS; 34 (UP LE), Brian J. Skerry/NGIC; 34 (CTR RT), Bigfoot Hostel/Barcroft Media/GI; 34 (LO LE), Annie Griffiths; 35, Grady Reese/IS

## Amazing Animals (36-89)
36-37, Ron Kimball/Kimball Stock; 38-39, PhonlamaiPhoto/IS; 40-41 (UP), Alexandra Young; 40 (CTR LE), Kreatiw/DRMS; 40 (LO RT), Action Sports Photography/SS; 40 (LO LE), OrangeGroup/SS; 41 (UP), Özlem Pınar Ivacu; 41 (LO RT), Stefan Rousseau/PA Wire/AP Images; 41 (LO LE), Express Newspapers Via AP Images; 42 (UP), Zara Palmer, Marketing Specialist - Toucan Rescue Ranch; 42 (LO), Michael Sharkey; 43 (UP), Mark Ralston/AFP/GI; 43 (LO), RSPCA Trading Ltd./RSPCA Photolibrary; 44 (UP), Grahm S. Jones/Columbus Zoo and Aquarium; 44 (LO), Taneile Hoare; 45 (UP), Leondra Schere; 45 (LO), Farm Sanctuary; 46 (UP), lifegallery/iStock/GI; 46 (CTR), DioGen/SS; 46 (LO), Nick Garbutt; 47 (UP LE), EyeEm/GI; 47 (UP RT), reptiles4all/SS; 47 (CTR LE), Hiroya Minakuchi/MP; 47 (CTR RT), FP media/SS; 47 (LO), Aleksandar Dickov/SS; 48 (UP CTR LE), Ingo Arndt/naturepl.com; 48 (UP CTR RT), Dr. James L. Castner/Visuals Unlimited, Inc.; 48 (LO CTR), Alex Hyde/naturepl.com; 48 (LO LE), NHPA/SuperStock; 48 (LO RT), Chris Mattison/FLPA/MP; 48 (UP), Cosmin Manci/SS; 49 (UP LE), Alex Hyde/naturepl.com/GI; 49 (UP RT), PREMAPHOTOS/naturepl.com; 49 (RT CTR), Kazuo Unno/Nature Production/MP; 49 (LE CTR), Christopher Smith/AL; 49 (LO), NH/SS; 50 (UP), Schafer & Hill/GI; 50 (LO LE), Chuck Graham; 50 (LO RT), Mel Melcon/GI; 51 (UP), Chuck Graham; 51 (CTR), Chuck Graham; 51 (LO), Chuck Graham; 52 (UP), Abby Wood/Smithsonian's National Zoo; 52 (LO), Anna Gowthorpe/PA Images via GI; 53 (LO LE), saad315/SS; 53 (UP LE), Andrea Izzotti/SS; 53 (UP RT), Sylvain Cordier/GI; 53 (LO RT), Dr. Axel Gebauer/Nature Picture Library; 54, Eric Baccega/NPL/MP; 55 (LO), Jordi Galbany/Dian Fossey Gorilla Fund International; 55 (UP LE), Stone Sub/GI; 55 (CTR RT), courtesy Dallas Zoo; 55 (UP RT), Martin Hale/FLPA/MP; 56 (UP), Klein and Hubert/MP; 56 (LO LE), Stephen Dalton/MP; 56 (LO RT), Christian Ziegler/MP; 57 (LO LE), Juan Carlos Muñoz/GI; 57 (UP RT), Paul Souders/GI; 57 (UP CTR), Ingo Arndt/MP; 57 (LO CTR LE), Ingo Arndt/MP; 57 (UP CTR LE), Ingo Arndt/MP; 57 (UP LE), Ingo Arndt/MP; 58 (UP), James Gourley/SS; 58 (CTR LE), Peter Murphy; 58 (LO LE), Kevin Schafer/GI; 58 (LO RT), Tom Reichner/SS; 58 (CTR RT), Purestock/GI; 59 (LO), Min-Soo Ahn/EyeEm/GI; 59 (UP), madmonkey0328/SS; 59 (UP CTR), LIMDQ/SS; 59 (CTR LE), AL-Travelpicture/iStock/GI; 59 (CTR RT), Alex Snyder; 60 (LO RT), 20th Century Fox/Entertainment Pictures/ZUMA PRESS; 60 (LO LE), Maria Diekmann/REST; 60 (LO CTR LE), Jamie Trueblood/©Columbia Pictures/Courtesy Everett Collection; 60 (LO CTR RT), Suzi Eszterhas/MP; 61 (LO CTR LE), imageBROKER/AL; 61 (UP), Christian Boix/Africa Geographic; 61 (UP CTR LE), J Dennis Nigel/GI; 61 (UP CTR RT), J Dennis Nigel/GI; 61 (LO CTR), © Walt Disney Studios Motion Pictures/Courtesy Everett Collection; 61, Everett Collection, Inc.; 62 (UP), Design Pics Inc/AL; 62 (LO), mauritius images GmbH/AL; 63 (UP LE), Kathryn Jeffs/Nature Picture Library; 63 (UP RT), Tony Wu/Nature Picture Library; 63 (LO), Tory Kallman/SS; 63 (CTR RT), Design Pics Inc/AL; 64 (UP LE), Donald M Jones/MP; 64 (LO LE), Doc White/Nature Picture Library; 64 (LO RT), Enrique R Aguirre Aves/GI; 64 (UP RT), Milo Burcham/Design Pics INC/AL; 65 (UP), John C. Lewis/SeaPics.com; 65 (LE CTR), Gary Bell/oceanwideimages.com; 65 (RT CTR), Gary Bell/oceanwideimages.com; 65 (LO LE), Jeff Rotman/SeaPics.com; 65 (LO RT), Doug Perrine/SeaPics.com; 66 (UP), Norbert Wu/MP; 66 (LO), Claudio Contreres/NPL/MP; 67 (UP), Doug Perrine/naturepl.com; 67 (CTR), SA Team/Foto Nature/MP; 67 (LO LE), Claudio Contreras/Nature Picture Library; 67 (LO RT), Doug Perrine/naturepl.com; 68 (UP), TLWilsonPhotography/SS; 68 (LO), Yuri Smityuk/TASS/AL Live News; 69 (LO LE), Action Sports Photography/SS; 69 (RT), Andrew Porter/GI; 69 (UP RT), Rudi Hulshhof/GI; 70 (UP), Photoshot License Ltd/AL; 70 (LO), Steve Winter/NGIC; 71 (LO LE), Tom Brakefield/CORBIS/GI; 71 (RT), James Kaiser; 72 (UP), Chris Butler/Science Photo Library/Photo Researchers, Inc.; 72 (CTR), Publiphoto/Photo Researchers, Inc.; 72 (LO), Pixeldust

Studios/NGIC; 73 (B), Laurie O'Keefe/Photo Researchers, Inc.; 73 (C), Chris Butler/Photo Researchers, Inc.; 73 (D), Publiphoto/Photo Researchers, Inc.; 73 (A), Publiphoto/Photo Researchers, Inc.; 73 (E), image courtesy of Project Exploration; 74 (LO), Andrea Meyer/SS; 75 (UP LE), Andrey Atuchin; 75 (UP RT), Mark Witton; 75 (LO), Jorge Gonzalez; 76 (UP), Franco Tempesta; 76 (CTR), Franco Tempesta; 76 (LO), Photo by Roderick Mickens, © American Museum of Natural History; 77 (LO LE), Julius Csotonyi; 77 (UP LE), Franco Tempesta; 77 (UP RT), Franco Tempesta; 77 (LO RT), Franco Tempesta; 78 (UP), Franco Tempesta; 78 (LO), Franco Tempesta; 79 (UP), Catmando/SS; 79 (CTR), Franco Tempesta; 79 (LO), Leonello Calvetti/SS; 80 (UP), Pete Oxford/MP; 80 (LO), Tui De Roy/MP; 81 (UP), Bernd von Jutrczenk/GI; 81 (LO LE), David Evison/SS; 81 (LO RT), Marion Vollborn/MP; 82 (LO LE), Piotr Naskrecki/MP; 82 (UP LE), Old Dog Photography/GI; 82 (RT), Keren Su/CORBIS; 83 (UP), Vicki Jauron/Moment RF/GI; 83 (LO), Ruaridh Connellan/BarcroftImages/GI; 84 (UP), Lubos Kovalik/GI; 84 (LO), Norbert Wu/MP; 85 (UP LE), Stephen Barnes/SS; 85 (UP RT), Jim Cumming/GI; 85 (LO LE), Mark Kostich/GI; 85 (LO RT), Ellende/GI; 86 (UP RT), Jonathan Androwski/GI; 86 (LO), Amanda Edwards/GI; 86 (UP LE), Patrick Endres/AGE Fotostock; 87 (UP), Kryssia Campos/GI; 87 (LO), Frank Lukasseck/GI; 88 (UP LE), Rudi Hulshof/GI; 88 (UP RT), James Gourley/SS; 88 (LO RT), John C. Lewis/SeaPics.com; 88 (LO LE), Design Pics Inc/AL; 89, GOLFX/SS

## Wonders of Nature (90–111)

90-91, Preto_perola/GI; 92-93 (UP), Jason Edwards/NGIC; 92 (LO LE), cbpix/SS; 92 (LO RT), Mike Hill/Photographer's Choice/GI; 93 (LO LE), Wil Meinderts/Buiten-beeld/MP; 93 (LO RT), Paul Nicklen/NGIC; 94-95, wildestanimal/GI; 96 (UP), AVTG/IS; 96 (LO), Brad Wynnyk/SS; 97 (UP LE), Rich Carey/SS; 97 (UP RT), Richard Walters/IS; 97 (LO LE), Karen Graham/IS; 97 (LO RT), Michio Hoshino/MP/NGIC; 98, Margarita Alshina; 99 (UP), Stephanie Sawyer/GI; 99 (LO), Grant Dixon/MP; 100 (UP), SS; 100 (LO RT), Spectrum Photofile.com; 100 (LO LE), Photo Researchers RM/GI; 101 (UP), U.S. Navy photo; 101 (LO LE), Sygma/Corbis; 101 (LO RT), AP Images; 101 (CTR), Jim Damaske/St. Petersburg Times/ZUMAPRESS.com/Newscom.com; 102 (UP), Stuart Armstrong; 102 (LO), Franco Tempesta; 103 (LO), Richard Peterson/SS; 103 (UP LE), Leonid Tit/SS; 103 (UP RT), Lars Christensen/SS; 103 (CTR LE), Frans Lanting/NGIC; 103 (CTR RT), Daniel Loretto/SS; 104-105, 3dmotus/SS; 106, Galen Rowell/CORBIS/GI; 107 (UP LE), Lori Mehmen/Associated Press; 107 (LO LE), Jim Reed; 107 (UP RT), Susan Law Cain/SS; 107 (LO UP CTR), Susan Law Cain/SS; 107 (RT CTR), Susan Law Cain/SS; 107 (CTR LE), Judy Kennamer/SS; 107 (LO RT), jam4travel/SS; 107 (LO CTR), jam4travel/SS; 108 (LE), Jeff Hill; 108 (UP RT), Jeff Hill; 108 (LO RT), Jeff Hill; 109 (UP), John Amis/EPA-EFE/SS; 109 (LO), Zoltán Csipke/AL; 110

(UP RT), Karen Graham/IS; 110 (UP LE), Galen Rowell/GI; 110 (LO RT), Jim Reed; 110 (LO LE), Wil Meinderts/Buiten-beeld/MP

## Space and Earth (112–133)

112-113, NASA/JPL; 114 (UP),NGIC; 115 (UP), Ralph Lee Hopkins/NGIC; 115 (UP LE and RT), Visuals Unlimited/GI; 115 (CTR LE), Visuals Unlimited/Corbis; 115 (CTR RT), Dirk Wiersma/Photo Researchers, Inc.; 115 (LO LE), Charles D. Winters/Photo Researchers, Inc.; 115 (LO RT), Theodore Clutter/Photo Researchers, Inc.; 116 (UP LE), raiwa/IS; 116 (LO LE), Albert Russ/SS; 116 (UP RT), MarcelC/IS; 116 (CTR RT), SS; 116 (LO RT), IS; 117 (UP LE), didyk/IS; 117 (UP RT), Mark A. Schneider/Science Source; 117 (LO LE), Ben Johnson/Science Source; 117 (LO CTR LE), Kazakovmaksim/DRMS; 117 (LO RT), oldeez/DRMS; 117 (LO CTR RT), Ingemar Magnusson/DRMS; 117 (UP CTR), Joel Arem/Science Source; 117 (UP LE), Meetchum/DRMS; 117 (UP CTR LE), Albertruss/DRMS; 117 (UP RT), 123dartist/DRMS; 117 (UP CTR RT), Igorkali/DRMS; 118-119 (BACKGROUND), GIPhotoStock/Science Source/GI; 119 (LE), Richard D. Norris; 119 (RT), Sven Sjöström/EyeEm/GI; 120, Illustration © Frank Ippolito; 121 (UP LE), All Canada Photos/AL; 121 (CTR LE), NASA; 121 (LO RT), Diane Cook & Len Jenshel/NGIC; 121 (LO LE), Image Science and Analysis Laboratory, NASA-Johnson Space Center. "The Gateway to Astronaut Photography of Earth."; 121 (LO RT), Douglas Peebles Photography/AL; 122-123, Naeblys/SS; 124-125 (CTR), Mark Garlick/Science Photo Library; 124 (LO), NASA/CXC/IOA/A FABIAN ETAL/Science Photo Library; 125 (UP), NASA, ESA and M.J. Jee (Johns Hopkins University); 125 (LO), M. MARKEVITCH/CXC/CFA/NASA/Science Photo Library; 126-127 (UP), David Aguilar; 128 (UP), David Aguilar; 128 (LO RT), NASA/JHUAPL/SwRI; 129 (UP), JPL/NASA; 129 (LO RT), Sommersby/DRMS; 129 (LO LE), Age FotoStock/SuperStock; 130 (CTR RT), Tony & Daphne Hallas/Photo Researchers, Inc.; 130 (BACKGROUND UP), Alexxandar/GI; 130 (UP RT), Walter Myers/Stocktrek Images/Corbis/GI; 130, Don Smith/GI; 131 (UP), NASA/Science Faction/SuperStock; 131 (LO), NASA; 132 (UP), NASA; 132 (CTR), IS; 132 (LO), All Canada Photos/AL; 133, pixhook/IS

## Fun and Games (134–153)

134-135, David Madison/GI; 136 (UP LE), Jak Wonderly; 136 (UP RT), Image99/Jupiter Images; 136 (CTR), gillmar/SS; 136 (LO LE), Erik Sampers/Jupiter Images; 136 (LO RT), Comstock/Jupiter Images; 137 (UP LE), Eising FoodPhotography/StockFood; 137 (UP RT), BananaStock/Jupiter Images; 137 (LE CTR), BananaStock/Jupiter Images; 137 (CTR), PhotoObjects.net/Jupiter Images; 137 (RT CTR), Stephen Frink Collection/AL; 137 (LO LE), James L. Amos/NGIC; 137 (LO CTR), Douglas Peebles/eStock Photo; 137 (LO RT), Siede Preis/GI; 138-139, Clayton Hanmer; 140, Dan Sipple; 141, James Yamasaki; 142 (A), DRMS; 142 (B), DRMS; 142 (C), DRMS; 142 (D), DRMS; 142 (E), DRMS; 142 (F), DRMS; 142 (G), DRMS; 142 (H), DRMS; 142 (I), DRMS; 143 (UP), Pierluigi .Palazzi/SS; 143 (CTR), Konrad Wothe/

naturepl.com; 143 (LO RT), S & D & K Maslowski/MP; 143 (RT CTR), Bradley Mason/GI; 144, James Yamasaki; 145 (UP LE), Gary Fields; 145 (UP RT), Gary Fields; 145 (CTR RT), Chris Ware; 145 (LO LE), Pat Moriarty; 145 (LO RT), Gary Fields; 146 (UP LE), Gerry Ellis/MP; 146 (UP RT), Michael & Patricia Fogden/MP; 146 (CTR RT), Fred Bavendam/MP; 146 (CTR LE), Julie Larsen Maher © Wildlife Conservation Society; 146 (LO LE), Gary K. Smith/MP; 146 (LO RT), Wild Wonders of Europe/Widstrand/Nature Picture Library; 147, Marty Bauman; 148, kuritafsheen/GI; 148 (RT CTR), Larry Lilac/AL; 148 (LO LE), GK Hart/Vikki Hart/GI; 148 (LE CTR), Stockbyte/GI; 149 (UP LE), David Wall/AL; 149 (LO LE), David Brownell/AL; 149 (CTR RT), Alexandr Grey/AL; 149 (LO RT), Thinkstock/Jupiter Images; 149 (UP RT), Index Stock/Jupiter Images/GI; 149 (UP CTR LE), Thinkstock/Jupiter Images; 149 (LO CTR LE), Medioimages/Jupiter Images; 150, James Yamasaki; 151 (UP), Suzi Eszterhas/MP; 151 (LO LE), Suzi Eszterhas/MP; 151 (RT CTR), Fotosearch/SuperStock; 151 (LO CTR), Stephen Dalton/NHPA/Collection/Photoshot; 151 (LO RT), Stephen Dalton/NHPA/Collection/Photoshot; 152-153, Strika Entertainment

## Science and Technology (154–179)

154-155, Alexander Miridonov/Kommersant Photo/Polaris/Newscom; 156 (UP), Mark Thiessen, NGP Staff; 156 (CTR), courtesy Wild Blue Media; 156 (LO), courtesy Wild Blue Media; 157 (UP), courtesy Wild Blue Media; 157 (CTR), courtesy Wild Blue Media; 157 (LO LE), courtesy Wild Blue Media; 157 (LO RT), courtesy Wild Blue Media; 158-159, Visual China Group/GI; 160-161, Mondolithic Studios; 162-163, Mondolithic Studios; 164, Ted Kinsman/Science Source; 165 (F), sgame/SS; 165 (A), Sebastian Kaulitzki/SS; 165 (B), Steve Gschmeissner/Photo Researchers, Inc.; 165 (C), Volker Steger/Christian Bardele/Photo Researchers, Inc.; 165 (LO CTR LE), ancelpics/GI; 165 (LO LE), puwanai/SS; 165 (LO RT), kwest/SS; 166 (UP), FotograFFF/SS; 166 (LO), Craig Tuttle/Corbis/GI; 167 (UP), Dave Bevan/AL; 167 (CTR), Brain light/AL; 167 (UP), Steven Russell Smith/AL; 167 (CTR RT), © Joseph Lacy/AL; 168 (UP), SS; 168 (LO), SS; 169, MedusArt/SS; 170 (LO), cobalt88/SS; 170 (UP), Cynthia Turner; 171 (LO), bgblue/IS/GI; 171 (CTR), Heritage Image Partnership Ltd/AL; 172 (UP), Roger Harris/Science Source; 172 (LO), Shaber/SS; 173, Tim Vernon/SPL/Science Source; 174 (UP LE), Dimarion/SS; 174 (LO LE), Microfield Scientific Ltd./Science Source; 174 (CTR), mrtza/SS; 174 (LO), iLexx/IS; 174 (UP RT), Eraxion/IS; 175 (UP), Jani Bryson/IS; 175 (CTR), MyImages - Micha/SS; 175 (LO), RapidEye/IS; 176, Matthew Rakola; 177 (UP LE), Matthew Rakola; 177 (CTR), Matthew Rakola; 177 (LO RT), Matthew Rakola; 178 (UP LE), courtesy Wild Blue Media; 178 (UP RT), Brain light/AL; 178, kwest/SS; 178 (LO RT), MedusArt/SS; 179, Klaus Vedfelt/GI

## Culture Connection (180–203)

180-181, Stefano Gentile/EyeEm/GI; 182 (UP), Dan Bergeron; 182 (LO), Xinhua/eyevine/Redux; 182 (UP LE), Rex Features via AP Images; 182 (UP RT), epa european press-photo agency b.v./AL; 183 (CTR LE), oakoak; 183 (LO LE), Rex Features via AP Images; 183 (CTR RT), Evening Standard/eyevine/Redux; 183 (LO RT), Mariusz Switulski/SS; 184-185, taveesak srisomthavil/SS; 186-187 (UP), foto-hunter/SS; 186 (UP LE), CreativeNature.nl/SS; 186 (LO LE), Tubol Evgeniya/SS; 186 (UP CTR), pattarastock/SS; 186 (LO RT), imageBROKER/AL; 187 (LO RT), wacpan/SS; 187 (RT CTR), Zee/AL; 187 (CTR), Dinodia/GI; 188 (LO LE), Timothy A. Clary/AFP/GI; 188 (LO LE), Splash News/NewsCom; 188 (LO RT), Timothy A. Clary/AFP/GI; 188 (UP RT), Fuse/GI; 189, Chonnanit/SS; 190 (UP), Rebecca Hale, NGP Staff; 190-191 (LO), Rebecca Hale, NGP Staff; 191 (UP), Jay Talbott, NGP Staff; 192 (LO RT), Ninette Maumus/AL; 192 (UP LE), Ivan Vdovin/AL; 192 (CTR LE), iStock/Mlenny; 192 (UP LE), maogg/GI; 192 (CTR RT), Jack Guez/AFP/GI; 192 (UP RT), Paul Poplis/GI; 192 (LO LE), Courtesy of The Banknote Book; 193 (LO CTR RT), D. Hurst/AL; 193 (UP RT), Comstock/GI; 193 (LO CTR LE), Splash News/Newscom; 193 (LO RT), Kelley Miller/NGP Staff; 193 (LO LE), 'Money Dress' with 'Colonial Dress' behind. Paper currency and frame, Lifesize ©Susan Stockwell 2010. ©photo Colin Hampden-White 2010.; 193 (UP CTR LE), Igor Stramyk/SS; 193 (UP LE), Numismatic Guaranty Corporation (NGC); 195 (RT), Oreolife/AL; 195 (UP LE), Subbotina Anna/SS; 196 (UP LE), John Hazard; 196 (UP RT), Jose Ignacio Soto/SS; 196 (LO), SS; 197 (UP LE), Corey Ford/DRMS; 197 (UP RT), Photosani/SS; 198, Christina Balit; 199, Christina Balit; 200 (UP), Randy Olson; 200 (LO LE), Martin Gray/NGIC; 200 (LO RT), Sam Panthaky/AFP/GI; 201 (LO LE), Reza/NGIC; 201 (LO RT), Richard Nowitz/NGIC; 201 (UP), Thierry Falise/LightRocket/GI; 202 (UP), Chonnanit/SS; 202 (CTR), Splash News/Newscom; 202 (LO), Christina Balit; 203 (UP LE), spatuletail/SS; 203 (UP RT), PictureLake/GI; 203 (CTR), cifotart/SS; 203 (LO), zydesign/SS

## Going Green (204–219)

204-205, Rana Sajid Hussain/Pacific Press/LightRocket/GI; 206-207, Rich Carey/SS; 208 (LE), Martin Fowler/SS; 209 (RT), AccentAlaska.com/AL; 210, Cnora/GI; 211 (UP), Rich Carey/SS; 211 (LO), Jimmy Cumming/GI; 212-213 (ALL), Mark Thiessen/NGP Staff; 214 (CTR), Sean Pavone/DRMS; 214 (UP), Scanrail/DRMS; 214 (LO), Rodrigo Kristensen/SS; 215 (UP RT), Jamie Squire/GI; 215 (CTR), Joao Sabino/Solent News/REX/SS; 215 (LO LE), Dirty Sugar Photography; 215 (LO RT), Courtesy of Austin-Mergold;215 (LE), Caters News Agency; 217 (UP), James Stone/Chasing Light/GI; 217 (LO), James Balog/NGIC; 218, Martin Fowler/SS; 218, AccentAlaska.com/AL; 218 (LO), James Balog/NGIC

## History Happens (220–251)

220-221, David Lazar/GI; 222-223, Tom Till/GI; 224 (LE), National Geographic; 224 (RT), The Print Collector/GI; 224-225, National Geographic; 225 (LO RT), © Look and Learn/Giovannini, Ruggero (1922-1983)/Italian/Bridgeman Images; 226, Wang da Gang; 227 (UP LE), O. Louis Mazzatenta/NGIC; 227 (LO LE), Wang da Gang; 227 (UP RT), O. Louis Mazzatenta/NGIC; 227 (RT CTR), O. Louis Mazzatenta; 227 (LO RT), O. Louis Mazzatenta/NGIC; 228-229, Pius Lee/SS; 229 (UP LE), © Providence Pictures; 229 (UP RT), HOPE PRODUCTIONS/Yann Arthus Bertrand/GI; 229 (LO RT), Hulton Archive/GI; 230 (UP RT), Christian Darkin/Science Source; 230, Arabes/DRMS; 230 (UP RT), Popperfoto/GI; 230 (LO CTR), Mark Newman/FLPA/MP; 230-231, paladin13/iStock/GI; 231 (CTR RT), William S. Kuta/AL; 231 (LO), Stock Montage/GI; 231 (UP LE), Khaled Desouki/AFP/GI; 232 (UP), Hilary Andrews/NGP Staff; 232 (UP LE), Leemage/GI; 232 (LO LE), Kaesler Media/SS; 232 (LO RT), Erlo Brown/SS; 233 (UP LE), spline_x/SS; 233 (UP LE), Photos.com/GI; 233 (UP RT), Margouillat/DRMS; 233 (CTR LE), revers/SS; 233 (LO CTR), Iakov Kalinin/SS; 233 (LO LE), Gtranquillity/SS; 233 (LO LE), Yvdavyd/DRMS; 233 (CTR RT), Hilary Andrews/NGP Staff; 233 (LO RT), Hilary Andrews/NGP Staff; 234, U.S. Air Force photo/Staff Sgt. Alexandra M. Boutte; 235, courtesy Navigea LTD.; 236 (UP), Scott Rothstein/SS; 237 (LO), Gary Blakely/SS; 237 (LO RT), Zack Frank/SS; 238 (LO), Education Images/UIG/GI; 238 (UP), AFP/GI; 238 (CTR), AFP/GI; 239 (alligator), Hln255/DRMS; 239 (ALL OTHERS), White House Historical Association; 240-242 (ALL), White House Historical Association; 243 (LO LE), SS; 243 (LO RT), Clint Spaulding/WWD/REX/SS; 243 (ALL OTHERS), White House Historical Association; 244-245, Adrian Lubbers; 246 (UP), Bettmann/CORBIS/GI; 246 (INSET), Science Source/GI; 247 (LO CTR), Charles Kogod/NGIC; 247 (LO LE), iStock Editorial/GI; 247 (LO RT), Chip Somodevilla/GI; 248, Bettmann Archive/GI; 249 (UP LE), Scott Eisen/GI; 249 (UP RT), Library of Congress Prints and Photographs Division; 249 (LO), Kirill Kudryavtsev/AFP/GI; 250 (UP), © Look and Learn/Giovannini, Ruggero (1922-1983)/Italian/Bridgeman Images; 250 (CTR), O. Louis Mazzatenta/NGIC; 250 (LO), Erlo Brown/SS; 251, Christopher Furlong/GI

## Geography Rocks (252–337)

252-253, Layne Kennedy/GI; 259, NASA; 259 (UP), Lori Epstein/NGP Staff; 260 (CTR CTR), Maria Stenzel/NGIC; 260 (LO CTR), Bill Hatcher/NGIC; 260 (UP), Carsten Peter/NGIC; 260 (RT CTR), Gordon Wiltsie/NGIC; 260 (LO LE), James P. Blair/NGIC; 260 (CTR LE), Thomas J. Abercrombie/NGIC; 260 (BACK), Fabiano Rebeque/GI; 261, Rosenberg Philip/Perspectives/GI; 262, iStock/GI; 263 (LE), keyvanchan/GI; 263 (UP RT), AdemarRangel/GI; 263 (CTR RT), Iko/SS; 263 (LO RT), Hugh Pearson/NPL/MP; 266, Yva Momatiuk and John Eastcott/MP; 267 (CTR RT), iCreative3D/SS; 267 (LE), Alex Tehrani; 267 (UP RT), Achim Baque/SS; 267 (LO RT), Stephen Nicol; 270, Nguyen Anh Tuan/SS; 271 (LO RT), Daniel Heuclin/NPL/MP; 271 (UP RT), Jon Arnold Images/DanitaDelimont.com; 271 (CTR RT), Nancy Brown/Photographer's Choice/GI; 271 (LE), John Downer/MP; 274, The Image Bank/GI; 275 (UP RT), Andrew Watson/John Warburton-Lee Photography Ltd/GI; 275, Matthew Williams-Ellis/GI; 275 (LO LE), Adam Fletcher/MP; 275 (CTR RT), David Wall Photo/GI; 278, Guillem Lopez/Cavan Images; 279 (UP RT), Roy Pedersen/SS; 279 (CTR RT), Annette Hopf/SS; 279 (UP LE), Afonso I of Portugal (litho)/The Stapleton Collection/Bridgeman Images/Bridgeman Images; 279 (UP RT), Anne-Christine Poujoulat/AFP/GI; 282, Gavriel Jecan/GI; 283 (LO RT), Janie Blanchard/GI; 283 (UP RT), Rodrigo Arangua/GI; 283 (LE), Beth Zaiken; 283 (CTR RT), Neirfy/SS; 287 (CTR RT), DC_Colombia/GI; 287 (CTR LE), David Tipling/AL; 287 (UP RT), SOBERKA Richard/hemis.fr/GI; 287 (LO RT), Keren Su/GI; 293, Kelly Cheng/GI; 294, Ondrej Prosicky/SS; 298, Renate Wefers/EyeEm/GI; 301, Tim Graham/GI; 302, EyeEm/GI; 306, Nikolai Sorokin/DRMS; 309, Peter Cade/GI; 314, Steve Lovegrove/SS; 326 (UP RT), Panoramic Images/GI; 326 (UP CTR LE), TexPhoto/SS; 326 (UP CTR RT), Harold G Herradura/SS; 326 (LO RT), PhotoDisc; 327, NASA; 327 (UP LE), Salama/SS; 327 (LO LE), Mint Images Limited/AL; 327 (LE), Evgeny Karandaev/SS; 327 (UP CTR), Corbis Historical/GI; 327 (UP CTR), Oku Okoko Photography/SS; 327 (LO LE), photka/SS; 327, DmitrySerbin/SS; 328-329, Blanscape/SS; 330 (UP), Shane Talbot/Solent News/REX/SS; 330 (LO), ZJAN/Canadian Tire Corporation/WENN/Newscom; 330 (CTR), Mario Armas/REUTERS/AL; 331, Supplied by WENN.com/Newscom; 332-333 (LO), Quaoar/SS; 333 (UP LE), Natchapon L./SS; 333 (RT), Subbotina Anna/SS; 333 (LE), Pola Damonte/SS; 333 (LO RT), Kononova Viktoriia/SS; 334 (BACKGROUND), John S Lander/LightRocket/GI; 334 (INSET UP), John S Lander/LightRocket/GI; 334 (INSET LOW), WENN Ltd/AL; 335 (LE), Ilona Ignatova/SS; 335 (LO RT), Brian Kinney/SS; 335 (LO CTR RT), lesapi images/SS; 335 (CTR RT), Roman Sigaev/SS; 335 (CTR), Bokic Bojan/SS; 335 (CTR LE), Songquan Deng/SS; 336 (UP LE), Pola Damonte/SS; 336 (UP RT), Rosenberg Philip/Perspectives/GI; 336 (LO LE), Blanscape/SS; 336 (LO RT), Hugh Pearson/NPL/MP

Boldface indicates illustration; **boldface** page spans include text and illustrations.

# E

Eagles **50**, 50–51
Earmuffs 322
Earth 114–121
 interior 114, **114**, 132
 layers 114, **114**, 132
 quiz 132
 rocks and minerals 115–119, 132, **132**
 in solar system 126, **126**
 see also Volcanoes
Earth-friendliness see Going green
Earthquakes 328, 329
East Timor (Timor-Leste) 313
Easter 186, **186**, 200, **200**
Eastern tiger swallowtail butterflies 167
Echinoderms 47
Eclipses 130
Ecuador 10, **10**, 80, **80**, 297
Eden Theatre, La Ciotat, France 279, **279**
Egypt
 Alexandria 222, 224–225, **225**, 250, **250**
 ancient bandages 223, 250
 moaning mummy 231, **231**
 overview 297
 pyramids 263, **263**, 333, 335, **335**
 Sphinx 228–229, **228–229**
 wars 235
Egyptian mythology 196, **196**
Eid Al-Fitr 186
Eiffel Tower, Paris, France
 height 332, **332–333**, 335, **335**
 leaning toward shade 278
 quiz 336, **336**
Éire (Ireland) 300
Eisenhower, Dwight D. 242, **242**
El Salvador 297
Electricity
 in human body 173, **173**
 power sources 216
 speed 216
 Strawscraper, Stockholm, Sweden 331, **331**
Elephant seals 134–135, 135
Elephants 103, **103**
Elizabeth I, Queen (England) 233
Emmons, Candice 63
Empire State Building, New York City 335, **335**
Emus 44, **44**
Endangered and threatened species 46
Endocrine system 168
Energy
 and climate change 217, **217**
 Strawscraper, Stockholm, Sweden 331, **331**
 waste energy 17
 world energy & minerals 216, **216**
Engineers 20, **20**, 156–157, **156–157**
England, U.K.
 London tourism 17, **17**, 279
 street art 182–183, **182–183**
 wars 234
Enhanced Fujita (EF) Scale 107, **107**
Environmental protection see Going green
Environments 260, **260**
Equatorial Guinea 297
Eris (dwarf planet) **127**, 128, **128**
Eritrea 297
Essays 35, 203

Estonia 297
Estuaries 96
Eswatini (Swaziland) 297
Ethiopia 297
Eukarya 165, **165**
Europe **278–281**
 map 280–281
 orange snow 98, **98**
 overview 278–280
European hares 146
Evaporation 102
Everest, Mount, China-Nepal 260, **260**, 261
Eve's Cone, Canada 121, **121**
Executive branch of government 237
Experiment design 133
Exploration **18–35**
 Almanac Challenge 24–25, **24–25**
 explorer profiles **20–22**, 156–157, **156–157**
 homework help 35
 no limits 30–31, **30–31**
 photography 32–33, **32–33**
 quiz 34
 wild adventure **26–29**
Explorer profiles
 exploration 20–22, **20–22**
 technology 156–157, **156–157**
Extinctions 72
Extreme sports 28–29, **28–29**
Eyes, frogs 57, **57**
Eyes, human 170–171, **170–171**

# F

Festivals and holidays **186–191**
 Bigfoot Festival, Oklahoma 324
 calendar 16, **16**, 186–187, **186–187**
 Chinese horoscope 189, **189**, 202, **202**
 Desert Festival, India 81, **81**
 Easter 186, **186**, 200, **200**
 gingerbread house activity 190–191, **190–191**
 Halloween 188, **188**
 kite festival, France **8–9**
 La Mercè festival, Barcelona, Spain **278**
 Navratri 200, **200**
 powwows **238**
 quiz 202
Fica, Haley 21
FIFA World Cup 286
Fiji, South Pacific Ocean 297
Fillmore, Millard 240, **240**
Finland 297
Fire coral 95
Fire rainbows 100, **100**
Fires 108
First aid 31
Fish
 clownfish 86, **86**, 92
 coral reefs 94
 definition 47
 discoveries 10, **10**
 endangered 46
 heat waves 109
 sharks 26–27, **26–27**, 34
 swirled picture 136
Fist bumps 175, **175**
Flamingos **136**
Florida
 cave divers **18–19**
 overview 321
 space shuttles 327, **327**

strawberries 283
Fluorite 116, **116**, 117, **117**
Flying foxes (bats) 109
Fog 282
Food
 ancient world 222, 223
 cultural aspects 184–185, **184–185**, 202, 334
 decomposition 176–177, **176–177**
 festivals and holidays 16, **16**
 fruit from Bangladesh 291
 fruitcake toss competition 320
 gingerbread house 190–191, **190–191**
 grilled squid teeth 334
 invisible ink from 233, **233**
 mustard museum 325
 pretzels **302**
 Vietnam 334
 waste 206
 watermelons shaped like pyramids 329
Ford, Gerald R. 243, **243**
Forests 96, **96**, 310
Fossil fuels 216, 217
Foxes 50–51, **50–51**, 86, **86**
France
 Eiffel Tower, Paris 278, 332, **332–333**, 335, **335**, 336, **336**
 festivals **8–9**
 King Louis XIV 279
 oldest cinemas 279, **279**
 overview 298
 street art 183, **183**
 tourism 279
 wars 234
Free riding 29, **29**
French and Indian War 234
Freshwater biomes 96, **96**
Frogs
 discoveries 10, **10**
 Javan gliding tree frog **148**
 poison dart frogs **47**
 red-eyed tree frogs 56–57, **56–57**, 85, **85**
Fruitcake toss competition 320
Fujita, T. Theodore 107
Fun and games **134–153**
 answers 338
 optical illusions 171, **171**
 see also Activities and projects
Fungi 165, **165**, 174, **174**
Future world **160–163**

# G

Gabon 298
Galápagos land iguanas 80, **80**
Galaxies 124–125, **124–125**
Galves, Jamal 22, **22**
Gambia 298
Games and puzzles **134–153**
 answers 338
 optical illusions 171, **171**
 see also Activities and projects
Garbage
 facts 206–207, **206–207**
 zero waste 11, **11**, 214, **214**, 218
 see also Recycling
Garbage Gone Glam 215, **215**
Garden snails **47**
Gardens 166–167, **166–167**
Garfield, James A. 241, **241**
Gastonia 78, **78**, 88
Geckos **46**
Geese 271, **271**

Gentoo penguins 266, **266**
Geographic Information System (GIS) 259, **259**
Geography **252–337**
 continents **262–289**
 countries **290–315**
 geographic features 260, **260**
 homework help 337
 maps 254–259
 quiz 336
 travel **328–335**
 United States **316–327**
 world maps 254–257
Georgia (republic) 298
Georgia (state) 321
Ger (portable huts) 271, **271**
Gerard, John 233
Gerenuks 82, **82**
Germany 182, **182**, 299
Germs 174–175, **174–175**
Ghana **298**, 299
Ghost slugs 263
Giant pandas 82, **82**
Giant's Causeway, Northern Ireland, U.K. 252, **252–253**
Gingerbread houses 190–191, **190–191**
Giraffe-necked weevils 48, **48**
Giraffes
 compared to quokkas 59, **59**
 jokes 145, **145**
 World Giraffe Day 16, **16**
GIS (Geographic Information System) 259, **259**
Giza, Egypt 229, **229**
Glaciers 260, **260**
Global warming
 dinosaur extinction 72
 overview 217, **217**
 quiz 218
 shrinking glaciers 260
 sources 216, 217
Goats 85, **85**
Going green **204–219**
 energy 216–217, **216–217**, 331, **331**
 fragile Earth **210–215**
 homework help 219
 human impact 206–207, **206–207**
 kids vs. plastic 212–213, **212–213**
 quiz 218
 save the ocean 208–209, **208–209**
 Strawscraper, Stockholm, Sweden 331, **331**
 zero-waste town 11, **11**
Gold 117, **117**, 192, **192**
Golden eagles 51
Goose, bar-headed 271, **271**
Gorillas 54–55, **54–55**
Government, U.S. **236–237**
Graham, Chuck 51
Grand Banks, Newfoundland, Canada 282
Grant, Ulysses S. 241, **241**
Grass, bridge made from 287, **287**
Grass-topped flip-flops 330, **330**
Grasshoppers 49, **49**, 146
Grasslands 97, **97**, 110, **110**
Gravity 124, 129
Gray, Cassyanna 59
Gray wolves 146, **282**
Great Britain see England; United Kingdom
Great Pyramid, Giza, Egypt 263, **263**, 333, 335, **335**

Since 1888, the National Geographic Society has funded more than 12,000 research,
exploration, and preservation projects around the world. The Society receives
funds from National Geographic Partners, LLC, funded in part by your purchase.
A portion of the proceeds from this book supports this vital work.
To learn more, visit natgeo.com/info.

NATIONAL GEOGRAPHIC and Yellow Border Design are trademarks of the
National Geographic Society, used under license.

For more information, visit nationalgeographic.com, call 1-877-873-6846,
or write to the following address:

National Geographic Partners
1145 17th Street N.W.
Washington, D.C. 20036-4688 U.S.A.

Visit us online at nationalgeographic.com/books

For librarians and teachers:
nationalgeographic.com/books/librarians-and-educators

More for kids from National Geographic: natgeokids.com

*National Geographic Kids* magazine inspires children to explore their world
with fun yet educational articles on animals, science, nature, and more.
Using fresh storytelling and amazing photography, *Nat Geo Kids* shows kids
ages 6 to 14 the fascinating truth about the world—and why they should care.
**kids.nationalgeographic.com/subscribe**

For rights or permissions inquiries, please contact National Geographic Books
Subsidiary Rights: bookrights@natgeo.com

Designed by Kathryn Robbins and Ruthie Thompson

National Geographic supports K–12 educators with ELA Common Core Resources.
Visit natgeoed.org/commoncore for more information.

Trade paperback ISBN: 978-1-4263-3671-3
Reinforced library binding ISBN: 978-1-4263-3672-0

Printed in the United States of America
20/WOR/1

The publisher would like to thank everyone who worked to make this book come
together: Angela Modany, associate editor; Mary Jones, project editor; Sarah
Wassner Flynn, writer; Michelle Harris, researcher; Lori Epstein, photo director;
Hillary Leo, photo editor; Mike McNey, map production; Chris Philpotts, illustrator;
Sean Philpotts, production director; Anne LeongSon and Gus Tello, design
production assistants; Joan Gossett, editorial production manager; and
Alix Inchausti and Molly Reid, production editors.